Institute of Cancer Research Library

Cancer and the Law

Cancer and the Law

A Medical Negligence Guide

Jonathan Waxman
BSc, MBBS, MD, FRCP
and
Daniel Simons
BA, JD

b
Blackwell
Science

Published in association with
Action for Victims of Medical Accidents

© J. Waxman and D. Simons 1999

Blackwell Science Ltd
Editorial Offices:
Osney Mead, Oxford OX2 0EL
25 John Street, London WC1N 2BL
23 Ainslie Place, Edinburgh EH3 6AJ
350 Main Street, Malden
  MA 02148 5018, USA
54 University Street, Carlton
  Victoria 3053, Australia
10, rue Casimir Delavigne
  75006 Paris, France

Other Editorial Offices:

Blackwell Wissenschafts-Verlag GmbH
Kurfürstendamm 57
10707 Berlin, Germany

Blackwell Science KK
MG Kodenmacho Building
7–10 Kodenmacho Nihombashi
Chuo-ku, Tokyo 104, Japan

The right of the Author to be identified as the
Author of this Work has been asserted in
accordance with the Copyright, Designs and
Patents Act 1988.

All rights reserved. No part of
this publication may be reproduced,
stored in a retrieval system, or
transmitted, in any form or by any
means, electronic, mechanical,
photocopying, recording or otherwise,
except as permitted by the UK
Copyright, Designs and Patents Act
1988, without the prior permission
of the publisher.

First published 1999

Set in 10/12.5 Palatino
by DP Photosetting, Aylesbury, Bucks
Printed and bound in Great Britain by
MPG Books Ltd, Bodmin, Cornwall

The Blackwell Science logo is a
trade mark of Blackwell Science Ltd,
registered at the United Kingdom
Trade Marks Registry

Disclaimer – The authors of this text have
provided information which they believe to be
accurate. No legal responsibility can be held for
any inaccuracies.

DISTRIBUTORS

Marston Book Services Ltd
PO Box 269
Abingdon
Oxon OX14 4YN
(*Orders:* Tel: 01235 465500
        Fax: 01235 465555)

USA
Blackwell Science, Inc.
Commerce Place
350 Main Street
Malden, MA 02148 5018
(*Orders:* Tel: 800 759 6102
           781 388 8250
       Fax: 781 388 8255)

Canada
Login Brothers Book Company
324 Saulteaux Crescent
Winnipeg, Manitoba R3J 3T2
(*Orders:* Tel: 204 837 2987
       Fax: 204 837 3116)

Australia
Blackwell Science Pty Ltd
54 University Street
Carlton, Victoria 3053
(*Orders:* Tel: 03 9347 0300
       Fax: 03 9347 5001)

A catalogue record for this title
is available from the British Library

ISBN 0-632-04852-2

Library of Congress
Cataloging-in-Publication Data
is available

For further information on
Blackwell Science, visit our website:
www.blackwell-science.com

For Clare, Thea and Freddie
                Jonathan

To Kay, Asher and Zack
With all my love
                Daniel

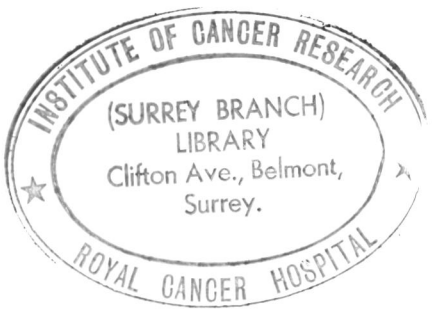

Contents

Preface		xv
Introduction		1
Chapter 1	**The Law of Medical Negligence**	**5**
	Duty of care	5
	Breach of duty	7
Chapter 2	**The Law of Causation**	**20**
	Loss of a chance	21
	Material contribution	25
	Duty and causation	28
Chapter 3	**The Cancer Patient as a Client**	**32**
	Strategies for managing the oncology client and the investigation	33
	Preparing to meet the client	36
	The first interview	41
Chapter 4	**Managing the Investigation**	**48**
	Pre-action disclosure	48
	Working with the disclosed records, notes and materials	53
	The medical brief	56
Chapter 5	**Instructing Experts in Oncology Cases**	**59**
	Example 1: case based on allegations of delay or failure to diagnose	60
	Example 2: case based on allegations of inappropriate or inaccurate radiotherapy	62
	The letter of instruction	65

	Introduction	65
	List of supporting documents	66
	Explanation of the records and documents	66
	Factual or medical history	67
	The expert's brief	67
	The opposing arguments	70
	Concluding the instructions	70
Chapter 6	**Damages**	**71**
	General damages	71
	Provisional damages	74
Chapter 7	**Cancer: Basic Facts and Background**	**78**
	Cancer and its causes	78
	Communicating	79
	Cancer and its symptoms	80
	Cancer and its signs	81
	Hospital referral	82
	Hospital assessment	82
	Hospital tests	84
	Treatment	84
Chapter 8	**Breast Cancer**	**88**
	Epidemiology	88
	Presentation	88
	Out-patient diagnosis	88
	Surgery	89
	Stage and grade	89
	Adjuvant radiotherapy	90
	Adjuvant hormonal therapy	91
	Adjuvant chemotherapy	91
	Treatment of metastatic breast cancer	91
	High-dose chemotherapy	92
Chapter 9	**Ovarian Cancer**	**93**
	Epidemiology	93
	Presentation	93
	Investigations	93
	Surgery	94
	Pathology	94
	Staging	94
	Treatment	94
	Second-look surgery	96
	Prognosis	96
	Tumour markers	96

Chapter 10	**Cervical Cancer**	**98**
	Epidemiology	98
	Symptoms and investigation	98
	Staging and grading	99
	Treatment	99
	Prognosis	99
	Terminal care	100
	Screening	100
Chapter 11	**Vulval Cancer**	**102**
	Introduction	102
	Symptoms	102
	Initial investigations and staging	103
	Treatment	103
	Grading and staging	103
	Prognosis	103
	Vulval intraepithelial neoplasia	103
Chapter 12	**Cancer of the Larynx**	**105**
	Epidemiology	105
	Presentation	105
	Investigation	105
	Grade and stage	106
	Treatment	107
	Prognosis	107
Chapter 13	**Lung Cancer**	**108**
	Epidemiology	108
	Presentation and investigations	108
	Staging	109
	Treatment	110
Chapter 14	**Cancer of the Tongue**	**112**
	Epidemiology	112
	Presentation	112
	Grading and staging	112
	Treatment	113
	Prognosis	114
	Complications of treatment	114
Chapter 15	**Cancer of the Oesophagus**	**115**
	Epidemiology	115
	Presentation	115
	Investigation	115

	Staging	116
	Pathology	116
	Treatment	117
	Prognosis	117
Chapter 16	**Gastric Cancer**	**118**
	Epidemiology	118
	Presentation	118
	Investigations	118
	Initial treatment	119
	Staging	119
	Adjuvant therapy	120
	Treatment of metastases in inoperable local disease	120
	Survival	121
Chapter 17	**Cancer of the Pancreas**	**122**
	Epidmiology	122
	Symptoms and investigations	122
	Staging and grading	123
	Treatment	123
	Treatment of inoperable disease	124
Chapter 18	**Cancer of the Colon**	**125**
	Epidemiology and presentation	125
	Surgical management	125
	Tumour grade and stage	126
	Adjuvant treatment	127
	Management of metastatic disease	127
Chapter 19	**Cancer of the Rectum**	**128**
	Epidemiology	128
	Presentation and initial assessment	128
	Surgery	128
	Staging and grading	129
	Complications of surgery	130
	Adjuvant treatment	130
	Prognosis	130
	Treatment of metastatic rectal cancer	130
Chapter 20	**Renal Cancer**	**131**
	Epidemiology	131
	Presentation	131
	Hospital investigation	131
	Surgery	132

	Staging	132
	Treatment of inoperable or metastatic tumour	132
	Prognosis	134
Chapter 21	**Bladder Cancer**	**135**
	Epidemiology	135
	Presentation and investigations	135
	Tumour grading and staging	136
	Treatment of superficial bladder cancer	137
	Treatment of invasive bladder cancer	137
	Treatment of metastatic bladder cancer	138
Chapter 22	**Prostate Cancer**	**139**
	Epidemiology	139
	Presentation and investigation	139
	Clinical staging and grading	139
	Prostate specific antigen	140
	Management	140
	Treatment	141
	Effects of treatment delay	141
	Prognosis	142
Chapter 23	**Testicular Cancer**	**143**
	Epidemiology and presentation	143
	Investigations	143
	Pathology and staging	143
	Treatment	144
	Side-effects of treatment	145
	Prognosis	146
Chapter 24	**Non-Hodgkin's Lymphoma**	**147**
	Epidemiology	147
	Presentation	147
	Initial investigations in hospital	147
	Staging	147
	Grading	148
	Treatment and prognosis	148
Chapter 25	**Hodgkin's Disease**	**150**
	Epidemiology	150
	Investigation and diagnosis	150
	Tumour grade	151
	Tumour staging	151
	Treatment and its side-effects	151
	Prognosis	153

Chapter 26	**Melanoma**	**154**
	Epidemiology	154
	Presentation	154
	Staging	155
	Treatment of metastatic melanoma	156
	Prognosis factors	157
Chapter 27	**Carcinoid Tumours**	**159**
	Epidemiology	159
	Presentation	159
	Investigations in hospital	159
	Management	160
	Prognosis	161
Chapter 28	**Mesothelioma**	**162**
	Epidemiology	162
	Presentation and referral	162
	Diagnosis and staging	163
	Treatment	163
	Prognosis	164
Chapter 29	**Myeloma**	**165**
	Epidemiology	165
	Presentation	165
	Hospital review	165
	Diagnosis	166
	Staging	166
	Treatment	166
	Response assessment	167
	Complications of myeloma	167
Chapter 30	**Soft Tissue Sarcomas**	**168**
	Epidemiology	168
	Presentation and initial investigations	168
	Pathology	168
	Staging	169
	Treatment of the primary tumour	169
	Treatment of metastatic sarcoma	170
Chapter 31	**Thyroid Cancer**	**171**
	Epidemiology	171
	Presentation	171
	Diagnosis	171
	Management	172

	Stage and grade	172
	Postoperative management	173
	Prognosis	173
Chapter 32	**Chemotherapy Extravasation**	**174**
Appendix	**Cases**	**176**
Glossary		200
Table of Cases		205
Index		207

Preface

The legal profession is currently undertaking the most radical procedural changes for 100 years. The Lord Chancellor's reforms are designed to ensure that the public has access to a faster, more user-friendly, and more just legal system.

Cancer is a significant cause of morbidity and mortality in our population. It affects 278,000 people and causes 150,000 deaths per year in England and Wales. Cancer used to be a disease that was little discussed between patients and doctors. However, nowadays every patient's expectation is that specialist care is given and that he is informed about the processes of his illness. There has been a corresponding change in litigation practice and, in contrast to the situation 20 years ago, patients are discussing and questioning standards of clinical practice more frequently.

This opening up of medicine has led to an increase in the number of claimants seeking legal attention. All litigants are entitled to receive not only the highest quality medical care, but the highest quality of legal care as well. The public expect their legal representatives to be familiar with the technical basis which underlies the dispute, as well as its legal basis. We write this book primarily for the medical negligence litigator and the medical practitioner interested in oncology claims, hoping to explain legal and medical practice in this increasingly busy area. It is hoped that the book will also be of use to hospital risk managers, individuals and organisations who oversee and fund medical claims, as well as to medical claimants themselves.

Jonathan Waxman
Daniel Simons

Introduction

Medical negligence litigation is on the increase. The number of incidents investigated, the number of legal practitioners representing patients, hospitals or doctors, the amount of money expended in legal fees and disbursements, and the total amount of damages awarded by settlement or trial are all burgeoning.

This increase in medical negligence litigation in the UK has brought with it positive lessons for the legal practitioner. Lawyers, whether acting for the defendants or the victims of medical accidents, appreciate that this area of the law is truly a discrete specialty with its own principles of practice. The aim of the professional practising in a specialty is to provide a higher quality of advice and service to the client. In medical negligence terms, this manifests itself in several key respects.

Specialist lawyers should have a developed understanding of the legal principles that underpin their specialty. This seems rather self-evident. Nevertheless, from time to time one still encounters a litigator new to medical litigation who will have overlooked that, in addition to considering the application of the Bolam[1] test, there is the matter of causation which must also be addressed.

The specialist must appreciate the procedural idiosyncrasies relevant to his area of law and be able to effectively utilise and exploit the process of case preparation. In medical negligence terms, this means knowing how medical investigations and litigation proceed. And, perhaps as important to the sub-specialty of oncology litigation, the litigator should understand and manage investigations and cases in order to ensure that the client achieves an accurate and expeditious resolution.

A word of caution is warranted here. As this text is being prepared, the government is well underway with proposing and implementing dramatic changes to the procedural face of all civil litigation, including medical

---

[1] *Bolam v. Friern Hospital Management Committee* [1957] 2 All ER 118, 1 WLR 582.

negligence. Many of these changes are in response to the findings of Lord Woolf's analysis of the civil justice system. This review, the landmark *Access to Justice Report* released in July of 1996, identified fundamental obstacles which victims of medical accidents face in litigating claims:

- excessive delay in progressing and resolving claims
- procedural complexity and dilatory lawyering
- the high cost of litigating such claims
- the unfairness to litigants which results from unequal financial positions.

Related issues for medical negligence litigators are the pursuance of unmeritorious claims and the defence of the indefensible claims.

The so-called 'Woolf Reforms' are being designed to take the complexity out of the process of litigation, accelerate the course of justice and level the financial playing field. These reforms are still effectively under construction, and their final shape remains uncertain. In particular, we still have yet to see the pre-action protocols being developed for medical claims. Nonetheless, what we do know is that the current government intends to alter the present system of litigation to encourage specialism as one method of alleviating many of the problems identified by Lord Woolf.

An example is the area of funding. The Lord Chancellor has announced an intention to end legal aid for civil cases where money damages are sought. Few would argue that, as legal aid has been the most widely used source of funding of medical negligence claims in the past, the impact of these funding changes on medical negligence litigation procedure is likely to be quite dramatic indeed.

At present the government's intention is that some degree of legal aid funding will remain intact for investigating medical claims and for claims involving minors and patients with a disability. However, it is equally apparent that any legal aid money made available for such litigation will likely only be afforded to litigators or firms of solicitors able to demonstrate a specialised skill in medical negligence litigation. These changes herald an end to the days when legal aid provided a source of subsidy for the inexperienced litigator.

Fast-track and multi-track litigation 'highways' have been designed and proposed as the inevitable procedural routes for all civil claims. In order to achieve the desired goal of faster and less expensive litigation, both are bound to contain some limit on profit costs and disbursements. When these tracks do become a reality, it is likely that the multi-track will be the mode of litigating most, if not all, medical negligence claims.

Even to attempt to second-guess the full impact and outcome of proposed major changes like these is seldom an accurate or wise exercise. However, it is clear that all of the changes are geared to ensure that complex legal work such as clinical negligence litigation is done by specialists, and that those specialists must 'front load' medical investigations and case preparations. The new focus on litigation is in the pre-action battlefield and not pre-trial. The necessity to develop an early understanding of the claimant's case is emphasized in Part I of the new civil procedures. Thus, in addition to medical issues related to cancer, this book considers aspects of pre-action case management in the context of currently existing procedures of oncology litigation and clinical negligence claims generally.

The medical negligence specialist practitioner must demonstrate an understanding of the medicine involved in his client's claim. This should not be interpreted as meaning that the lawyer should become the medical expert; indeed, far from it. Nonetheless, there must be some difference between the medical negligence 'specialist' and other lawyers or litigators engaged in acting for injured people generally. Certainly a large part of that difference must be at least a rudimentary knowledge of the medicine and medical issues which underpin the client's complaint. How else would the 'specialist' be able even to begin to plan the pre-action investigation.

A commonality of language is key to a considered knowledge of the ethos and practices of any society. The world of medicine and its population of doctors, surgeons, nurses, midwives, radiologists, physiotherapists and countless other allied specialists is no different. Therefore it is critical that specialists acquire a working knowledge of the terminology, structure and practice of the medical profession. Insight into patient problems has always been a fundamental requirement of the patient's legal advisor.

However, what often makes a good medical negligence litigator a great one is the ability to understand, appreciate and evaluate the clinical setting within which the care in question was delivered. Often all of the medical textbooks in the lawyer's library combined will not be able to describe this perspective of the delivery of care.

The inevitability of the continually diminishing pool of legal aid recipients has over the past two years seen the rapid development of alternative sources of funding. In the main, medical negligence litigation is now looking to conditional fee agreements, the so-called 'no win, no fee' arrangements, and after-the-event legal expenses insurance to fund claims. Conditional fee agreements and, to a lesser extent, legal expenses cover mandate that the lawyer assume great risk in the selection and preparation of a case. The extent to which the lawyer is familiar with the terminology, ethos and medical bases of the proposed claim is the extent to which that lawyer will be in a position to evaluate effectively which cases should or should not be risked.

Although currently only a relative few medical negligence cases have been funded on either a conditional fee or after-the-event insurance basis, there are already valuable lessons for the litigator to take on board. Firstly, if either of these two vehicles is to be used to fund the potential claim, then insurance cover should underpin them in order to protect the client in the event of an adverse costs award. Secondly, the insurers will only underwrite these cases after a full and accurate investigation into the merits of all of the legal issues has been completed. Thirdly, the client will usually be responsible for funding the investigation needed to get to the point where a cogent decision can be made as to whether further funding is feasible.

Investigations into potential medical negligence cases have always been long and expensive exercises. They are labour intensive. Obtaining volumes of case notes, reviewing and organising them, instructing experts and evaluating risk in view of the independent reports all takes many hours of detailed and careful work. Without the relative security of legal aid to pick up the cost and cover the risk, how are medical negligence practitioners as a profession to effect necessary change in the manner in which they practise to reduce cost and risk to their clients?

The answer is 'specialisation'. This means creating an environment where the practice of clinical negligence claims is largely restricted to lawyers so used to it, so familiar with the law and language of medical litigation, that there are reductions in cost, time and other uncertainties in the investigation of proposed claims. In short, fast-track litigation and the death of legal aid must, by necessity, further encourage the development of the litigators. The new procedural and funding changes, which are at the forefront of the changes in the civil justice system, are driving the legal profession even more towards specialisation.

This book is intended as a guide for all medical negligence practitioners, for whom we hope it is useful.

Note

Throughout this book 'he' is used when discussing patients, doctors and lawyers in general, unless the individual is specifically female, instead of the more cumbersome 'he/she'.

Medical statistics quoted are for England and Wales, as no UK-wide figures are published to the authors' knowledge, but issues are discussed from a UK perspective.

Chapter 1
The Law of Medical Negligence

As with all forms of negligence actions, medical negligence claims require the plaintiff or, as they are now known under the new rules of civil procedure, the 'claimant', to prove all three of the following propositions:

(1) the existence of a duty of care;
(2) a breach of the duty of care; and
(3) a causative link between the breach of duty and any personal injury suffered by the patient.

While there may be nothing particularly unique about these legal elements, they do acquire particular characteristics in the context of medical negligence litigation generally, and oncology claims specifically.

Duty of care

Establishing a duty of care between the claimant as patient and the defendant as health care professional or organisation is rarely an obstacle when litigating medical negligence claims. Whether the defendant is a hospital or National Health Service (NHS) trust (institutional defendants) or a doctor or health care professional (individual defendants), the existence of a duty of care is rarely disputed. Whenever a therapeutic relationship exists between a patient and clinician, hospital or health care professional, a duty of care should be presumed.

One of the best descriptions of the scope of the duty of care owed by a physician to a patient is that of Lord Chief Justice Hewitt in *R v. Bateman*[1]:

---

[1] [1925] 94 LJKB 791, at 794.

'If a doctor holds himself out as possessing special skill and knowledge and he is consulted, as possessing such skill and knowledge, by or on behalf of a patient, he owes a duty to the patient to use due caution in undertaking the treatment. If he accepts the responsibility and undertakes the treatment and the patient submits to his direction and treatment accordingly, he owes a duty to the patient to use diligence, care, knowledge, skill and caution in administering the treatment. No contractual relationship is necessary, nor is it necessary that the service be rendered for reward.'

Among the multitude of situations giving rise to this duty of care is the duty to inform patients of test results. This duty is particularly important in cases where the patient alleges that biopsy or other histopathological testing results were not communicated to the patient at all, or where it is alleged that the reporting was insufficient to warn the patient of the true nature of his illness. Failures in communication and the duty to communicate are an important factor in a large number of cancer cases.

The duty of care owed by hospitals, health authorities and NHS trusts exists in two forms: a vicarious duty and a so-called direct duty. Hospitals are vicariously responsible for the negligent acts and omissions of their individual employees and staff. As Lord Justice Denning said in *Cassidy* v. *Ministry of Health*[2]:

'In my opinion authorities who run a hospital ... are in the law under the self same duty as the humblest doctor; whenever they accept a patient for treatment, they must use reasonable care and skill to cure him of his ailment. The hospital authorities cannot, of course, do it by themselves: they have no ears to listen through the stethoscope, and no hands to hold the surgeon's knife. They must do it by the staff which they employ; and if their staff are negligent in giving the treatment, they are just as liable for that negligence as is anyone else who employs others to do his duties for him.'[3]

There is nothing unusual or unique about this form of vicarious liability. It is fundamental that the employee's or employees' actions or omissions in question were committed in the course and scope of their employment.

One exception to this rule is where a patient has contracted with a health care professional for private treatment. If the patient subsequently receives privately contracted care from the clinician within a hospital setting, that hospital is not then vicariously liable for the acts or omissions.

In addition to a duty of care owed vicariously through the acts or

---
[2] [1951] 2 KB 343.
[3] *ibid*, at 356.

omissions of its employees, it is now settled law that a hospital owes a direct duty of care to the patient – a duty that exists independently of any negligent conduct by individual members of staff. The scope of this duty is that a hospital is obligated to select or employ suitably competent and qualified staff, appropriately instruct and supervise them, provide proper facilities and equipment, and establish safe systems. The best expression of the breadth of this duty is still found in the words of Lord Browne-Wilkinson, the Vice Chancellor, in *Wilsher v. Essex Area Health Authority*[4].

> 'I agree with the comments of Lord Justice Mustill as to the confusion which has been caused in this case ... which blurred the distinction between the vicarious liability of the health authority for the negligence of its doctors and the direct liability of the health authority for negligently failing to provide skilled treatment of the kind that it was offering to the public. In my judgment, a health authority which so conducts its hospital that it fails to provide doctors of sufficient skill and experience to give the treatment offered at the hospital may be directly liable in negligence to the patient. Although we are told in argument that no case has ever been decided on this ground and that it is not the practice to formulate claims in this way, I can see no reason why, in principle, the health authority should not be so liable if its organisation is at fault.'[5]

We shall return to *Wilsher* later. However, before leaving duty of care, there is one perhaps less obvious form of vicarious duty which is critically important to a growing number of oncology cases: the duty which the defendant assumes for the actions of independent testing laboratories and facilities. A recent spate of incidents involving a large number of inaccurately interpreted test results, most often Pap smears for cervical cellular anomalies, has brought heightened media and medico-legal attention to the quality of the staff and facilities independently employed by hospitals or physicians to screen samples, biopsies, tests and the patient whose sample is under review. The claimant's legal advisor should appreciate that in these circumstances the defendant, most often a hospital, area health authority or NHS trust, is vicariously responsible for any negligent errors.

Breach of duty

Every negligence claim must demonstrate a breach in the relevant duty of care owed in order to be successful. Forty years after Mr Justice McNair

---
[4] [1986] 3 All ER 801.
[5] *ibid*, at 833.

instructed the jury in *Bolam v. Friern Hospital Management Committee*[6], the 'Bolam test' remains the cornerstone by which the standard of care is measured in medical negligence claims.

> 'Where you get a situation which involves the use of some special skill or competence, then the test as to whether there has been negligence or not is not the test of the man on top of a Clapham omnibus, because he has not got this special skill. The test is the standard of the ordinary skilled man exercising and professing to have that special skill. A man need not possess the highest expert skill; it is well-established law that it is sufficient if he exercises the ordinary skill of an ordinary competent man exercising that particular art.
>
> 'A doctor is not guilty of negligence if he has acted in accordance with a practice accepted as proper by a responsible body of medical men skilled in that particular art... Putting it the other way round, a doctor is not negligent, if he has acted in accordance with such a practice, merely because there is a body of opinion which takes a contrary view.'[7]

Although promulgated via instructions to a jury, the House of Lords has accepted *Bolam*[8] in several important decisions, including, most recently, the decision in *Bolitho v. City and Hackney Health Authority*[9], which will be discussed further below. *Bolam* establishes that the standard of care expected of the heath care professional need only be 'ordinary'. The law neither requires the health care professional to be the best, nor even one of the best, to be at risk of being successfully sued for professional negligence. Ordinary care is enough. *Bolam* also confirms that this 'ordinariness' is to be judged by 'a responsible body of medical men' practising in any given branch of medicine.

In short, if the defendant is able to prove that his actions are accepted as proper by a responsible body of medical opinion in that particular art, the defendant is to be exonerated from allegations of medical negligence. But what if the court is presented with two bodies of medical opinion; one for the plaintiff maintaining that the care in question is not acceptable by a responsible body, and one by the defence to the contrary? Did *Bolam* intend that in determining what level of care was 'ordinary' or 'reasonable' the court must, by necessity, exonerate any defendant able to muster a body of supporting and reasonable medical men? The answer is most assuredly 'No': *Bolam* does have some limits. There are practitioners and commen-

---

[6] [1957] 2 All ER 118, 1 WLR 582.
[7] *ibid*, at 122.
[8] *Maynard v. West Midlands Regional Health Authority*[1984] 1 WLR 634; *Whitehouse v. Jordan* [1981] 1 WRL 246.
[9] *New Law Digest* Commercial Communication 163, 13 November 1997; *Times Law Report*, 27 November 1997.

tators who express concern that the Bolam test focuses the determination of negligence on what medical practice or action was performed on the patient, rather than what medical practice or action should have been performed. However, a slender, yet important, thread of case law makes clear that the court can, in limited circumstances, reject the body of evidence offered by the defendant as not satisfying the Bolam test. Equally clear is that the court will only reject in rare circumstances such evidence as being *Bolam* incompetent.

For example, when cases of conflicting expert evidence are presented by the parties, the court is charged with the authority and responsibility to scrutinise that evidence in order to determine whether the opinions are based on sound logic. In *Hucks v Cole*[10], a case from 1968, a general practitioner (GP) failed to use penicillin to treat a maternity patient who was suffering from septic skin spots. The plaintiff, Mrs Hucks, suffered puerperal fever and significant residual health problems as a result. At trial experts for the defendant gave evidence that they too would have failed to treat Mrs Hucks with penicillin if they had been presented with the same problems as the defendant, Dr Cole. A question arose on appeal as to whether the trial judge was bound to accept this expert evidence and exonerate the defendant.

The Court of Appeal examined the reasonableness or logical basis of this evidence. In this case, the court recognised that the trial judge was entitled to approach the determination of the reasonableness of the experts' opinions by weighing up the respective risks against the benefits of treatment:

'When the evidence shows that a lacuna in professional practice exists by which risks of grave danger are knowingly taken, then, however small the risk, the court must anxiously examine that lacuna particularly if the risk can be easily and inexpensively avoided. If the court finds, on an analysis of the reasons given for not taking those precautions that, in the light of current professional knowledge, there is no proper basis for the lacuna, and that it is definitely not reasonable that those risks should have been taken, its function is to state that fact and where necessary to state that it constitutes negligence. In such a case the practice will no doubt thereafter be altered to the benefit of patients. On such occasions the fact that other practitioners would have done the same thing as the defendant practitioner is a very weighty matter to be put on the scales on his behalf; but it is not ... conclusive. The court must be vigilant to see whether the reasons given for putting a patient at risk are valid in light of any well-known advance in medical knowledge, or whether they stem from a residual adherence to out-of-date ideas.'[11]

---

[10] [1968] 4 Med LR 393.
[11] *ibid*, at 397.

Whilst an analysis of the logic underpinning a body of expert evidence may well result in one view prevailing over another in court, what the court is not at liberty to do is 'prefer' one body of 'reasonable care' over another. As *Bolam* says, a defendant is not negligent if he has acted in accordance with a responsible body simply because there may be other equally responsible views.

In *Maynard v. West Midlands Regional Health Authority*[12], the Bolam test was extended to medical diagnosis. Both a physician and a surgeon saw Mrs Maynard when she presented with symptoms of tuberculosis. In view of their interpretation of the presenting symptoms, both included differential diagnoses of Hodgkin's disease, carcinoma and sarcoidosis. Concerned that the Hodgkin's disease might prove fatal if left untreated, both doctors agreed to perform a biopsy by way of mediastinoscopy, rather than await the results of a sputum test.

Mediastinoscopy carries a risk of injury to the laryngeal nerve. As with a great number of medical procedures, this injury can occasionally occur even when the procedure is performed with the utmost care by the most experienced of operators. Indeed, in Mrs Maynard's case, her laryngeal nerve was in fact injured, even though the operation was found to have been performed appropriately and reasonably.

The biopsy taken via the mediastinoscopy was negative, and Mrs Maynard brought proceedings alleging negligence for the doctors' decision to have used the more invasive biopsy in the first instance rather than the less invasive sputum test. The defendant health authority presented distinguished expert opinion at trial that confirmed the appropriateness of the mediastinoscopy.

Despite the quality of the evidence proffered by the defendant, the judge found for the plaintiff. In doing so, the trial judge effectively discounted the defendant's evidence in preference of the evidence of Mrs Maynard's expert. His opinion was that, insofar as the diagnosis of tuberculosis should have been made *ab initio*, to perform an unnecessary and potentially dangerous biopsy was negligent. The case went on appeal.

As recently as in the *Bolitho* decision, the House of Lords cited with approval the following often-quoted passage from Lord Scarman's speech in *Maynard*:

> '...I have to say that a judge's "preference" for one body of distinguished professional opinion to another also professionally distinguished is not sufficient to establish negligence in a practitioner whose actions have received the seal of approval of those whose opinions, truthfully expressed, honestly held, were not preferred. If this was the real reason for the judge's finding, he erred in law even though else-

---

[12] [1984] 1 WLR 634.

where in his judgment he stated the law correctly. For in the realm of diagnosis and treatment negligence is not established by preferring one **respectable** body of professional opinion to another. Failure to exercise the ordinary skill of a doctor (in the appropriate specialty, if he be a specialist) is necessary.' (emphasis added)[13]

This issue is particularly important in cancer cases. Often doctors who treat cancer patients will have available to them a number of treatment options for any given pathology. The decision on whether surgical intervention is desirable, the amount of radiation to prescribe, the number of fractions or the chemotherapeutic regimen to employ may, to a large extent, represent personal opinion or the philosophy of the institutional health care provider. Some doctors, like some hospitals, may choose more aggressive treatment protocols than others. This decision is often based on the doctor's views and judgements.

Treatments of cancers, be they by surgery, radiation or chemotherapy, are being developed, tested and improved daily. In any field of medicine as dynamic as this – and this is one of the most dynamic – it will often happen that second opinions may differ. Does the simple fact that one physician would treat a patient with a particular cancer in one way, while another physician would treat the same patient differently, indicate that *ipso facto* at least one must be proposing negligent treatment? According to *Maynard* the answer is resoundingly 'No'. Equally, this does not mean that one or both of the two recommendations might not be negligent. The key is whether either one individually complies with practice which is *Bolam* acceptable.

This 'dynamism' raises a second critical point when evaluating the quality of care rendered in cancer cases: the time when the care was delivered. The court will assess ordinary care in the context of the time when the claim is brought. The court will seek to establish the standard of care in the context of the state of medical knowledge at the time the treatment in question was administered:

> 'Advances in medical science or medical knowledge between the date of the alleged negligence and the date of trial should be ignored when determining whether the defendant exercised reasonable skill and care.'[14]

In the words of Lord Justice Denning in *Roe* v. *Minister of Health*[15]: 'We must not look at the 1947 accident with 1954 spectacles.'

---

[13] *New Law Digest* Commercial Communication 163, 13 November 1997, p. 4.
[14] Goldrein, I.S. and deHass, M.R. (1997) *Medical Negligence: Cost Effective Case Management*, p. 85. Butterworths, London.
[15] [1954] 2 QB 66, at 84.

When considering the appropriateness of care given to a cancer patient, the legal advisor, the medical expert and the court must view that care through the 'spectacles' of the time that the care was given or not given, whichever the case may be. This principle will become increasingly more important as a growing population of 'survivors' of cancers become aware of long-term side-effects which were perhaps unknown or not appreciated at the time of their treatment.

While not aware of any body of decided case law on these situations, we are aware of several potential claims where former cancer patients have sought to investigate this point exactly. Typically, these patients become aware of the sequelae of certain forms of radiation or chemotherapeutic protocols many years after they received the treatment. Very often the treatments originally administered have long since been relegated to obsolescence by medical or scientific advancement. With equal frequency, many of those treatments were developed well before medical knowledge and circumstance could have possibly predicted all of the potential side-effects. Looking at the appropriateness of the care in such cases yields quite different views, depending on the 'spectacles'. The litigator must resist the temptation to consider these cases in the light of current knowledge and practice. In addition to the emotional toll which unsuccessful litigation has on the client as well as the defendant, the failure to do so may well have dramatic cost consequences to that growing number of non-legally aided clients.

Other less obvious aspects of *Bolam* are worth noting at this point. First, let us briefly consider the requisite size of the 'responsible body of opinion' necessary to present an adequate defence to allegations of medical negligence. This is important in a relatively small medical community like that of oncology where one may only find a handful of specialists or facilities performing certain treatments and procedures, such as allogeneic bone marrow transplantation. Where the area of medicine involved in the plaintiff's care is so specialised as to be limited to only a few practitioners, the court will look beyond a mere 'head counting' exercise in determining whether the defendant's experts comprise a 'body' of opinion. This issue arose in the recent case of *Defrietas* v. *O'Brien*[16], where Lord Justice Otton said:

'...There was evidence before the learned judge which he clearly accepted to justify his conclusion that a small number of tertiary specialists could constitute a responsible body of medical opinion. It is a matter for the learned judge to assess whether or not he accepted the evidence as to what that opinion was... It was open to him to find as a fact that a small number of specialists constituted a responsible body and

---

[16] [1995] 6 Med LR 108, CA.

that the body would have considered the first defendant's position justified, or more succinctly, as the learned judge put it, that the plaintiff had failed to discharge the burden of proof that the first defendant was negligent...'[17]

Following through on the topic of specialists raises a further corollary of *Bolam*. We have previously discussed the following passage from Mr Justice McNair's instructions to the jury[18]:

'A doctor is not guilty of negligence if he has acted in accordance with a practice accepted as proper by a responsible body of medical men skilled in that particular art...'

Implied in these words is that a specialist is held to the same higher standard of expertise expected of other ordinary and competent specialists skilled in that specialism.[19] The higher the degree of expertise, the higher the standard of care owed to the patient.

Some breaches of duty are by omission rather than commission. Although not particularly common, these cases can present an extra layer of complexity to a determination of whether the defendant's action or lack of action constitutes grounds for a claim in negligence. The leading case on this point has rapidly become *Bolitho* v. *City and Hackney Health Authority*, with the House of Lords decision now reported in full[20], more fully discussed below. Briefly, *Bolitho* involved doctors who failed to attend a very ill child. The child, Patrick Bolitho, suffered a respiratory failure and a secondary cardiac arrest. It was accepted that the omission by the doctors to attend Patrick when requested on two separate occasions by the nurse constituted a breach of duty.

However, in order to evaluate the consequences of this breach of duty, the court rightly had to speculate as to what would have happened had the omission not occurred and, as here the omission involved patient care, whether that hypothetical care would have constituted acceptable practice:

'But in cases where the breach of duty consists of an omission to do an act that ought to have been done (e.g. the failure by a doctor to attend) that factual inquiry is, by definition, in the realms of hypothesis. The question is what would have happened if an event which by definition did not occur had occurred... Therefore in the present case, the first relevant

---

[17] *ibid*, at p. 115.
[18] [1957] 2 All ER 118, at p. 122.
[19] See, for example, *Sidaway* v. *Governors of the Bethlem Royal Hospital* [1985] 1 All ER 643, at p. 660.
[20] *New Law Digest* Commercial Communication 163, 13 November 1997.

question is "what would [either the SHO or the registrar] have done had they attended?" As to [the registrar] the judge accepted her evidence that she would not have intubated... Therefore the Bolam test had no part to play in determining the first question, viz. what would have happened? Nor can I see any circumstance in which the Bolam test could be relevant to such a question.'

Thus a kind of second, hypothetical yet critical, duty arises from the omission which by necessity had to be dealt with in order to allow the court to decide the issue of causation.

'There were, therefore, two questions for the judge to decide on causation:
(1) What would [the registrar] have done or authorised to be done, if she had attended Patrick? and
(2) If she would not have intubated, would that have been negligent?
The Bolam test has no relevance to the first of those questions but is central to the second.
There can be no doubt that, as a majority of the Court of Appeal held, the judge had directed himself correctly in accordance with that approach.'[21]

In considering the second question, both parties had presented expert medical evidence at trial. The plaintiff's experts were of the view that a reasonable and responsible doctor would have intubated Patrick if they had attended. The defendant countered with experts who took the contrary view, and in essence agreed with the registrar that even if she had attended, it would have been reasonable and responsible not to intubate.

Counsel for the plaintiff argued to both the Court of Appeal and the House of Lords that the view expressed by the defendant's experts against intubation was not internally logical or sensible given Patrick Bolitho's medical history. Thus, the trial judge erred in accepting the defendant's case when he himself seemed to question its logical basis. While agreeing that the court must by necessity scrutinise the inherent logic in the medical opinion, Lord Browne-Wilkinson, the Vice Chancellor, was nonetheless of the view that the trial judge had approached the evidence correctly before accepting the defendants' expert opinions.

In this way, the judgment reaffirms that the risk/benefit rationale described in *Hucks* v. *Cole* remains a means of demonstrating whether a medical opinion adduced by the defendant from a responsible and respectable body of medical expertise does in fact present a viable defence to the plaintiff's case:

---

[21] p. 7.

'The use of these adjectives responsible, reasonable and respectable all show that the court has to be satisfied that the exponents of the body of opinion relied upon can demonstrate that such opinion has a logical basis. In particular in cases involving, as they often do, the weighing of risks against benefits, the judge before accepting a body of opinion as being responsible, reasonable and respectable, will need to be satisfied that, in forming their views, the experts have directed their minds to the question of comparative risks and benefits and have reached a defensible conclusion on the matter.

I emphasise that in my view it will seldom be right for a judge to reach the conclusion that views genuinely held by a competent medical expert are unreasonable. The assessment of medical risks and benefits is a matter of clinical judgment which the judge would not normally make without expert evidence... It is only where a judge can be satisfied that the body of expert evidence cannot logically be supported at all that such opinion will not provide the bench mark by reference to which the defendant's conduct falls to be assessed.

I turn to consider whether this is one of those rare cases. Like the Court of Appeal, in my judgment it plainly is not.'[22]

Therefore, ultimately *Bolitho* continues the trend of judicial reluctance to interfere with the medical profession's assessment of the reasonableness of their actions. The Law Lords were of the view that, regardless of the trial judge's suggested concerns 'as a layman' about the decision not to intubate Patrick Bolitho, he had nonetheless applied the correct test in deciding that this was a case where the views of the defendant's experts should not be dismissed as illogical. In short, this was not a case where the court was prepared to allow the views of the judiciary as to what should have been done to interfere with the views of the medical experts as to what was done. Hence the appeal was dismissed.

Consent to treatment

The *Bolam* principle was extended beyond the realms of diagnosis and treatment to one of the last frontiers in the doctor–patient relationship – patient advice and consent – in the landmark case of *Sidaway v. Board of Governors of the Bethlem Royal Hospital*[23]. *Sidaway* presented the House of Lords with its first opportunity to consider whether the law of negligence imposed a duty of care on the quality and quantity of disclosure of information from doctor to patient, and, if so, what level of standard was to be

---

[22] p. 8.
[23] [1985] AC 871, HL.

applied to this duty. What information is the doctor obligated to share with the patient prior to any given procedure? How much detail must be given? These questions, which have formed a significant part of medico-legal practice in the 1990s were being asked for the first time only a little more than a decade ago.

Five different Law Lords prepared speeches; each with a slightly different focus. Rehearsing the individual nuances of the separate approaches is beyond the scope of this study. Suffice it to say that the majority adopted a *Bolam*-style standard of care phrased in the following, now well-known terms:

(1) The standard by which English law measures the doctor's duty of care to his patient when advising him about a particular course of treatment is the standard of the ordinary skilled man exercising and professing to have the special skill which that doctor is exercising and professing to have.
(2) The decision what degree of disclosure of risks is best calculated to assist a particular patient to make a rational choice as to whether or not to undergo a particular treatment must primarily be a matter of clinical judgment.
(3) An issue whether non-disclosure of a particular risk or cluster of risks in a particular case should be condemned as a breach of the doctor's duty of care is an issue to be decided primarily on the basis of expert medical evidence. In the event of a conflict of evidence, the judge will have to decide whether a responsible body of medical opinion would have approved of non-disclosures in the case before him.
(4) A judge might, in certain circumstances, come to the conclusion that disclosure of a particular risk was so obviously necessary to an informed choice on the part of the patient that no reasonably prudent medical practitioner would fail to make it, even in a case where no expert witness in the relevant medical field condemned the non-disclosure as being in conflict with accepted and responsible care.

Thus, in the first instance the court will accept the parameters for material disclosure established by a responsible body of medical professionals in that field of medicine. However, this arguably paternalistic view of the role of the doctor is clearly not without limit. The court will ordinarily accept that whether to disclose certain risks is a matter of clinical judgment. However, the fourth point explicitly anticipates the possibility of the court exercising the right to reject unreasonable views on disclosure, no matter how responsible the body of opinion against it might be.

Critical to this analysis are the words of Lord Justice Denning in *Roe v. Minister of Health*, discussed previously. As with any area of medicine, standards of care are expected to, and do, change. In few areas of medicine has the standard of care altered as quickly as with consent and the disclosure of information. One of the authors assisted in the investigation of allegations of negligence made by a number of women against one particular hospital in the UK. These women had all undergone the same or similar forms of a new technique of radiotherapy. Their treatments had all been administered over a period of several years from the late 1970s through the mid 1980s.

The clients were concerned that the new form of radiotherapy they received had associated risks and complications of which they were not previously advised. Although inevitably there were some disadvantages to it, the older alternative treatment protocol had a proven rate of morbidity and mortality generally far less than that of the new treatment. None of these women had been given the option of whether to undergo the new treatment or to have the older, more established treatment. Indeed most, if any, were not even aware that options existed.

When complications associated with the new treatment started to develop, the extent of the duty to inform the women at the time when their treatments were administered came into question. If the litigator made the mistake of viewing this investigation through the 'spectacles' and standards of the late 1990s, the need for such an investigation would almost beggar belief. Of course patients should be informed of treatment options and choices. Of course the doctor owes a duty to give the level and standard of advice set out in *Sidaway*. However, as the author discovered when these cases were being investigated, one would be wrong to assume that this same level of detail and disclosure was practised by reasonable and responsible clinical oncologists only 15 or 20 years ago.

In conclusion, the Bolam test continues to steer the analysis of breach of duty of care in a medical negligence case. The simple fact that the defendant advances a reasonable, respectable and/or responsible body of opinion in support of his case does not preclude the judge from finding for the plaintiff. The judge is empowered to accept the defendant's case once he is satisfied that the opinions expressed are inherently logical. The court is not at liberty to find against the defendant by relying on a 'preference' for the plaintiff's expert evidence where the defendant's expert opinion is logical and reasonable. On rare occasions there may be bodies of expert medical opinion not capable of withstanding logical analysis. This may be possible where the medical opinion ignores questions of the relative risks and benefits of adopting a particular medical practice.

This review of breach of duty concludes by summarising some of the more common breaches of duty the litigator can expect to encounter when considering, investigating and preparing a medical negligence case arising from oncology management.

I. *Common breaches of duty associated with delays or failures to diagnose cancer*

(1) Failure to take a relevant history from the patient given the patient's presenting symptoms and complaints.

(2) Failure to take a complete history from the patient given the patient's presenting symptoms and complaints.

(3) Failure to conduct the physical examination required or necessitated by the patient's history and presenting symptoms.

(4) Failure to conduct further investigations or tests required or necessitated by the patient's history, presenting symptoms or examination.

(5) Failure to refer the patient to an appropriate specialist or facility for necessary and appropriate further testing or investigation.

(6) Failure to arrange appropriately timed follow-up appointments with the patient in light of the patient's history and/or examination.

(7) Failure to arrange any follow-up with the patient when, given the history, symptoms or examination, a further appointment(s) was appropriate.

(8) Failure to communicate suspicious or adverse test results at all to the referring medical practitioner or health care professional.

(9) Failure to accurately communicate suspicious or adverse test results to the referring medical practitioner or health care professional.

(10) Failure to communicate adequate recommendations to the referring medical practitioner or health care professional in view of suspicious or adverse test results.

(11) Failure to perform an adequate biopsy in terms of size, quality or general selection of tissue.

(12) Failure to re-biopsy when circumstances necessitate a further specimen for examination.

(13) Failure to accurately and appropriately interpret the histopathology (i.e. biopsy sample), resulting in no diagnosis (i.e. false negative) of cancer – a missed pathological diagnosis.

(14) Failure to accurately and appropriately interpret the histopathology resulting in an over-pathological diagnosis (i.e. false positive) of non-existent cancer.

(15) Failure by clinician and/or histopathologist to relate pathological diagnosis to clinical diagnosis.

(16) Failure to act upon pathologist's advice.

II. *Common breaches of duty associated with treatment or clinical management of cancer patients*

(1) Failure to take an adequate consent from the patient in advance of treatment.

(2) Failure to administer the appropriate chemotherapeutic medication(s).

(3) Failure to administer chemotherapy through the appropriate route (i.e. intramuscular or intrathecal, instead of intravenous).

(4) Failure to administer the appropriate dose of chemotherapy.

(5) Failure to ensure quality assurance procedures maintained in radiotherapeutic equipment.

(6) Failure to appropriately or adequately plan radiation therapy or treatment in advance.

(7) Failure to ensure that the appropriate dose of radiation is delivered to the patient.

(8) Failure to ensure that the appropriate dose of radiation is delivered to the patient in the appropriate loci.

(9) Failure to await the results of histopathologic tests or examinations when appropriate before undertaking what becomes unnecessary chemotherapeutic, radiotherapeutic or surgical intervention.

(10) Failure to perform salvage surgery appropriately, resulting in further or unnecessary damage to the patient.

Chapter 2
The Law of Causation

The issue of causation is very often the front line of the legal battlefield in medical negligence cases, and this is particularly true in cancer.

A legal claim for compensation based on allegations of negligence must demonstrate damage or injury to the claimant. Thus, it has to be shown that a clinician's negligence has led to a loss to his patient; in other words, that the clinical outcome would probably have been different if the negligence had not occurred. The burden of proof is on the claimant to show that this is the case.[1] In many instances outcome and treatment may have been the same, whether or not there had been negligence.

As we will see, this inquiry is most critical to oncology cases, and indeed most difficult to answer. It is almost inconceivable to imagine a medical negligence case in oncology where this issue should not be foremost in the legal advisor's mind from the outset. The wise litigator will not hesitate to seek appropriate expert opinion on causation as soon as possible in the investigation of the client's case.

The classic expression of causation in a medical negligence case is found in the case of *Barnett* v. *Chelsea and Kensington Hospital Management Committee*[2]. The facts of *Barnett* are well known. After drinking some tea in the early hours of New Year's Day 1966, three night watchmen fell ill. They presented at the casualty department of the defendant's hospital some three hours later at approximately 8 AM. Mr Barnett lay on some armless chairs in the casualty department while one of his colleagues reported to the nurse on duty that the men had fallen ill after drinking some tea. The nurse contacted a casualty doctor. He told the nurse that he himself was unwell and that the men should go home and contact their own doctors. The three men left, and Mr Barnett died some hours later from what was found to be arsenical poisoning.

---
[1] *Bonnington Castings Limited* v. *Wardlow* [1956] 1 All ER 615.
[2] [1969] 1 QB 428, [1968] 1 All ER 1068.

The defendant admitted that a duty of care was owed to the plaintiff and that the duty was breached by virtue of the inaction by the defendant's staff. However, it took the view through the trial that Mr Barnett would have died from the poisoning in any event; that this breach did not cause the death. Mr Justice Nield concluded:

> 'It remains to consider whether it is shown that the deceased's death was caused by negligence or whether, as the defendants have said, the deceased must have died in any event... If Dr Banerjee had got up and dressed and come to see the three men and decided to admit them, the deceased (and Dr Lockett agreed with this) could not have been in a bed in a ward before 11 AM ... an intravenous drip would not have been set up before 12 noon, and if potassium loss was suspected it could not have been discovered until 12.30 PM. Dr Lockett, dealing with this, said "If [the deceased] had not been treated until after 12 noon the chances of survival were not good" ... I find that the plaintiff has failed to establish, on the grounds of probability, that the defendant's negligence caused the death of the deceased.'[3]

In short, even if the deceased had been examined and admitted, there was little, if any, chance that the only effective antidote would have been administered to him before the time at which he died. Not only did the breach in duty not cause the patient's death, the evidence was that it could not have caused the patient's death.

Loss of a chance

Medicine is an art and not an exact science. In recognition, the court does not require a medical expert to predict outcomes and causative results of breaches of duty to a certain degree of likelihood or reliability. The 'balance of probabilities', greater than 50% certainty, is the required element of proof in the plaintiff's case. The application of this principle is demonstrated in *Hotson* v. *East Berkshire Area Health Authority*[4], a case involving a claim for loss of a chance for a better medical recovery.

In *Hotson*, a young boy fell from a tree and suffered a fracture near the top, or head, of his left femur. The fracture unfortunately extended into the epiphysis, or growth plate. The trauma itself severely damaged the blood vessels responsible for vascularising the epiphysis. This injury presents an orthopaedic emergency. Immediate revascularisation is critical if death to the bone is to be avoided.

---

[3] [1969] 1 QB 428, at p.439.
[4] [1987] AC 750, 2 All ER 909, HL.

The boy was examined in hospital shortly after the fall; however, no diagnosis of the fracture was made. This failure to diagnose was later deemed a breach of duty. When the plaintiff returned to hospital several days later, the fracture was at last detected and he underwent surgery in an effort to revascularise the top of the femur. Unfortunately, the period of delay in diagnosing and operating on the damaged femur had caused the epiphysis to go too long without blood. As a result, the plaintiff had developed avascular necrosis, an immediate disability, with a risk of future development of osteoarthritis.

Expert medical evidence at the trial indicated that the plaintiff had a 75% chance of developing avascular necrosis even if his fracture had been diagnosed and surgical intervention undertaken at the first hospital attendance shortly after the fall. The court therefore found that there was a 25% chance that the defendant's negligence had adversely affected the clinical outcome, i.e. had caused the plaintiff to develop avascular necrosis; the defendant was therefore only responsible for 25% of the total damages which the plaintiff had sustained.

Although the Court of Appeal approved of this approach, the House of Lords reversed it. In allowing the defendant's appeal, their Lordships were of the view that the plaintiff had failed to prove on the balance of probabilities, i.e. 51% or greater, that the negligent care had resulted in a lost chance of a better medical result. The plaintiff was therefore not entitled to any damages. Conversely, if a plaintiff establishes a causative nexus between negligence and damage by a mere 51% or greater, he is entitled to full damages.

This approach to the relationship between causation and quantum is referred to as 'all-or-nothing'. On this basis, their Lordships found that the trial judge erred in awarding proportional damages rather than no damages:

> 'But if the plaintiff had proved on the balance of probabilities that the authority's negligent failure to diagnose and treat his injury promptly had materially contributed to the development of avascular necrosis, I know of no principle of English law which would have entitled the authority to a discount from the full measure of damage to reflect the chance that, even given prompt treatment, the avascular necrosis might well still have developed.'[5]

Many commentators have expressed concern over the apparent inequities that appear to flow from this 'all-or-nothing' approach. However, this mixing of the concepts of causation and quantum arose again recently in

---

[5] *ibid*, at 783.

the 1994 decision of *Judge v. Huntingdon Health Authority*[6], with a rather different and surprising result.

Mrs Judge brought a claim against the Huntingdon Health Authority for alleged negligence in delaying the diagnosis of her breast cancer. She alleged negligence in failing to properly investigate and excise the cancer lump. It was the plaintiff's case that the failure to promptly diagnose and treat her tumour effectively meant a change in predicted clinical outcome from an 80% chance of surviving the cancer down to a 0% chance.

The case was heard by Mr R. Thitheridge QC sitting as a Deputy High Court Judge. As to liability, he found that the surgeon was negligent in failing to pay sufficient attention to the plaintiff's complaint of a 5 mm lump, the GP's referral letter and all of the circumstances of her case. Furthermore, the surgeon should have arranged to follow up the patient. There was no negligence in the surgeon's assertion that the health authority failed to make either fine needle biopsy or ultrasound facilities available to him. However, this non-availability made it more important to ensure that there was no error or mistake in the surgeon's diagnosis.

The court accepted that on the balance of probabilities the delay had resulted in the plaintiff's chances of a successful, disease-free recovery plummeting from 80%, on the basis that there was no nodal involvement at the time the diagnosis should have been made. As to the assessment on quantum, the judge used this analysis to justify an award of 80% of full damages. In doing so the judge relied, *inter alia*, on the judgment of Lord Diplock in *Mallett v. McMonagle*[7]. In support, he cited the following passage from that opinion[8]:

> 'The role of the court in making an assessment of damages which depends upon its views as to what will be and what would have been is to be contrasted with its ordinary function in civil action of determining what was. In determining what did happen in the past a court decides on the "balance of probabilities". Anything which is more probable than not it treats as certain. But in assessing damages, which depend upon its view as to what will happen in the future, or what would have happened in the future if something had not happened in the past, the court must make an estimate as to what are the chances that a particular thing will or would have happened and reflect those chances whether they are more or less than even in the amount of damages which it awards.'[9]

---

[6] [1995] 6 Med LR 223.
[7] [1970] AC 166.
[8] *ibid*, at p. 176.
[9] [1995] 6 Med LR 223, at p. 230.

This approach may be seen as hard to reconcile with the approach accepted in *Hotson*. Clearly, whether for purposes of quantum or causation, both cases involve the court taking a 'view as to what will happen in the future, or what would have happened in the future if something had not happened in the past'. However, the digression in views seems to result from the court in *Judge* equating the reduction in cure itself as constituting damage, regardless of the chances of cure in any event. It is indeed difficult to understand the failure of the court to factor into the assessment of quantum the effect on the plaintiff's survivability of the treatment that the plaintiff did have.

Some effort toward simplifying the relationship between loss of chance and causation was recently made by the Court of Appeal in *Doyle v. Wallace*[10]. One question considered in the judgment was whether the claimant there was entitled to an award of 50% of her past lost wages, where the trial judge found that she only had a 50–50 chance of becoming a drama teacher. Counsel for the defendant appealed on the ground that it was less than probable (i.e. less than 51%) that the plaintiff would have become a drama teacher, and that therefore these losses should have been disregarded. Lord Justice Otton noted:

'There is a key distinction between a plaintiff who has to prove on the balance of probabilities that a particular result would have come about and when he needs to prove only that a chance, which may be less than a probability, of achieving that particularj result has been lost. In his speech in *Davis v. Taylor* [1974] AC 207 Lord Justice Reid said "When the question is whether a certain thing is or is not true – whether a certain event did or did not happen – the court must decide one way or the other... Thus with matters past, the court has to determine on the balance of probabilities whether the defendant's act caused the plaintiff's loss, and if the answer is in the affirmative there is full recovery, will if in the negative there is none." ... *Hotson* was concerned with causation and liability and not with the quantification of chance.'

In affirming the trial judge's assessment of 50% of the loss, Lord Justice Otton also noted the comments of Mr Roger Bell QC (now Mr Justice Bell) in *Anderson v. Davis*[11]. In finding that had it not been for the injuries the plaintiff would have had a two-thirds chance of obtaining promotion as a principal lecturer, he wrote:

'Where the question is one of what might have been the situation in a hypothetical state of facts, then, to the extent that a chance of the event

---

[10] CA 18 June 1998.
[11] [1993] PIQR 287.

necessary to an award of damages falls significantly below 100%, the award should be discounted in my view.'

It would appear therefore that 'loss of chance' is a misnomer when considering causation. Causation remains an issue of fact resolved by an evaluation of the balance of probabilities. Once the probability of loss is established then percentages of loss of chance apply to proportional assessment and quantification of damages.

Material contribution

The concept of 'material contribution' mentioned in *Hotson* continues to cause confusion when causation is considered. Ever since *Bonnington Castings Limited* v. *Wardlaw*[12] employed the term, a defendant's 'material contribution' to the plaintiff's injury has meant that the defendant bears legal responsibility for the damage, even if the defendant's negligence was not the sole cause of the injury. In *Bonnington*, Lord Justice Reid said:

'What is a material contribution must be a question of degree. A contribution which comes within the exception of *de minimis non curat lex* is not material, but I think that any contribution which does not fall within that exception must be material. I do not see how there can be something too large to come within the *de minimis* principle but yet too small to be material.'[13]

The 1988 decision in *Wilsher* v. *Essex Area Health Authority*[14] considered a complex application of the principle of material contribution. The plaintiff, Martin Wilsher, was born three months prematurely with a correspondingly low birth weight. In addition to Martin's general premature condition, or perhaps more accurately, in association with this condition, he suffered further complications, including difficulties with breathing, intraventricular haemorrhage leading to hydrocephalus, a structural cardiac anomaly known as patent ductus arteriosus, and suspected pneumonia. Even in the relatively advanced world of today's neonatology, the care and well-being of such infants presents a tremendous medical challenge. The sequelae of Martin's prematurity made his immediate neonatal condition very worrying, and shortly after birth he was transferred for treatment to a special care baby unit (SCBU).

---

[12] [1956] AC 613; [1956] 1 All ER, HL.
[13] [1956] AC 613 at 621.
[14] [1988] AC 1074, HL.

Once on the neonatal SCBU, Martin was placed on oxygen to assist with stabilising his blood gases and acid balances. It was well known at that time that too much oxygen administered to a premature newborn can damage the infant's retinas – a condition then known as retrolental fibroplasia (RLF), now known as retinopathy of prematurity (ROP). This condition leads to permanent blindness. In order to avoid this potential medical catastrophe, a monitor was used to measure Martin's oxygen saturation. Unfortunately, owing perhaps to the inexperience of the doctor who placed the device, the catheter which fed information on oxygen content from the peripheral blood to the monitor was placed in the plaintiff's vein rather than in the artery. A more senior doctor also attempted to insert the catheter, with the same unfortunate and unrecognised result. Despite concerns over the monitor readings, the error was not recognised until the next day, when it was realised that the plaintiff had been over-saturated with oxygen for many hours.

Although Martin survived his stormy neonatal course, he sadly developed RLF that left him totally blind. At trial, the plaintiff and his legal team were left with the difficult task of proving that 'but for' the incorrect placement of the catheter the damage would not have occurred. While the over-saturation of oxygen that resulted from the incorrectly placed catheter might have caused RLF, when considered along with Martin's other medical problems it was not the only possible cause. In view of the number of serious problems Martin was suffering as a newborn, he faced an uphill struggle to prove that this error was either the sole cause or the material cause of his blindness.

The trial judge found that the senior doctor's failure to detect the misplaced catheter amounted to negligence, and that the burden of proof shifted to the defendant to demonstrate why there was no breach of duty. As to causation, the judge associated the material risk of blindness, which is intended to be avoided by the correct placement of the catheter, with the actual material contribution to Martin's injury. In essence, the judge took the view that since the damage which occurred (RLF) was precisely the risk which the exercise of due care would have avoided, the burden of proof then shifted to the defendant to establish that the negligence did not cause the injury. In so ruling, the judge relied heavily on the decision in *McGhee v. National Coal Board*[15].

In *McGhee*, the plaintiff contracted dermatitis as a result of exposure to brick dust at his employer's (the defendant's) brick kilns. The court found the defendant negligent in not providing adequate facilities for workers to wash the dust off after completing their shifts. They were not negligent, however, for actually exposing the plaintiff and the other workers to the brick dust during the course of the work day itself.

---

[15] [1973] 1 WLR 1.

The difficulty the plaintiff faced was in establishing the causal link between the dermatitis and the negligent failure to provide washing facilities which increased his exposure to brick dust. Logically, in order to succeed, this causative nexus had to be proven to the exclusion of the argument that he would have developed dermatitis in any event from his being exposed non-negligently to brick dust on the job. At the time it was not possible for the plaintiff to prove that 'but for' the lack of washing facilities he would not have contracted dermatitis. However, the court was satisfied that the inability of the plaintiff to wash materially increased the risk and development of the dermatitis, even if it was not the sole cause of it. The court accepted this increase as a 'material contribution'.

While the court in *McGhee* may have had the luxury of not having to consider and evaluate more than one mechanism for the plaintiff's injury, this was surely not the case in *Wilsher*, where several factors could possibly have lead to RLF. Nonetheless, in reliance on *McGhee* and another decision in the medical negligence case of *Clark* v. *MacLennan*[16], the court found for the plaintiff. The Court of Appeal dismissed the defendant's appeal and the case went before the House of Lords.

The Law Lords allowed the defendant's appeal. In doing so they attempted to distinguish *Wilsher* from *McGhee*. The latter involved only one possible cause of the injury – brick dust – for which the breach of duty had increased the risk. However, in *Wilsher* there were effectively five possible causative sources. While the negligence increased the risk of the injury, there had been no showing that this was to the exclusion of the other possible causes. In short, it is the plaintiff's burden of proof to show on the balance of probabilities that the negligence caused or materially contributed to the injury, to the exclusion of other possible causes.

How are practitioners to understand this sometimes-confused *mélange* of phrases variously employed to describe the legal basis of causation? Does *Hotson* tell us something about the law of causation that *Bonnington* and *Wilsher* do not, or vice versa? The simple answer is probably not. In reconciling the cases, it could be suggested that the court in *Hotson* employed the terms 'material contribution' and 'balance of probabilities' similarly, i.e. the nexus between the breaches in duty and the damages alleged to have resulted must be established by a greater than 50% likelihood.

---

[16] [1983] 1 All ER 416. It was held that where a gynaecological procedure was alleged to have been performed too soon following childbirth and thereafter the plaintiff suffered from stress incontinence, the sort of damage which is likely to result if the procedure is done too soon, then the burden shifted to the defendant to explain why his departure from the practice designed to avoid the plaintiff's injury was not negligent. It is the view of the author that this decision is as close as one can get to applying the doctrine of *res ipsa loquitur* without actually calling it such.

Duty and causation

Bolitho v. City and Hackney Health Authority

On occasion, the distinction between duty of care and causation can seemingly become blurred, as in the recent case of Bolitho, already discussed in some detail in Chapter 1. In Bolitho, negligence was established by omission – the doctors failed to attend the young patient. The judge then considered how best to evaluate the consequences of this breach in duty: did the failure of the medical staff to attend Patrick, after having been requested to do so on two occasions, cause his injuries? To an extent the facts belie the apparent complexity of the legal issues involved and deserve a reasonably full recital.

Patrick Bolitho was admitted to St Bartholomew's Hospital on 11 January 1983, suffering from croup. On 12 January, his condition deteriorated and Patrick was having difficulty breathing. On the following day he appeared to be cyanosed; however, he was discharged to home on 15 January. Patrick was readmitted on the following evening. His parents were concerned that his condition had deteriorated at home. He had not slept well and seemed to be having increased difficulty in breathing. That night, 16 January, the paediatric senior house officer (SHO) arranged for Patrick to have one-to-one nursing. The next morning, 17 January, Patrick was seen briefly on a ward round and was noted to have improved.

At about 12.40 PM the nurse assigned to Patrick became concerned at what she thought was a deterioration in his condition. She summoned the sister, who bleeped the registrar instead of going through the usual route of summoning the SHO first. The sister discussed this situation with the registrar directly. The registrar expressed surprise at Patrick's apparent sudden change of condition since the morning round, and said she would attend as soon as possible. Despite this assurance, neither the registrar nor the SHO came to visit Patrick. When the sister returned to Patrick she was surprised to find that he had 'pinked up' and was walking.

Approximately an hour and a half later, at around 2 PM the sister was again summoned back to Patrick by the observation nurse. He was experiencing the same symptoms as at 12.40 PM. The sister again called the registrar. While they were discussing the situation a nurse reported that Patrick had again become pink. The registrar asked that the SHO be called to see Patrick. The SHO gave evidence that her bleeper was not working and she therefore never received the message to attend.

Approximately half an hour later Patrick's condition again changed. The sister instructed the nurse to again call the doctors. While this was taking place, Patrick suffered a respiratory failure which led to a cardiac arrest. There was a period of some nine to ten minutes before his respiratory and cardiac functions resumed. Unfortunately, that period of time was sufficient for Patrick to have suffered severe brain damage. He has subsequently died.

At trial, Mr Justice Hutchinson accepted the sister's version of what was discussed between her and the registrar, and the parties then agreed that the failure of the doctors to attend to Patrick either at 12.40 PM or at 2 PM constituted a breach in the duty which the defendant owed to Patrick. It was further accepted that had Patrick been intubated either at 12.40 PM or at 2 PM, the critical arrest would have been avoided.

As the breach of duty constituted an omission, a two-step approach was employed by the court to allow it to consider what consequences flowed from the breach. The first step was to delve into the realm of the hypothetical, by determining what would or should have happened if the doctor had attended to Patrick at either 12.40 PM or 2 PM. Once the judge accepted the doctor's evidence that she would not have intubated Patrick even had she attended, the court examined whether this hypothetical action in and of itself constituted a breach of duty of care. Counsel for the plaintiff contended that this approach incorrectly injected *Bolam* principles into the consideration of causation. In dismissing the appeal, Lord Browne-Wilkinson, the Vice Chancellor, writing for the House of Lords, approved of the approach taken by the trial judge:

> 'Where, as in the present case, a breach of duty of care is proved or admitted, the burden still lies on the plaintiff to prove that such a breach caused the injury suffered... In all cases the primary question is one of fact: did the wrongful act cause the injury? But in all cases where the breach of duty consists of an omission to do an act which ought to be done (e.g. the failure by a doctor to attend) the factual inquiry is, by definition, in the realms of hypothesis. The question is what would have happened if an event which by definition did not occur had occurred...
>
> 'However in the present case the answer to the question "what would have happened?" is not determinative of the issue of causation. At the trial the defendants accepted that if the professional standard of care required any doctor who attended to intubate Patrick, Patrick's claim must succeed. [The registrar] could not escape liability by proving that she would have failed to take the course which any competent doctor would have adopted. A defendant cannot escape liability by saying that the damage would have occurred in any event because he would have committed some other breach of duty thereafter.'[17]

It is difficult to predict what effect in practice this decision will have on the litigation of medical negligence claims. Clearly, in those relatively rare situations where a claim is based on alleged failure of a doctor, nurse,

---

[17] p. 6.

midwife or other health care provider to attend the patient, then the approach taken by Mr Justice Hutchinson in deciding the causation issues is likely to be urged on the court. Less clear are the circumstances when this approach would apply other than in a case where it is alleged that the omission is the failure of medical staff to attend and treat. Certainly there are many instances of omissions that do not require such an approach. An example is a failure or omission by a surgeon to perform a fine needle aspiration cytology on a woman with a breast lesion appropriate for further investigation.

Assume that the failure itself caused a compromised clinical outcome. Although, strictly speaking, the failure constitutes an omission (that is, a failure to take an action), there need be no intermediate stage between this omission and the outcome that needs to be examined before an evidentiary consideration of the nexus between the clinical management and the damage. Even if the surgeon gives evidence that he never even considered doing a fine needle biopsy, and with the benefit of hindsight would still not have done one, then evaluating breach of duty would seemingly still only involve the consideration of that single omission before considering causation. It is difficult to see how the extra layer of hypothetical duty that emerged in *Bolitho* would apply in as common an oncology example as this.

Many of the difficulties associated with the application of these complex principles of causation to cancer cases are nicely summarised in the following passage:

> 'In light of that test [*Hotson*'s so-called "all-or-nothing" approach], it will be obvious how the estimation of prospects of recovery or the prospects of avoiding death or injury takes on predominating importance in many cases. This exercise has to be gone through firstly on the assumption that the allegedly negligent acts did happen and then on the assumption that they did not. If the prospects of injury or recovery lie on the same side of probability whichever assumption is made, then there is no cause of action. The medicine of such calculations is often of forbidding difficulty.'[18]

The assessment of quantum in cancer cases typically mirrors the words of Lord Bridge in *Hotson* when he said:

> 'In some cases, perhaps particularly medical negligence cases, causation may be so shrouded in mystery that the court can only measure statistical chances.'

---

[18] Irwin, S., Fazan, C. and Allfrey, R. (1995) *Medical Negligence Litigation: a Practitioner's Guide.* Legal Action Group, London.

Causation in cancer cases almost always involves statistical speculation on the likelihood that the negligence affected the chances of survival. Both issues presuppose that 'but for' the negligence the percentage chance of either outcome is calculable. In addition, even when survival is not an issue – where the victim's illness is terminal – questions can arise as to the statistical likelihood that the alleged negligence has affected the length, degree and quality of palliative treatment. Some practical examples of causation issues in cancer cases follow:

(1) Has the patient's prospect of recovery or chance of survival been affected by the failure in diagnosis, care or treatment? If so, would the patient's prospect of recovery have been greater than 50% 'but for' the negligence? If yes, is it more likely than not (i.e. greater than 50%) that the increased risk to the patient resulting from the negligence led to the reduced prospect of recovery?

(2) Was the patient's prospect of recovery or survivability less than 50% even if the negligence had not occurred? If so, has any delay or failure in diagnosis or treatment, i.e. any negligence, affected patient outcome in terms of length of survival and quality of life? If yes, is it more likely than not (i.e. greater than 50%) that the negligence contributed to these effects?

If a woman with breast cancer has had a negligent delay in diagnosis, and if the expert evidence suggests that her chance of disease-free survival has been reduced to 30% from 60%, is she entitled to recover 100% of her proven damages, as *Hotson* would indicate, or only 60% of her damages, as *Judge* would suggest? Just how far does *Doyle* go to resolving these issues? One fact seems certain: for the moment it appears that the rationale in *Hotson* prevails when considering issues of causation.

Chapter 3
The Cancer Patient as a Client

Very few illnesses evoke such a sense of doom and gloom as cancer. This reality presents the medical negligence practitioner with one of the most arduous personal and professional challenges. The legal practitioner will find himself acting as advisor and counsellor, supporting both his client and the client's family.

In this chapter, we consider ways in which the cancer patient and his claim can best be managed to help achieve the desired goals from the legal process. By definition, therefore, much of this chapter is devoted to issues faced by claimants' lawyers. However, case management should be an area of keen interest to litigators acting for medical defence organisations and NHS trusts in our world of low profit margins and competitive tendering for contracts.

Although case management is a tool which good litigators employ throughout the entire life of a case, it is not the intention of the authors to use this book as an oppportunity to consider the entire process of litigating medical negligence claims. Indeed the next three chapters deal with managing the pre-action investigation of cancer cases. This is because it is primarily in the investigation that cancer cases distinguish themselves from other medical negligence cases. Recent moves to standardise the process of litigation of clinical negligence claims[1], while at the same time 'front loading' case preparation, require the successful medical negligence litigator more than ever to focus case management and preparation on pre-action tasks. Again, the reader is reminded that the remarks which follow will help supplement the soon to be published pre-action protocols.

---

[1] Practice Direction Medical/Clinical Negligence No 49/1997. *NLJ Practitioner*, 16 January 1998, p. 59.

Strategies for managing the oncology client and the investigation

The legal advisor does well to understand the exhausting effects that the physical and mental stress can have on even the most optimistic and robust of cancer victims.

Of course, this battle weariness is not solely the province of the cancer patient. There are countless other areas of medicine and medical mishap which involve similar stresses and strains on patients. Equally, lawyers defending claims brought by cancer victims would be wrong to interpret this as implying that the resolution of these clients can usually be worn down by protracted litigation. Although generalisations can indeed be unfair, the cancer patient usually wishes to 'see justice done before I die'.

Another, perhaps less obvious, consideration for the newly instructed lawyer is the role that the cultural background of the client can play. Although thankfully an increasing rarity, there are nevertheless some individuals, family units and cultures who, even at the end of the twentieth century, still shun the victims of cancer as social outcasts. It can therefore happen that in addition to all of the stress of the treatment and the prospect of facing the legal process, the client may actually have the added trauma of having to shoulder these burdens alone.

When cultural issues play a role in the response of the client's family or social group to the client's cancer, the lawyer will need to be careful to understand from the initial instructions with whom they will be dealing. Will the lawyer in effect be prevented from meeting or seeking support from the family? If it is the victim who wishes to avoid contact with the lawyer, from whom is the lawyer authorised to take instructions?

It is axiomatic that all medical negligence practitioners should strive to complete claims as quickly as possible given the particular circumstances of their case. It would be neither too unfair nor too inaccurate to observe that, until recently, unfocused and undirected litigation of medical negligence claims has been the rule rather than the exception. Arguably, no class of medical negligence victim is more needy in terms of an early and expeditious resolution or disposition of his claim than the cancer victim.

It would be simplistic to suggest that the client is generally desirous of seeing the matter to an end before succumbing to what he may understand to be a fatal illness. His motivation for seeking legal redress may be almost entirely due to concerns for family he will be leaving behind.

Although perhaps trite, it still bears remembering that victims of medical negligence generally approach compensation claims with motives quite different from those seen by legal consumers in other areas of the profession. Few scientifically valid studies have been conducted into the reasons why such clients ultimately approach a legal representative for advice or assistance. Nonetheless, most practitioners report empirically that rarely do such client's motives *ab initio* involve the recovery of compensation.

Indeed, one very recent study into this issue confirms that compensation and punishment ranked down the list of motivations behind medical litigation. The study considered the goal- and non-goal-oriented reasons for litigating medical negligence claims. Over 100 medical negligence plaintiffs or their families responded to detailed questionnaires regarding their completed cases. The case types related to a wide range of medical specialties. The most frequently given reason for litigation was medical accountability (28%) – acknowledgement of a mistake, investigation and disciplinary action. The second most frequently cited reason for litigation was the patient's desire for an explanation or apology (22%). Not far behind this was the patient's desire to see an improvement in care, to prevent the same thing happening again (19%). At the very bottom of the list are compensation (12%) and punishment (2%).

It is in many ways a reflection of the problems encountered by cancer patients generally that their concerns often go far beyond the usual motives which characterise the victims of medical accidents. With such clients the need for quick investigation and, if appropriate, litigation becomes paramount.

The most critical factor in ensuring the speedy completion of any medical negligence claim is the extent to which the lawyer for the victim is able to enlist the assistance of the legal representative for the defendant. Despite popular perceptions amongst many plaintiffs' lawyers, very few defence lawyers would be unwilling to help expedite disclosure of case notes, lab reports, histopathology sections or slides, radiography studies and the like if they are made aware that a client's prognosis is not good.

Recently, one of the authors was instructed to investigate the case of a 53-year-old woman with stomach cancer. The client had been under the care of a team of general surgeons for nearly three years. It was only after she sought a second opinion at another hospital that her cancer was discovered. Not surprisingly, the client expressed concerns from the outset that her cancer went undiagnosed for a period of several years, despite repeated visits to the hospital with a myriad of gastric complaints. At the time of initial instructions her prognosis was poor, and in terms of undertaking and completing a full investigation, time clearly was not on her side.

In addition to regular hospital attendance with various members of the medical team, during this three-year period the client underwent numerous radioisotope, ultrasonic and biochemical investigations, all without a positive result. Not only were the records required to ensure a complete investigation voluminous, they were spread throughout the four corners of the hospital. To make matters slightly more complex, since her cancer had eventually been diagnosed and operated on at another hospital within the same NHS trust, it was necessary to obtain voluntary third-party disclosure from that facility as well.

By sharing the client's plight with the lawyer for the trust, full disclosure of the notes and investigations from both hospitals was achieved within four weeks of initial notification. Even more noteworthy was that this initial contact with the trust's legal advisor was made by telephone. As a result of that solicitor's willingness to co-operate, the requests for the client's records preceded the arrival of the letter before action by some two days.

Three experts, a general surgeon, a radiologist and an oncologist, were contacted during the four-week hiatus while the records were being prepared for disclosure. All agreed in the circumstances to provide expedited reports. The records were sorted and paginated within days of arrival. Instructions to the experts were completed shortly thereafter, and the last of these preliminary reports was received four months to the day from the first meeting with the client. Although the expert reports firmly stated that the claim was unsupportable, the client had the satisfaction of discussing the circumstances of her treatment with the experts and counsel in conference four weeks later. She expressed a feeling of great solace in the fact that her concerns had been thoroughly and independently investigated.

A similar example of appropriate, expedited case management in a tragic case is *Cathryn Shorrock* v. *Crewe Health Authority*.[2] Mrs Shorrock underwent a cervical biopsy and Pap smear in May 1989. Although the biopsy showed no evidence of malignant disease, the smear test was strongly indicative of carcinoma of the cervix. The result was not communicated to either Mrs Shorrock or her GP. Her symptoms persisted and Mrs Shorrock was finally readmitted to hospital one year later, in May 1990. She was then diagnosed with adenocarcinoma of the cervix with lymph node metastases. Despite surgical, chemotherapeutic and radiation treatment, Mrs Shorrock's prognosis was extremely poor, and her condition was gradually deteriorating.

Mrs Shorrock was referred by Action for Victims of Medical Accidents (AVMA), a UK-based organisation dedicated to patients' rights, to one of their panel solicitors in August 1991. A well planned approach to the early investigation of the case, along with the co-operation of the solicitors for the defendant health authority, facilitated relatively rapid disclosure of the necessary medical records in addition to expert evidence from both an oncologist as well as a gynaecologist. Armed with positive evidence and a co-operative opponent, the solicitor for the plaintiff was not only able to extract an admission of liability from the defendant prior to Mrs Shorrock's death, but an interim payment as well.

Regardless of whether the cancer victim's case is or is not successful, the

---

[2] (1993) *AVMA Medical and Legal Journal* (2), p. 13; *PMIL Letter* 9 (5), p. 36.

simple fact that he is able to realise a result in his lifetime gives a sense of justice done. These results would not have been achieved were it not for effective and carefully planned case management. Let us focus on what is meant by 'case management'. Like any project, a medical negligence case involves a series of sequential and parallel tasks which need to be completed in order to achieve a stated objective or outcome.

The initial question posed by an experienced case manager is: 'Should I take this case?' This is something all lawyers ask themselves when they consider taking on a new case. The legal advisor must be sufficiently confident in this area of law to identify appropriate outcomes and to understand the various stages of dispute management involved in achieving those outcomes. The client's first and most fundamental questions, 'How much will it cost?' and 'What happens next?', can only be answered by a medical negligence litigator with experience of case management.

Meandering, undirected medical negligence cases slowly grinding their way over a period of years through the courts will surely soon become museum pieces of a bygone age of litigation. The reforms envisaged by Lord Woolf, and the changes to funding and procedure likely to be adopted over the next few years, will work to the great advantage of lawyers able to understand how to manage cases effectively. Streamlined procedures and preparation will help keep costs and time within defined limits while expediting the resolution of the legal issues: fundamental needs of both society and the cancer patient. We next look at possible suggestions and strategies for improving the effectiveness of early case preparation in cancer claims.

Preparing to meet the cancer client

Taking initial details

We have already discussed in some detail the fundamental changes afoot in the funding and process of civil litigation. All of these changes revolve around the principles that litigation generally, and for our purposes medical negligence litigation, must proceed more expeditiously and be less costly if the interests of and access to justice are to be extended to as wide a portion of the population as possible. For litigators, and medical negligence litigators in particular, managing risk begins with the very first client contact and starts with the basic question: 'Do we want this case?'

In virtually every area of civil litigation, careful preparation before the first attendance with the client is imperative. In view of the complexity of the technical aspects of medicine there is a great need here for pre-attendance preparation. The new client is tremendously supported by the observation that his legal advisor not only has a grasp of the legal issues but also of the medical issues. There are two steps involved in preparing for the first attendance: obtaining the necessary information from the client in advance to know what to research, and then performing the necessary research itself.

In recognition of the importance of gathering relevant information as early as possible in the investigation, more and more specialist medical firms or practitioners are identifying and specially training members of staff to field initial client inquiries. Increasingly this person is medically trained and qualified.

'In-house' nurses, midwives and physicians now have several vital roles in terms of case preparation. Their training and experience at taking patient histories in a clinical setting make them the obvious choice for amassing the necessary pre-attendance information for the potential client. In fact, it is the experience of several practices that many patients are relieved to speak with a nurse or non-legal member of staff on the occasion of the first contact. Often prospective clients will experience conflict about discussing their problems with a lawyer. They realise that they will need to deal with the lawyer in order to explore fully their concerns, yet there may be a subconscious apprehension about becoming involved in the legal process. The nurse is an ideal 'halfway house' to helping the patient overcome these anxieties.

However, regardless of whether or not the person dealing with the potential client at this stage is medically qualified, certain information is of critical importance if the legal team is going to be able to adequately prepare. In addition to routine questions, the following queries should be addressed:

What is the basis of the patient's complaint?

Why is the patient contacting a legal advisor? What is it about his care or treatment that caused him concern? The most common concern expressed by cancer patients is whether there was a possible delay in the diagnosis or a failure to diagnose the illness. Less frequently, patients will be primarily concerned that the treatment was in some way inappropriate.

What is the best description, name or understanding of the nature of the cancer?

Do not be surprised if the patient is unable to give an answer to the most obvious question of all: 'What cancer have you been diagnosed with?' Remember that a sizeable majority of the non-medical population has very little understanding that 'cancer' is a descriptive title for approximately 200 pathologies. Owing to the different treatments and outcomes for different cancers, it is absolutely crucial to identify the primary site of the cancer.

Knowing the identity of the patient's cancer will help focus the pre-interview research on the signs, symptoms, diagnostic and treatment parameters of that specific disease. Even where the patient is unable to describe anything other than the generic name of the cancer, for example 'skin cancer', this should provide a platform from which the research can commence. Needless to say, this general description does not facilitate the more focused preparation that would be possible if it was known precisely which form of skin cancer the patient suffered.

When did the care in question occur?

This is a necessary inquiry, not just in oncology but in all medical negligence cases. However, in few areas of medicine has there been as much scientific, technological and medical advancement than in oncology. Treatment has changed dramatically and many of the treatments employed a few years ago seem, with the unerring vision of hindsight, today to be primitive. So in this area it is crucially important that the lawyer must take into account the care available at the time of the treatment, and not that available at the time of the investigation or litigation.

What does the patient understand to be his current condition?

'How are you doing now?' It can be very distressing and upsetting to a cancer patient or a member of that patient's family to answer questions about prognosis over the telephone, and before the first meeting. Of course it is important in any event to know how the patient is doing, and it also allows the litigator to learn a little more about the course of the illness and the likely pace of the investigation.

Who will be attending the first meeting, and what is their relationship to the client?

Anticipate that much of what will be discussed at the first interview will be difficult for the patient and the patient's family. It is important to be sensitive to the social dynamic of the patient's family unit. If it is not the patient, who is it within the family unit that you will be relying on for information? And with whom are you able to discuss difficult and emotive issues of prognosis and life expectancy?

Case screening

An increasing number of specialist medical negligence practices now routinely 'screen' their cases after considering the information adduced from the initial client contact. The principle behind case screening is a simple one: lawyers should be focusing their time and effort on cases that have sufficient merit to warrant the commitment of the human and financial resources of the practice. Not every prospective client that seeks help could or should have his case accepted. To do so would dilute the efforts which are required on behalf of other, perhaps more meritorious, claims.

Screening, therefore, is the process by which lawyers consider and decide which cases to accept for further investigation and possible litigation. The process itself is as varied as the number of firms who employ it. What follows is one proven and successful model.

General criteria or guidelines are first agreed which help define those types of cases and areas of practice where instructions will be accepted. It is important to note that these guidelines are intentionally flexible to allow for special consideration to be given to the unusual or particularly challenging case. Initial details are taken from the prospective client by one of the in-house medical assistants. These facts are then edited down to the essential, relevant information that addresses the acceptance criteria, and then entered onto a computer presentation system.

The fee earners then all meet on one appointed day per week, when the medico-legal assistants then present the potential new matters they have received details on during the previous week. Each potential case is presented separately with discussion and debate. A group decision is then reached as to whether the practice is in a position to assist the potential client. Once that decision is reached, a brief discussion ensues identifying which fee earner would be best suited to deal with the new case. This allows the team to direct particular cases, like oncology cases, to those who have previous experience of managing these claims. The client, the Legal Aid board or any other funder should not have to pay unnecessarily for the medical lawyer to learn his trade.

Background reading

The fee earner should now focus on the initial client meeting. The specialist legal practitioner will undertake some medical research which will assist in preparing critically important questions dealing with the merits of negligence and causation. It is important to remember that each of the dozens of diseases that fall under the general name 'cancer' have their own presenting symptoms, their own natural histories and different prognoses. In short, specific questions tailored to the patient's specific form of cancer must be asked if the litigator is to be in any position to help progress the pre-action investigation.

The reader will appreciate that the medical chapters of this volume have been designed to facilitate easy reference to much of the needed background material on the more common cancers. Let us briefly review the importance of the information, as it will be set out in those chapters: epidemiology; presentation and investigation; staging and grading; treatment.

Epidemiological details assist the lawyer in understanding the frequency and social characteristics of a given cancer. This can, and often does, provide clues to what the standard of informed care should have been in recognising and treating any given cancer, and these are as follows:

(1) Was the cancer so rare that a GP would not likely have been expected to ever encounter it?

(2) If so, is it likely that a body of reasonable and responsible opinion will be found to defend the failure to diagnose or treat?

(3) To what extent does the client fit the description of the sort of person more likely to have developed this cancer?

(4) How does this relationship between the epidemiological profile and the plaintiff's characteristics affect the expected standard of care in diagnosis and treatment?

Understanding presentations and investigations almost invariably strikes at the heart of the litigator's consideration of negligence or breach of duty:

(1) What were the presenting symptoms?

(2) How well do they mirror the symptoms usually described for the cancer?

(3) What tests or investigations should have been undertaken?

(4) What follow-up was appropriate in the circumstances?

Understanding the stage or grading of the tumour or cancer is the most critical piece of evidence to evaluating causation. However, it should not be forgotten that this information might also play a key role in determining whether a breach of duty has occurred.

(1) What was the stage of the tumour or cancer at the time of diagnosis?

(2) What treatment is accepted as appropriate for that stage or grade of cancer?

(3) What inferences can be drawn about the natural history of the cancer from its staging or grading at the time of diagnosis, i.e. at what stage was the cancer likely to have been at a specified time prior to diagnosis?

(4) What does the staging of the cancer tell us about the patient's prognosis?

Finally, a discussion of the treatment used for any given cancer not only helps the litigator to understand whether that care itself has been acceptable, but also how the treatment may affect patient condition and prognosis, or mortality and morbidity in the short, medium and long terms. This information is likely to feature prominently in decisions related to heads of damage and calculations of damages:

(1) What treatment has the patient/client undergone?

(2) How closely does the treatment correspond with those described treatments for the patient/client's given stage or grade of cancer?

(3) To what extent is treatment for the patient/client's particular cancer related to the stage or grade of the illness? In other words, does the patient suffer from a form of cancer where earlier diagnosis might have resulted in less invasive or extensive treatment?

(4) What short-, medium- and long-term side-effects are reported for the treatment carried out on the patient/client?

In addition to a general text of medical diagnosis and treatment, such as *The Merck Manual*[3] and a medical dictionary suitable for the lawyer's level of medical acumen, the litigator should have a least one general medical text in his office related to principles of diagnosing and treating cancer. As the legal practitioner is instructed in more and more medical negligence oncology claims, his 'medical library' will be supplemented by more specialised texts.

Whichever texts are used, it is fundamental that before the client arrives for the first appointment, the litigator should be prepared to ask not only general questions, but specific questions as well. These specific or focused questions should be designed to obtain more specific information to assess both negligence and causation aspects of the client's diagnosis, treatment and prognosis.

The first interview

A successful interview is one that has a plan, a direction. The practitioner starts by determining the purpose of the meeting, what needs to be achieved, and how best to achieve this. The first meeting between the client and the lawyer serves many purposes: an opportunity to meet, a chance to discover and exchange important background information, a time to

---

[3] Published by Merck, Sharpe & Dohme Research Laboratories, a division of Merck & Co., Inc., and found in many general bookshops as well as nearly all medical or academic bookshops.

explain funding options and consequences, and an occasion to discuss the management of the case, to name just a few.

Many of the general rules of so-called 'best practice' of managing the initial client interview apply to all medical negligence cases, not just those involving oncology patients. First, and in many ways foremost, is the importance of putting the client and/or family as much at ease as possible. The extent to which the legal advisor is able to achieve this often difficult objective is the extent to which the necessary information and detail will flow from the prospective client or the family.

Many practitioners wrongly believe that assuming a sympathetic demeanour will both relax and reassure the client. In truth, clients who have endured real hardship can find sympathy from the lawyer to be insincere, superficial and unproductive. What reassures clients and puts them at ease is a professional and confident approach, and a demeanour which convinces the client that the litigator knows this area of the law, is comfortable with the basic concepts of the medicine and understands or empathises with the client's plight.

It is unwise for the litigator to ever cross the line between sympathy and empathy. At the same time, the lawyer must resist setting too much of a commanding tone. This is more difficult to avoid than one might think, and the litigator's questioning technique is an important, but often overlooked, factor.

When conducting the first interview, it is critical that the litigator's knowledge of the medical issues, however extensive, should not be imposed upon the prospective client. For example, avoid telling clients in closed, leading questions what their symptoms should have been. Begin by asking open-ended questions to elicit from the client what, in fact, the symptoms were. Open-ended questions begin with: 'Who', 'What', 'Where', 'When', 'Why', 'How', 'Please describe...' or 'Tell me...'. The object of using this form of questioning is to get patients to tell their stories in their own words, rather than the litigator 'suggesting' to the patient what really happened or should have happened. Equally, if the legal advisor is of the view that during the questioning there may have been some important details which were either glossed over or ignored by the patient, then more direct, leading questioning may be appropriate.

Consider this example: you have been asked to meet with a prospective client who has recently undergone extensive treatment for breast cancer. At the initial interview she expresses concern that her treatment was more invasive and extensive than it should have been. Although she knows little about the medicine of breast cancer, she explains that in her mind there has possibly been a delay in diagnosis of several months. Because your background reading on the epidemiology and diagnosis has taught you that a family history of breast cancer is a diagnostic risk indicator, you have asked the prospective client whether there is such a history in her family. The client answers that in fact both her mother and her mother's mother suffered from breast cancer.

You should of course now be focused on trying to establish with the client whether the doctor elicited this history. At the appropriate time during the interview it is advisable in the first instance to ask the open-ended question, 'What history did the doctor take from you?' Conversely, to begin by asking a leading question such as, 'You told the doctor about your family history of breast cancer, didn't you?' is very likely to produce at least two negative outcomes. First, the question alone, the unspoken 'Of course you did! Any sensible person would have!' places enormous and unnecessary pressure on the lay person. It has the effect of somehow imputing blame on the patient if the information was not offered. Second, and equally important, the question may consciously or subconsciously shape or suggest a response from the prospective client.

There can be little doubt that the open-ended question is more apt to evince full and accurate information with less aggression. When answering open-ended questions there is always the possibility that the client will unintentionally avoid volunteering relevant details. If, after having asked the non-leading question about the history taken, the lawyer notices the absence of any mention of the family history, then slightly more directive questions can assist in teasing out the desired information: 'Did you or your doctor discuss either your mother or grandmother's cancer? If so, what was said?'

One of the characteristics of the inexperienced litigator is the inability to listen. No one person in the 'litigation team' is ignored more often than the client is. The good lawyer seeks to ask questions which will get the client talking and then listens and notes the answers carefully. Open-ended questions are designed to force the litigator to listen and not speak.

One of the most important pieces of information which any litigator should attempt to elicit is the answer to the following rarely asked question: what would the prospective client like to achieve? Litigators assume, quite dangerously at times, that when prospective clients appear in their office for the first time, they obviously are there to litigate for monetary compensation. This is perhaps not an unreasonable assumption, but nonetheless is of course one of the major avoidable misunderstandings in medical negligence litigation today; avoidable because it results purely from the lawyer's failure to address this issue with the client early in the initial interview.

Often the prospective client is only seeking an apology or an explanation. He may actually have no interest whatsoever in litigation, and has simply come to the lawyer's office because he has no idea what the options are or where else he can turn for assistance. The litigator must be prepared to discuss alternatives to litigation and to advise the prospective client as to where else to turn if litigation is not the preferred route of redress for the complaint. The legal advisor should consider whether other avenues of investigation, such as the complaints procedure or referral to other agencies like the Community Health Council, are more appropriate to achieve the patient's desired result.

With this approach to the conduct of the initial interview in mind, what follows are a few areas or issues to focus on when interviewing clients in cases involving missed or delayed diagnoses in the more common types of cancer cases. It is hoped that this section will provide a useful starting point for developing a standardised approach to obtaining information from the cancer patient at the first meeting.

Information to obtain from the client

(1) Patient's date of birth.

(2) Patient's age.

(3) Current address and, if different, address at the time of treatment.

(4) Take details of any other names the patient may have used during the course of the treatment.

(5) The defendant may require the patient's National Insurance number for the Compensation Recovery Unit (CRU) or for identification.

(6) General explanation from the client as to why he has sought legal advice and what damage he has suffered.

(7) Age of the patient at the time of the onset of symptoms.

(8) Significant medical history, including any and all hospitalisations.

(9) General review of the patient's fitness and health.

(10) Review of any family history of cancer or serious illness.

(11) Detailed list of all symptoms that pre-dated the diagnosis of cancer.

(12) Detailed history of any possible exposure to environmental carcinogens.

(13) Obtain detailed history from the patient of each symptom, including when it was first detected, how it first appeared, how long it lasted, and how it has progressed.

(14) List of names and addresses of all involved doctors and hospitals and any other allied health care professionals.

(15) When did patient first seek medical advice and from whom?

(16) When was the patient first seen by a health care professional?

For each attendance with a doctor or at a hospital:

(17) Who was present during the consultation or examination i.e. witnesses?

(18) Full description of history given at the attendance.

(19) Which medical or nursing staff examined or consulted with the client?

(20) Full description of examination performed and tests carried out.

(21) What advice was given regarding prescription or follow-up?

(22) What did the medical staff discuss regarding the patient's condition and prognosis?

(23) How was patient told of the diagnosis? How did the patient react?

(24) Describe the progress of symptoms after the examination.

(25) Describe fully all treatments undergone; if the patient underwent radiation therapy, how many fractions did the patient undergo, dose per fraction and total dose?

(26) Discuss what support, emotional or otherwise, the patient has received from outside agencies, counsellors, family, etc.

(27) Description of the patient's physical and psychological response and recovery to the treatments.

(28) How compliant was the patient in adhering to medical advice?

(29) Describe fully what, if anything, the client has been told about his current condition and prognosis.

(30) What further treatment or consultations have been or are to be arranged?

(31) Has the patient employed any complaint procedure and, if so, with what result?

(32) What is the patient's desired outcome? What relief does he seek?

Whatever the format of the interview, the legal advisor must of course pay careful attention to note all relevant information related from the client or the family. This detailed note will form the basis of a preliminary client statement around which the initial investigation will evolve. By the conclusion, the legal advisor must have obtained enough information to prepare a statement which should be forwarded to the client for approval and signature as soon as possible following the interview.

The preliminary statement, or written version of the relevant details, should be prepared as soon as possible after the conclusion of the interview. The format should add structure, not substance, to the client's history. It is usual, but not mandatory, that the statement relates the events described by the client in a chronological order. The legal advisor should use numbered paragraphs, with each paragraph containing only one idea.

In addition to being able to fashion the statement, by the end of the first interview the legal advisor must obtain enough information to make an informed decision as to whether the potential claim has sufficient merit to warrant further investigation. If the decision is that the complaint should progress to full investigation, then the litigator must explain to the client the way forward – what is the plan of action?

No interview should be completed without the client knowing precisely what steps need to be taken to ensure the completion of the investigation, how long it is likely to take and, most importantly, how much it is likely to cost. The likely impact of the changes in funding arrangements already underway has been discussed earlier. Cost restraints imposed by fast-track litigation, or clients funding their own investigations prior to an underwriter agreeing to insure their legal action, will require litigators in all areas of medical negligence litigation to budget their investigations and litigation in advance. This exercise can only be satisfactorily completed if the litigator is familiar with the concepts of case management discussed earlier in this chapter.

If the client is likely to qualify for legal aid then it is of course necessary that the appropriate forms are explained to the client and completed. Clients unable to qualify will need to be advised carefully of the financial risks and burdens of undertaking expensive litigation. They will need to know that the complex nature of medical negligence litigation is such that, before any decisions can be made on the relative risks of litigation, a full investigation will have to be undertaken. The lawyer should also explain that the investigation itself will at the very least include disclosure of the case notes and obtaining preliminary opinions from independent experts.

In case planning and budgeting, the fee earner should attempt to think laterally in considering what steps of the investigation run in parallel in order to save time and money. For example, must you always await the receipt of the medical notes before making an initial approach to an expert inquiring whether he will be willing to provide an opinion when the notes have been received? The answer is of course 'No'. Overlapping two stages of investigation may result in a cancer patient/client who is able to know the results of the investigation rather than die not knowing.

In short, these initial contacts with the client are critical to establish both the lawyer's credibility and the client's confidence in the process of investigation and litigation. Care must be given to ensure that all of the client's concerns are fully addressed, and that all necessary information has been explained to the client in simple terms. A detailed note of the client's answers will provide the basis of the preliminary statement of proof which will help drive the investigation forward.

All of this can only be achieved through preparation. Preparation even before the client enters the lawyer's office for the first time may well mean the difference between a quick and accurate investigation, and one which is protracted, filled with errors and ultimately produces incorrect advice to the cancer patient. The next chapter examines how to avoid these problems by considering some specific ways of managing the investigation.

Chapter 4
Managing the Investigation

Chapter 3 considered strategies for managing the early investigation of the potential merits of the oncology case by obtaining as much relevant information about the progress, diagnosis and prognosis of the client's disease at the initial client interview. Although the litigator should always look to the experts to provide the material, if not definitive, answers to questions of negligence and causation, there is much the litigator can do to make the job of the expert easier and help the expert focus on critical issues.

In the new age of cost-effective litigation, the ability of the litigator to assist the expert in the expeditious preparation of a fair and impartial report is not only a luxury for the expert, it is a necessity for the financial success of the litigator's practice. The key to cost- and time-effective investigations and litigation is early preparation. 'Front loading' of the preparation of the claim is just another way of saying what good lawyers have known for many years: success comes from early and thorough investigation.

The first step is ensuring that disclosure from the potential defendants and any third parties is both appropriate and as complete as possible. What materials, documents and information should be disclosed and how is disclosure best undertaken?

After considering disclosure, attention is focused on methods for obtaining competent expert opinion on issues of both a breach of duty and a causative nexus between any breach and the resultant damage.

Pre-action disclosure

The Civil Litigation Committee of the Law Society has now issued a revised edition[1] of *Medical Negligence and Personal Injury Claims: A Protocol for Obtaining Hospital Medical Records*. Along with the Clinical Disputes Forum

---
[1] June 1998.

report on pre-action protocols[2], this voluntary procedure for obtaining medical records in medical negligence cases is, in theory, designed to avoid the lengthy and expensive disclosure described by Lord Woolf in his inquiry into the civil justice system. As has been stated previously, at the time of writing the final version of the protocol mandated by the new rules of civil procedure is not yet available.

However, the present protocol utilises standard application and response forms. The purpose of the forms is to standardise and streamline the disclosure of records and other documents and materials from hospitals to the patient's legal advisors. It was anticipated that the use of a relatively simple form would reduce time and costs principally by reducing the need for sometimes lengthy letters before action and responses.

Although the use of such forms is voluntary, many practitioners have used them over the past two years and have met with mixed results. Nearly as many plaintiffs' legal advisors have found the protocols ineffective as have found them effective. Much of the variation in results would seem to be due to regional factors with variable responses from different area health authorities or trusts.

Voluntary forms aside, several key steps in these pre-action procedures, such as the preparation and disclosure of detailed case summaries and relevant chronologies, are already becoming the standard foundation of pre-action notification of a potential claim. Indeed the medical/clinical negligence practice direction specifies that the plaintiff should serve a letter before action at least three months before issue of the writ setting out 'the fullest available information as to the basis of the claim'[3]. In the absence of compliance, the court is empowered to grant the defendant 'an appropriate extension of time' within which to serve a defence.

Because the demise of the current methods of investigating medico-legal claims is not a *fait accompli* and much of what exists currently will be retained in one form or another, a review of the *status quo* is more than justified. Indeed, under any system the goals of disclosure must invariably be the delivery to the patient or the patient's legal advisor of all relevant medical records, radiology and imaging materials and documents to all parties as quickly and inexpensively as possible.

There now exists more than one method of obtaining pre-action discovery of a client's medical records. Use of the Access to Health Records Act 1990 facilitates relatively rapid and inexpensive disclosure of defined medical records. Disclosure can be made either to the patient/client directly by applying at the hospital, or through a nominated person

---

[2] *Pre-Action Protocol for the Resolution of Clinical Disputes*, Version 1, July 1998.
[3] Practice Direction No 49/1997 Medical/Clinical Negligence. *NLJ Practitioner*, 16 January 1998, p. 59.

authorised by the patient/client to obtain the records[4]. This nominated person is usually the patient/client's legal advisor.

Quite apart from the perceived time and cost benefits associated with this procedure of statutory disclosure, many litigators would argue that access under the 1990 Act has potential strategic benefits as well. Primary in this regard is the probability that a request by the patient for access to his medical records is not likely to arouse the suspicions of the defendant health authority or NHS trust or their legal advisors. The reality is that so many patients are now asking for access, and the request forms themselves are so routine, that it is extremely difficult for the hospital staff responsible for handling these requests to actually give any more thought to these applications than the administrative task allows. Exceptions can occur when the administration staff responsible for dealing with patients' requests for access to their records have been alerted to potential problems in the clinical management.

Although an increasing number of hospital trusts now operate some form of clinical risk management scheme, the majority simply do not have the human and financial resources to fully review all of the medical care and treatment involved in every request for access to records under the 1990 Act. If the hospital simply provides the patient with the records, it of course has no idea whether that patient intends to forward them on to a lawyer. Some litigators see this lacuna in the health authority or trust's awareness of a medico-legal investigation as an opportunity to exploit its inability to prepare a defence strategy to the potential claim.

With respect to litigators who employ this tactic, the implementation of this approach to the investigation of medical negligence claims can be counter-productive. This is because under the 1990 Act patients are not entitled as a matter of right to all their records. First, the Act as a whole only relates to records that came into existence after the date that the Act came into effect – 1 November 1991. Any necessary records which pre-date 1 November 1991 will not be disclosed under the Act unless the hospital voluntarily chooses otherwise. Second, the holders of the records have the right to withhold disclosure of notes in circumstances where they feel disclosure might not be in the best interests of the patient[5].

Thus, if this approach is followed the patient's legal advisor can have no real assurance of the extent to which the medical records disclosed form a complete and full record of the clinical care and management.

Currently, the traditional letter before action from the plaintiff's legal advisor to either the defendant or the defendant's legal advisor still remains one of the best ways to ensure maximum disclosure of relevant documents and materials at the earliest possible stage. The schedule of documents that accompanies the letter before action should request both general information and items specific to the case type. The should provide a basic outline of the facts entitling the applicant to disclosure to comply

---

[4] See the Access to Health Records Act 1990, section 3.
[5] See Access to Health Records Act 1991, section 5.

with the language and intent of section 33(2) of the Supreme Court Act 1981 and Order 24, rule 7(A) of the Rules of the Supreme Court 1965. The facts should be sufficient to set the basis for the potential claim, the possibility that both the patient and the hospital are likely to be parties to an action for damage, and the fact that the records in possession of the latter are needed to investigate the merits of the claim.

What follows, therefore, is intended as a guide to items which should form part of the litigator's standard list for pre-action discovery in cancer cases. In the event that the Woolf reforms bring about the demise of the letter before action, it is hoped that this list will maintain its relevance as a guide for the sorts of documents the plaintiff's lawyer should be seeking during disclosure or discovery.

PRE-ACTION DISCLOSURE SCHEDULE IN AN ONCOLOGY CASE: HOSPITAL

Any and all surgical, medical, nursing and drug records, chemotherapy, radiotherapy or other treatment and investigation notes, test results, correspondence and any other documents related to the treatment of [PATIENT NAME] *including but not limited to* the following items:

(1) Accident and emergency department card and records

(2) Letter of referral from GP

(3) Doctor's notes on admission

(4) Nurses' notes and cardex from admission

(5) Medical or nursing patient care and/or treatment plans

(6) Nurses' records

(7) Clinical and medical records and notes

(8) Medical and nursing records from out-patient clinics

(9) Operation records and notes

(10) Anaesthetic records and notes

(11) Intensive care charts, records and notes

(12) Consent forms

(13) Test requests, including blood, biochemistry and other studies, along with all results

(14) Full schedule of all tissue and bodily samples retained in pathology including your undertaking to preserve the same

(15) Fluid balance charts

(16) Drug charts

(17) Prescriptions

(18) Temperature, blood pressure, pulse and respiration charts

(19) Electrocardiogram (ECG) reports

(20) Electroencephalogram (EEG) reports

(21) Blood transfusion record

(22) Copies of any and all radiographic studies, diagnostic or planning, along with request forms, reports and results, including:
  (a) X-rays (plain and enhanced);
  (b) computerised tomography (CT) scans;
  (c) magnetic resonance imaging (MRI) or nuclear magnetic resonance (NMR) studies;
  (d) mammography;
  (e) ultrasonography;
  (f) bone scans.

(23) Dosimetry charts and plans

(24) Radiotherapy prescription charts

(25) All quality assurance manuals for the radiotherapy equipment and software employed in the treatment of the patient

(26) All quality assurance and maintenance records, reports and documents for the radiotherapy equipment and software employed in the treatment of the patient

(27) Quality assurance manuals, procedures, records and protocols for pathology and cytology labs employed or used to examine, read or interpret the patient's histology or cytology samples

(28) Documents related to any untoward incident or accident investigation by the hospital, NHS trust, area or regional health authority

(29) Copies of any and all documents created for or used by any risk management or peer committee reviews including statements, correspondence, transcripts, evaluation forms and results

(30) All correspondence between other doctors, hospitals and health care professionals.

Often oncology clients raise concerns about the care and treatment they received from their GP. But, regardless of whether the GP's care is alleged to be negligent, his records must also be obtained. Remember to have the client sign appropriate authorisations for the disclosure of the medical notes before the first interview is completed. This is often overlooked and can lead to an extra week or more of wasted time.

Requests for the GP's records should be addressed to him specifically and need only be in the form of a letter. The letter should make it clear whether the GP's care is in question, or whether the focus of the investigation is elsewhere and the records are required for the sake of completeness. As with hospital trusts, it is best to specify what documents are sought. Advise the GP that you require 'copies of any and all documents, including cardex, correspondence with other doctors and hospitals, test requests and reports, including but not limited to the documents and materials contained on the enclosed schedule.' Then enclose a copy of the schedule of documents as above.

An additional circumstance that merits mention is the need to obtain disclosure of quality assurance records, reports and protocols from cytology labs employed by health authorities or NHS trusts. This information is often voluminous and can be tedious to review. Nonetheless, the success of numerous claims has rested on violations of protocols and quality assurance procedures.

The protocols ordinarily contain invaluable information on matters such as the number of slides one laboratory technician is permitted to review in a given period. One need only recall the increasing numbers of incidents reported in the last two to three years of mass errors in cytology reporting to know how important this information can potentially be in establishing a breach or breaches of duty.

It is accepted that in the vast majority of such incidents the health authority or trust has usually accepted the existence of a breach of duty, and claims are generally contested over the issue of causation. Nonetheless, if the litigator finds himself in the position of having to press forward in the investigation of breach of duty, then pressure can be brought to bear by requesting the laboratory protocols and guidelines.

In the first instance, the litigator should request this information directly from the potential defendant. In the event of non-disclosure from the potential defendant, and in the unusual circumstance that liability appears to be in issue, the litigator should then not hesitate to send a letter before action to the laboratory as a potential defendant requesting disclosure directly from it.

Third-party disclosure is disclosure sought from hospitals or doctors who are not at the time of disclosure intended or potential defendants. Pre-action disclosure in these circumstances is voluntary. Be sure to include in your letter of request that the care that party delivered to the potential plaintiff is not in issue, and that no proceedings are being actively investigated or considered against that party.

Working with the disclosed records, notes and materials

Once the records have arrived, the litigator must satisfy himself that the disclosure is complete. This does not mean that he could or should be able to identify every relevant record that may be missing. However, the litigator should know enough about cancer to ensure that there are no overt omissions. Nothing slows the pace of a medico-legal investigation more than instructing an expert with an incomplete set of documents. While it is accepted that the expert is often the only person who can properly advise whether disclosure is complete, the litigator assuming responsibility for a preliminary check in the first instance should limit the risk of this happening.

Even in the original, medical records are a challenge for any lay person, but photocopies make the job more difficult. Any practitioner with experience of even one medical negligence investigation will know that photocopied notes disclosed through pre-action discovery are invariably in an order other than that required to make any sense of them. More often than not they appear to have been forwarded after a brief stop at the local casino for a croupier to practise shuffling techniques. Regardless of this, it is essential that the notes be appropriately ordered. Nothing is more infuriating to an expert than to start work on a file by ordering disorganised, randomly assembled medical bundles.

Employing in-house nursing or medico-legal staff in the process of sorting and paginating the records disclosed can save many hours of medical experts' and legal practitioners' time. Their backgrounds will allow them to identify records and help with the chronological organisation of the copies. In any event, regardless of whether the fee earner or the medico-legal assistant sorts and paginates the notes, the end result should be records separated into logical subsections such as clinical notes, nurses' records, test results, temperature, pulse and respiration (TPR) charts, fluid balance charts, prescriptions, etc., all arranged chronologically within those sections. X-rays, MRIs, CT scans and other radiographic plates should be listed in a comprehensive schedule. Now the notes can be inspected properly.

The job of reviewing the records and documents for completion is not one that should ordinarily be delegated. The fee earner responsible for the conduct of the investigation should review the prepared bundles. While nurses or other staff can help by organising the notes, the fee earner will be the individual preparing or supervising the preparation of the expert instructions, meeting with the client and attending the conferences with counsel. All of these tasks can only be done effectively if the litigator understands the basics of his case and is familiar with the records.

A close check should be made that the photocopies do not have any crucial dates, times or entries partially or totally cropped off in the copying process. Are there requests for tests or studies without the corresponding results? Are there X-ray requests for which no copies have been provided? Incompleteness of disclosure may well require the issuance of an originating application for discovery through the use of the Rules of the Supreme Court, Order 24, rule 7A (see earlier). However, more often than not, incomplete disclosure is remedied by contacting the solicitor acting for the defendant.

There are matters that warrant specific attention when seeking discovery in an oncology case. Below are highlighted some of the more important items of information the litigator may wish to look for while considering the discovery provided.

Histopathology

It is axiomatic that the only method of definitively diagnosing any tumour or cancer is by histological examination of biopsy material. Whenever the diagnosis or staging of a cancer is in doubt, it is critical that the legal advisors have access to the histopathology samples. Requesting this material from the outset will potentially shave weeks off the time needed to investigate the claim.

Tissue samples will have been removed and sent to the pathology laboratory for both gross and microscopic examination. Once received and examined, the selected tissues may be fixed in paraffin blocks. Very thin slices of these blocks, called sections, are then prepared for microscopic examination. Examination of the cells on the slides helps to confirm the type, the grade, and ultimately the prognosis of the tumour.

Confirmation of these details is critical for a consideration of negligence and causation. The grade will give valuable evidence as to the aggressiveness of the cancer. Evidence of a high mitotic or division rate is very often an indication that the cancer is fast growing. This evidence is critical for the expert oncologist to consider when providing an indication of the stage of development the cancer or tumour was likely to have been at when it is alleged that it should have been diagnosed. In other words, this information is central to answering the question of what the clinical outcome would have been but for the negligence.

In terms of breach of duty itself, the histological samples, along with the reports from the pathologists or histopathologists, may in and of themselves be evidence of negligence. Does a review of the samples provide confirmatory evidence of a mistake by the pathologist, a false positive or false negative? Has the pathologist correctly identified and graded the cancer?

The litigator must carefully examine the clinical records and consider whether they are consistent with the histopathology findings. Have the doctors confirmed clinically the accuracy of the pathological diagnosis? Below are two examples of this forensic approach to the review of the medical notes:

Breast cancer cases

Carefully review the records, looking for any descriptions or diagrams of a palpable lump or mass. If detectable, it should have been measured and described by shape and mobility of tumour, all of which are essential indicators for both diagnosis and prognosis. Look for descriptions of the examination of the breast, lump or node. Any history of a persistent mass, discharging duct or unexplained nipple discharge should be noted.

Also, be sure to inspect the records, particularly those of the GP, for any evidence of instruction on breast self-examination. This could form an important part of the liability case.

Lung cancer cases

Examine the notes carefully for details of the presenting symptoms at the early attendances. Is there a constellation of diagnostic indicators such as a history of smoking, weight loss, blood in the sputum and bone pain? Has the chest been examined for abnormalities or the fingers for clubbing?

If lung cancer figures in the differential diagnosis, then the lawyer should examine the notes for evidence of further tests such as blood tests, X-rays and sputum cytology. Most important is the possibility that bronchoscopy has been used to further investigate a possible lesion. Check to see whether it has been ordered, and whether the histological results of any biopsies and samples taken during the course of the procedure have been disclosed. Many lung cancer patients receive radiotherapy or chemotherapy. Ensure that you have requested and received the radiotherapy and chemotherapy prescriptions.

The medical brief

Specialist medical negligence practitioners are increasingly discovering the value of preparing a 'medical brief' at the outset of the investigation. This brief can take various forms, but is essentially intended to be a working document to help the lay legal advisor understand and prepare the claim. Most commonly the brief will include an introduction to the claim, a chronology, a discussion of the basic medical principles and issues, and a conclusion which applies the facts to the medical principles with informal conclusions as to the merits of the claim.

The 'introduction' should be a brief (one paragraph of no more than half a page of A4) summary of the basis of the investigation. It will ordinarily identify the potential parties, the incident giving rise to the claim and the outcome to the victim. Strictly imposed limits on the length of the introduction are a valuable tool in training the litigator to focus on and identify the real core of the potential claim.

The preparation of the chronology requires more than just an ability to transfer dates, times and events from the records onto a new sheet of paper.

All medical records contain an enormous amount of detail, but very little is usually relevant to the negligence claim. A proper chronology is one that separates the 'wheat from the chaff' and includes only those facts likely to be relevant to the issues under investigation. Thus, whoever prepares the chronology must know in advance what the claim is about in order to identify what information is important to note.

The chronology contained in the medical brief should be based entirely on the version of events and history contained within the medical records. After it is compiled, the fee earner must review the chronology carefully to see whether there are any major inconsistencies between what is contained in the records and what history the client has given in interview or statement. Inconsistencies must be addressed as soon as possible with the client.

Regardless of whether inconsistencies exist, the client should be given the opportunity to consider the chronology and the medical records with the lawyer before instructions to the expert are finalised. Often this is done at a second appointment with the client which, owing to the time ordinarily involved in disclosure, may be several months after the first interview. This second meeting not only gives the client the chance to see that the investigation is progressing, but allows him to participate actively in the process of preparing for the instructions to the expert. For the vast majority of clients this meeting will be the first time they have had a chance to see the clinical records. This can often be a distressing visit for the client and must be handled sensitively, with particular reference to comments regarding prognosis.

It is important to note that far more than constituting 'best practice' in investigating potential claims, the preparation of the introduction and chronology now forms an important component of the litigation process as well. Practice Direction 49, issued by the Queen's Bench Division first in October 1996 and revised in December 1997[6], regulates the management of medical/clinical negligence litigation. Paragraphs 3(b)(i) and (ii) and 3(c)(i) and (ii) require the parties to medical negligence litigation to have summaries and chronologies of the claim available prior to the appointment for the summons for directions. The appropriate use of the medical brief 'front loads' the preparation of these requirements.

The discussion section of the medical brief focuses on the basic principles of medicine. It is not only intended to familiarise the practitioner with the medical basis of the client's claim, but in doing so it provides a guide of clinical practice in the context of which the care delivered can be compared and analysed. Perhaps as lay persons most medical negligence lawyers will only be able to undertake a basic or rudimentary comparison of the medical standards and the actual care. However, this discussion section sets the

---

[6] *NLJ Practitioner*. 16 January 1998, p. 59.

foundations for the concluding part of the brief where the outcome of this analysis, the potential merits of the claim, is summarised.

Traditionally, medical negligence practitioners have been reluctant to express their view on the potential merits of the claim. The usual explanation is that this in some way usurps the role of the expert. However, as litigators become increasingly more experienced and familiar with medicine, they become increasingly less inhibited about suggesting views to their experts. In fact, often the litigator's view of the focus of the case can be extremely helpful to the expert. This is particularly so when the litigator is offering a preliminary view on the medical issues in order to explain the context of the instructions.

Indeed, the litigator's views on the merit of the case may impact directly on how the investigation is managed. If, for example, it appears that duty of care is relatively indefensible and funding is somewhat restricted either by a limited legal aid certificate or because a private client is carefully budgeting the investigation, then the litigator may choose to first approach an expert on the issue of causation. If, on the other hand, the care appears to reasonably accord with what the medical research appears to describe as acceptable, then it might be appropriate to approach a liability expert first.

Lastly, a review of the medical records allows the litigator to decide which experts are most appropriate for the investigation. It is understandable that clients cannot always accurately identify exactly where or when during the course of their illness suboptimal care may have occurred. Often the records will reveal areas of investigation far beyond what the client is able to appreciate.

When reviewing the notes, it is the litigator's job to attempt to ascertain precisely what areas of care require investigation and the corresponding areas of medical expertise. Armed with this knowledge it is now time to approach the expert.

Chapter 5
Instructing Experts in Oncology Cases

You have now completed disclosure. The records have been reviewed and you are confident that they are as complete as you can determine. You have decided which areas of expertise must be approached for independent opinions. The notes have been organised and paginated. The medical brief, including a relevant chronology, has been prepared. A preliminary proof of evidence has been drafted from the details taken from the client during your early meetings. In short, the documents that support the investigation are now ready to be examined by independent experts. Are you ready to instruct your expert? Please note that what follows is based on current best practice. Since Part 35 of the new rules of civil procedure has yet to be implemented, it is impossible to know whether it will have any impact on existing practice regarding medical experts.

The answer to this question depends on whether the litigator has used the early stages of the investigation not only in identifying which experts to instruct but in what order as well. Is it appropriate or necessary to initially investigate liability? Alternatively, have your investigations revealed problems with causation which require this issue to be investigated first? Often it is appropriate to examine both issues simultaneously. It is more commonly the case that separate experts will be required to consider whether there has been a breach in the duty of care owed to the cancer patient, and whether that breach of duty has caused damage. One of the exciting challenges of litigating oncology cases is that, unlike most areas of medical negligence litigation, there are no particular areas of medical specialty regularly or routinely called upon to establish breach of duty. Although the majority of cancer claims are against GPs and radiologists, in theory the patient with cancer is just as likely to be alleging negligence against a gastroenterologist as against a physiotherapist. Contrast this with litigation arising out of birth traumas: with very little exception, the expert on breach of duty is likely to be an obstetrician; less often, the legal advisor may need to employ an expert midwife or a GP. Very few birth trauma cases require expertise beyond these three specialties to resolve issues of breach of duty. Litigators who act for cancer patients must develop a familiarity or working knowledge with a wider number of the medical specialties in order to effectively manage their case-load and investigate liability.

The reason for the variety in approach is both the variety of cancers and the number of different types of clinicians involved in diagnosis and care. The practitioner will ordinarily look to establish breach of duty by obtaining the opinion of an expert in the same specialty as the individual responsible for the care of the plaintiff at the time of the alleged failure to diagnose or treat.

The legal practitioner should also expect that the correct specialty of expert to consider liability, or breach of duty, may vary widely depending on the basis of the proposed cause of action, the theory of negligence. Below are two examples of the possible variety of liability experts in an oncology case dependent on the theory of negligence. Legal practitioners should note that, in contrast to the variety of possible liability experts, the range of causation experts in cancer cases tends to remain the same.

Example 1: case based on allegations of delay or failure to diagnose

Liability experts

Possible defendants, and hence possible liability experts with some common areas of inquiry of the expert:

1. General practitioner

A discussion of

- whether the patient's symptoms were appropriately appreciated;
- whether appropriate testing or investigations of the patient were undertaken;
- whether there was an appropriate time-scale for the investigations undertaken;
- whether appropriate referrals were made for further patient testing;
- whether the provision for follow-up with the patient was adequate.

2. Radiologist

A discussion of

- whether the scope of the radiology studies conducted on the patient was appropriate;

- whether the interpretation of the patient's radiology was accurate;
- whether the patient's clinical findings were sufficiently considered when the interpretation of the radiology was made;
- whether the patient's results were reported or communicated within an acceptable time-scale.

3. Pathologist

A discussion of

- whether the interpretation of the patient's histopathology or cytology was accurate;
- whether the patient's clinical findings were sufficiently considered when the interpretation of the histopathology or cytology was made;
- whether the patient's results were reported or communicated to the patient within an acceptable time-scale.

4. Surgeon

A discussion of

- whether the patient's referral information was given due attention when treatment or investigation was planned;
- whether the biopsies were appropriately performed to ensure accurate diagnosis;
- whether, given the patient's symptoms and history, appropriate investigations were ordered and performed;
- was the definitive surgery carried out according to an acceptable standard?

Causation experts

Generally, regardless of the wide variety of possible liability experts, the causation experts will very likely include the following specialists and issues:

1. Pathologist

- Confirmation of the precise diagnosis of cancer;
- a description of the grading or classification of the cancer.

2. Oncologist

- .Given the diagnosis and staging, a description of the natural history of the patient's cancer;

- an extrapolation as to what stage the cancer was likely to have been at the time it is alleged the cancer should have been diagnosed;
- a discussion of the client's general medical history and health profile, and a description of the likely treatments and clinical outcomes if the cancer had been diagnosed at an appropriate time;
- a discussion of how the alleged delay in diagnosis altered the treatment which the patient eventually received;
- a discussion of how the delay in diagnosis affected the patient's chance of survivability and general prognosis.

3. Psychologist

- A description of the patient's psychological history and current diagnosis;
- a discussion of the extent to which the patient's condition has been adversely affected or exacerbated by the consequences of the delayed diagnosis of the cancer;
- given the likely progress and outcome of the patient's cancer, a description of the patient's psychological prognosis.

4. Surgeon

- A discussion of whether the patient will now require more extensive surgery as a result of the delay in diagnosis.
- if so, a description of the likely consequences of this surgery;
- have complications arisen from negligent surgical practice?

Example 2: case based on allegations of inappropriate or inaccurate radiotherapy

Liability experts

Possible defendants, and hence possible liability experts with some common areas of inquiry of the expert:

1. Clinical oncologist or radiotherapist

A discussion of

- whether the prescription of radiation was appropriate in duration, amount and location;
- whether the patient's treatment was appropriately planned, e.g. whether the planning CT scans were accurate or dosimetry plans were accurately mapped;

- whether the patient's consent to the radiotherapy was appropriate and adequate;
- treatment alternatives available to the patient other than the radiotherapy in question.

2. Radiation physicist

A description of

- the nature of the radiotherapy error giving rise to the patient's claim.
- all checking or safety mechanisms which were in place to deal with calibration or planning errors.

Causation experts

Despite the difference in the theory of liability between Examples 1 and 2, the causation experts and their areas of inquiry look unsurprisingly similar:

1. Pathologist

- Description and confirmation of the precise diagnosis of cancer;
- description and discussion of the exact grading or classification of the cancer.

2. Oncologist

- Given the diagnosis and staging, a description of the natural history of the patient's cancer;
- an extrapolation as to what stage the cancer was likely to have been at the time it is alleged the cancer should have been appropriately treated with radiotherapy;
- a discussion of the client's general medical history and health profile, and a description of the likely treatments and clinical outcomes if the cancer had been appropriately radiated;
- a discussion of how the inaccurate or inappropriate radiation altered the treatment which the patient eventually received;
- a discussion of how the inaccurate or inappropriate radiation affected the patient's chance of survivability and general prognosis.

3. Psychologist

- A full description of the patient's psychological history and current diagnosis;

- a discussion of the extent to which the patient's condition has been adversely affected or exacerbated by the inaccurate or inappropriate radiation of the cancer;
- given the likely progress and outcome of the patient's cancer, a description of the patient's psychological prognosis.

4. Surgeon

- A discussion of whether the patient now requires more extensive surgery as a result of the inaccurate or inappropriate radiation;
- if so, a description of the likely consequences of this surgery.

After determining which experts to instruct, a letter of approach should be prepared. The letter of approach is the important first step in working with the expert. It is the expert's first exposure to your client's case, and should be both brief and informative. The legal advisor would be wise to *never* instruct an expert until after this initial approach and confirmation of the expert's willingness to assist.

It is best practice for the litigator to obtain this confirmation of intention to accept his instructions in writing. The initial approach to the expert should be sufficiently detailed to allow the expert to determine:

(1) Whether he is expert in the area of medicine at issue.

(2) Whether this is a matter in which another party has already instructed him. This is particularly important in oncology litigation, which has relatively few specialists and correspondingly few medico-legal experts.

(3) Whether he is in a position to undertake the necessary investigations within any time and/or cost parameters which are required.

Case management has been discussed previously. The initial approach to the expert need not await completion of the sorting and paginating of the records and the preparation of the medical brief. After the litigator has reviewed the records and confirmed which specialties are required, he should enlist the experts early. This simple short cut saves valuable time. Once the records have been organised and paginated, the lawyer can prepare the instructions to the experts. Again, one need not waste time by waiting for the response to the letter of introduction to the expert before preparing at least a draft of the detailed letter of instruction.

Those practitioners who have acted in medical negligence cases for several years will remember a time, not that long ago, when the standard letter of instruction to a medical expert read:

> Dear Dr Waxman,
> I am instructed by a patient in this potential medical negligence. Enclosed are photocopies of the records. Please review the same and advise me as soon as possible whether there are good grounds for a legal case.
> Yours sincerely,
>
> A. Lawyer

As with medicine, the standard of care owed by the litigator to the client is dynamic, an evolving concept. And in medical negligence litigation it has now evolved far beyond this sort of terse, uniform blind reliance on the thoughts and views of others.

Many experts will tell you that no single document says more about the quality and expertise of their instructing lawyer than the expert's letter of instruction. Get it right and you save the expert, counsel, yourself and the client hours of valuable preparation and investigation time. Get it wrong and you may set your expert off on a wild goose chase, a fruitless examination of irrelevancies and incidentals.

Below is considered one approach to instructing the expert. As with all of the practice tips contained in this volume, the reader will feel free to take or adopt from this proposed structure what he wishes. What is important is that the instructions have some logical structure or format which actually assists the expert in preparing the report.

The letter of instruction

As with all aspects of representing clients, effectiveness and success depend almost entirely on preparation and planning. Preparation and planning of a set of expert instructions is assisted greatly through a workable structure which can be 'transported' and used in different types of medical negligence cases.

Several elements make a useful structure. First, the organisation should assist the fee earner drafting the instructions by focusing preparation on discrete blocks of necessary information. Second, segmenting the instructions into logical sections of information and discussion assists the expert in digesting precisely what the brief is. The following format provides a useful, user-friendly framework that can easily be employed in most, if not all, medical negligence cases.

Introduction

Begin by thanking the expert for agreeing to assist in the preparation of the report. Remind the expert of the date of your earlier letter of introduction and the expert's responding correspondence agreeing to act. Remind the expert of the identity of your client, and briefly review in one or two sentences whether you require the expert's opinion on breach of duty, causation or both.

List of supporting documents

All of the documents, or bundles of medical records, which accompany the set of instructions to the expert should be listed early in the instructions. There should be no doubt as to the exact information you wish the expert to consider in preparing the opinion. Indeed it is also wise to ask the expert to confirm by telephone or otherwise upon receipt of the instructions that he has received all of the enclosures as well. All too often experts have used the incompleteness of the supporting documents as an excuse for not progressing with the investigations and report.

Only in the rarest of circumstances will the practitioner fail to provide a copy of the client's first proof of evidence, his witness statement, along with the instructions. This should of course be listed in the supporting documents. By the time the expert has been instructed, the client will have had the opportunity of not only checking the statement for accuracy and completeness, but also of comparing it with the medical chronology and the medical records. However, inconsistencies can still exist.

It should never be assumed that inconsistencies between the records and the client's version of events mean the client's story is inaccurate. Unless the practitioner has reason to think otherwise, the expert should assume that the client's version does indeed represent the truth as he knows and recalls it. The expert should therefore be instructed to assume the accuracy of the client's version of events when preparing the report. The expert may find technical reasons why the client's version of the events is inherently unreliable. In that event, the expert should be invited to explain those reasons, and which portion of the client's statement he is unable to accept.

Explanation of the records and documents

Explain your system of pagination and bundling for those experts who may be unfamiliar with it. Equally explain to the expert whether there are any problems with the records or notes which he should be made aware of from the outset. Although the practitioner should always strive to instruct the expert with a full and complete set of records, this is not always achievable. Any documents for which discovery is outstanding or any questions you may have about the relevancy or authorship of certain notes should be mentioned in this section.

Factual or medical history

It is fundamental that the expert's final conclusions are only as inherently reliable as the medicine referred to and the history relied on. The expert should be asked to succinctly describe the medical history relevant to the issues he has been asked to address. Some litigators include a copy of the chronology from the medical brief in with the instructions to the expert. If this is done, the expert should be cautioned not to rely on this document as a substitute for his own review of the records and interpretation of the relevant events that form the basis of the claim.

The expert's brief

After the formalities comes the most important section of the set of instructions, the expert's brief. Begin by telling the expert precisely which of the issues he is to consider and what legal tests he is to apply (e.g. *Bolam*).

If the expert is experienced at medico-legal investigations then the legal advisor may wish to dispense with a rehearsal of legal tests which he feels the expert may already be well acquainted with. If there is ever any doubt about the expert's degree of familiarity, the tests should be restated and explained simply. Even where the expert is experienced, the instructing litigator should always invite the expert to contact him if the expert has any questions about the application of the legal requirements to prove or defend a claim of medical negligence.

After including the necessary information on the legal tests, the instructing lawyer can pose questions to the expert. This is the heart of the instructions. The questions should be carefully prepared to prompt the expert into considering those areas of the case which the litigator and his team will have identified as being critical to a thorough examination of the issues raised.

The experienced medical negligence litigator will feel no hesitation to include questions for the expert. Careful questions, even when perhaps misplaced, show a litigator's interest in the progress of the investigation. They show a willingness to work with the expert by attempting to understand the possible bases of the claim at an early stage. Provided that they are phrased in this spirit, no credible expert should resent addressing the lawyer's queries.

The questions themselves can be both general and specific, and it is best to begin with the former. As previously mentioned, questions should be phrased in an open-ended format in order to encourage the expert to provide thorough answers.

Breach of duty

Examples of general questions on breach of duty

'Please comment on the standard of care of the management and treatment given to my client by Dr Jones and/or the Grimethorpe NHS Trust. In summarising those aspects of the care and/or treatment which are relevant to this claim, please discuss any failures by the doctor and/or hospital staff in:

(1) administering treatment which, in the circumstances, they should not have (if so, identify what treatment should not have been administered and why not);

(2) failing to adminster treatment which, in the circumstances, they should have (if so, identify what treatment should have been administered and why); or

(3) failing to diagnose my client's condition (if so, identify the length of delay and reason why the condition should have been recognised earlier).'

Examples of specific questions on breach of duty

'In addition to addressing the general questions above, please address the following specific queries:

(4) Discuss the appropriateness of the decision by the GP to resist referring Mrs Johnson to a surgeon for biopsy. In doing so, please refer specifically to Mrs Johnson's presenting symptoms at the time of the GP's examination, and their relevance to a diagnosis of breast cancer.

(5) Please discuss whether it was appropriate for the GP to fail to arrange a follow-up appointment with Mrs Johnson until five months after the initial visit. In answering, please explain acceptable and appropriate parameters for scheduling follow-up appointments for patients such as Mrs Johnson.'

Causation

Proving causation in cancer litigation is often an exercise reduced to percentages and medical estimation. A consistent and structured approach to the proof of causation will not only help abbreviate the time and cost, but will also increase the accuracy of your investigation.

Again, the legal advisor should seek to work from the general to the specific.

Examples of general causation questions

'(1) Please discuss what outcome would have been expected on the balance of probabilities but for the negligence.

(2) Describe how this ideal outcome compares with the patient's actual outcome. In other words, on the balance of probabilities, how has the alleged negligence altered the clinical outcome?

(3) If there has been a negligent delay in treatment, and if you have not already done so above, please discuss whether and to what extent that delay has affected my client's clinical outcome.'

Examples of specific causation questions

'(4) Describe the precise form of cancer which the patient has acquired as confirmed by histopathological diagnosis.

(5) Explain the expected natural history of this cancer. In doing so, please address the following:

    (a) How long and well do people live with it?
    (b) What is its doubling time or growth rate?
    (c) Most importantly, is it amenable to screening – what is the duration of its detectable, but pre-clinical, phase?

(6) Please describe the goal of treating this cancer. Please consider whether it is to cure or to palliate the cancer.

(7) On the balance of probabilities, describe how advanced or widespread was the cancer at the time when the alleged negligence occurred.

(8) If the claim is based on failed diagnosis or misdiagnosis, describe how the answer to the previous question compares with the extent or stage of the cancer at the time of diagnosis.

(9) Please explain the likely clinical progress of the disease if an appropriate diagnosis had been made, or the appropriate treatment commenced, at the time when the negligence was alleged to have occurred.

(10) Please describe the treatment options available at the time when the diagnosis should have been made.

(11) Explain the treatment administered to my client and how it differed

from what would likely have been employed in the absence of the alleged negligence.'

The opposing arguments

The lawyer should always seek the expert's own advice on possible counter-arguments to the expert's opinions and conclusions. Anticipating your opponent's position is critical to ensuring that both the lawyer and the expert have fully considered all of the issues raised by the investigation of the client's position.

In addition, an expert owes a duty to the court and the parties to act independently. In his review of the civil justice system, Lord Woolf considered that where there are diverging opinions in two reports the parties and the judge should be able to see the basis on which an expert has been instructed. There are reports already of this trend toward 'transparency' of instructions. If this position continues to be adopted, it will become increasingly more important that the instructions themselves be seen to be assisting the expert in achieving this independence.

What follows are two examples of questions which seek to elicit this information from the expert:

'(1) What reasoning might the other side advance to support the argument that the care in question either was or was not appropriate?

(2) Please anticipate what arguments the other side could credibly advance in opposition to the opinions which you have formed.'

Concluding the instructions

Complete the instructions by specifically asking that the expert or the expert's assistant confirm safe receipt of the instructions and all of the enclosures as soon as possible. This should be diarised, and if the lawyer has not heard from the expert within a week of having forwarded the instructions, then the lawyer should contact the expert as soon as possible.

This is the safest method of ensuring not only that the expert has received the instructions, but also all of the enclosures and supporting documents as well. Any litigator who has waited months on end for a report from an expert, only finally to be advised by the expert that the instructions or documents were never received, will appreciate that this simple procedure may well save months of senseless delay.

Chapter 6
Damages

It is axiomatic that in order to recover financial damages any injuries that the patient has suffered must have been caused by the negligence complained of. With the exception of those cases where the plaintiff is alleging that inappropriate medical treatment caused the cancer, oncology cases almost invariably involve patients who would have suffered their cancer irrespective of the alleged negligent conduct. In most cases such as these, the advisors for the defendant can be expected to argue that the plaintiff has suffered no greater or lesser injury by virtue of any negligence than he would have suffered as a result of the illness in any event. In other words, the clinical outcome to the patient would have been unchanged regardless of negligent care, and hence there is no injury which the patient should be compensated for.

To the extent that the plaintiff is able to prove that he has suffered injury as a result of the negligence, the plaintiff will of course be entitled to claim compensatory damages. Of the damages available to the victims of negligence, it is in the area of general damages that we see the most idiosyncratic treatment from the courts. In this chapter we consider the application of such damages to cancer cases. Any legal advisor who has been presented with the challenge of quantifying a claim for a cancer patient will have found that the task of assessing compensation for additional pain, suffering and loss of a percentage chance for survival is not straightforward.

General damages

General damages are awarded for a plaintiff's past and future suffering which can be shown to be consequential to the injury which resulted from the alleged negligence. The type and quality of a cancer patient's pain and suffering is related to the nature of the alleged negligence. For example, in a case where the plaintiff claims damage for negligent delay in diagnosis of his cancer, pain and suffering may well include:

(1) The physical suffering associated with chemotherapy which would otherwise not have been needed 'but for' the delay.

(2) The physical suffering associated with radiotherapy which would otherwise not have been needed 'but for' the delay.

(3) The physical suffering associated with surgical salvage which either would not have been required 'but for' the delay, or was more extensive because of the delay.

Damages for pain and suffering also includes compensation for mental anguish. While all injuries cause some degree of emotional distress to the victim, in cancer cases this can far exceed what one might otherwise anticipate. Indeed, often in claims based on alleged negligence in failing to diagnose the disease, the patient will have evidence that the acts and omissions complained of have resulted in a decreased life expectancy. The anguish caused by this awareness is amenable to an award of compensation under this head of damage.

Equally, the plaintiff may be entitled to recover under this head for the probability that the negligent treatment has resulted in an increased likelihood of an early recurrence of the cancer or an increased likelihood of death – a death which will now occur earlier than otherwise as a result of inappropriate treatment. As with the other heads, this claim is predicated on the patient's awareness of his change of circumstances.

In *Sutton* v. *PSFBP*[1] the plaintiff's cancer was diagnosed late as a result of negligence. The cancer was highly aggressive. In the circumstances, the evidence was that earlier surgical intervention, had it been carried out, would not have been curative: the cancer was bound to recur. However, an earlier attempt to remove the tumour would have delayed its recurrence by approximately four years. It was proven that the plaintiff would have worked and lived as normal during this remission. Thus, the plaintiff was awarded damages for four years' loss of future earnings and four years' life expectation.

In the following year, the Administration of Justice Act 1982 abolished the right to claim damages for loss of expectation of life. However, section 1(1)(b) of the act requires that suffering caused by an awareness that expectation of life has been reduced be taken into account when assessing damages for pain and suffering:

---

[1] [1981] *Times Law Report*, 7 November 1981.

'... If the injured person's expectation of life has been reduced by the injuries, the court, in assessing damages in respect of pain and suffering caused by the injury, shall take account of any suffering caused or likely to be caused by him by awareness that his expectation of life has been so reduced.'

This principle was recognised recently in *Taylor v. West Kent Health Authority*[2]. In *Taylor*, the plaintiff alleged failures by the defendant to interpret cytology reports to exclude malignancy, to report on the suspected malignancy and to provide adjuvant chemotherapy. While Mr Justice Kay accepted that all three amounted to negligence, i.e. breach of duty, none caused the plaintiff's breast cancer. Further, since her tumour was particularly aggressive, the judge concluded that the plaintiff would not have survived her illness in any event. However, the court ruled that on the balance of probabilities the negligent failure to provide the plaintiff with adjuvant chemotherapy caused her to die 18 months before she would have died anyway. This was clearly damage for which compensation was allowed. At the time of the report of the decision, the assessment of quantum was outstanding.

Similar, but slightly different, are those rare cases involving a loss of opportunity to receive palliative care resulting from negligence. The authors have only seen two of these cases. Both involved male plaintiffs with terminal lung cancer where it was alleged that negligent delays in diagnosis meant months of unrelenting and under-treated pain. Both cases are still pending. Clearly, to the extent that negligence has caused a delay or failure to provide palliative care, the resulting pain and suffering which the patient would not have experienced 'but for' the lack of appropriate therapy must be recoverable. This principle of damage should apply whether the failure to provide palliative care happens to a patient with or without a terminal illness.

Also included within general damages is loss of amenities. These damages include injuries that have deprived the plaintiff of some element of enjoyment of life, for example a hobby or particular recreational activity. The objective component of loss of amenity would include loss of bodily capacity. Thus, the cancer patient who, for example, alleges that the failure or delay in diagnosing his cancer resulted in more extensive surgery would claim under this head for the additional damage done by the surgery which would not have occurred 'but for' the alleged negligence. A woman who required a full mastectomy instead of a lumpectomy would claim damage for the effect of the more extensive procedure under this head.

One does not have to be a victim of cancer to be aware that the treatment alone can, and often does, have devastating consequences on the patient's

---

[2] [1997] 8 Med LR 251.

appearance and self-esteem. The effects of chemotherapy, radiation and surgery are very often transparent and difficult to cover up. While it is always easy for friends and family to reassure the patient that these side-effects are relatively benign, the patient's subjective assessment is almost always far more critical. Indeed, there are times when the patient's appearance or lack of personal esteem as a result of this appearance can irrevocably affect their personal relationships. In the unfortunate event that a client is made to endure the double tragedy of having a marriage breakdown which can be causally related to the negligence and not the cancer in the first instance, then this also forms a component of the claim for general damages.[3]

The award of general damages is usually a single figure, or lump sum, which incorporates the past and future pain and suffering, and loss of amenities. General damages, and hence its constituent parts, are available for all personal injury plaintiffs for both mental as well as physical injury. It is now accepted that recovery of psychological damage need not require physical injury as well[4] provided the plaintiff can prove that he has suffered from a recognised psychiatric illness. Whenever psychological injury is alleged, the litigator must be careful to differentiate the psychological trauma which the cancer patient would likely have undergone as a result of the illness itself from the additional anguish and suffering caused by the negligence. Additional psychological trauma may result from a risk of recurrence of cancer, accelerated death, enhanced disfigurement, or additional treatment and surgery.

Provisional damages

Provisional damage awards occur more frequently in cancer cases than in other areas of medical and personal injury litigation. The reason for this relates to the nature of cancer treatment itself. The principle which underpins many cancer treatments is to destroy tumour cells by either removing them or altering their development processes. Inevitably, healthy as well as diseased cells can be injured in the process of administering chemotherapy, radiotherapy or surgery. These treatments have short-, medium- and long-term sequelae which require the litigator to ensure that provisional damages feature in the relief pleaded.

Historically, it has been the rule that a plaintiff can only recover damages from a defendant on a 'once and for all' basis. In other words, the plaintiff does not have the right to commence a second action at some indeterminate

---
[3] See for example *Thurman v. Wiltshire and Bath Health Authority* (1997) 36 BMLR 63, discussed below.
[4] *Page v. Smith* [1995] 2 All ER 907, HL.

time in the future to recover additional damages if it turns out that the injury is greater or more seriously thought than at the time of the original action. Clearly these principles raise difficulties in the context of oncology-related issues where the full extent of the alleged acts or omissions may not be known until many years after the treatment, or indeed the completion of the legal process. The Supreme Court Act 1981, section 32(a), gives courts the authority to order provisional damages in situations where:

> 'there is proved or admitted to be a chance that at some definite or indefinite time in the future the injured person will as a result of the act or omission which gave rise to the cause of action, develop serious disease or suffer some serious deterioration in his physical or mental condition.'

An order awarding provisional damages makes possible the plaintiff's ability to claim damages again in the future in the event that he develops the contemplated serious disease or deterioration. An excellent example of the application of provisional damages to an oncology case is seen in the recent case of *Thurman* v. *Wiltshire and Bath Health Authority*[5].

The plaintiff, Mrs Thurman, was aged 24 when a routine cervical smear in 1988 was reported as normal. She had her first child in June 1990, and in January 1991 she began to have heavy and frequent vaginal bleeding. Mrs Thurman was referred for a dilatation and curettage (D&C) in March 1991, after which she was told that the histology results were clear. From January 1992 she again noticed some vaginal blood loss, but did not consider it serious. In May 1992, she was confirmed as pregnant. Bleeding continued during the early stages of her pregnancy.

In June 1992, Mrs Thurman saw a gynaecologist, as the bleeding had become heavier. Following a colposcopy and biopsy, the diagnosis revealed that her cervix was 'almost completely destroyed by a tumour'. The only treatment was a termination of her 12-week pregnancy, a Wertheim's hysterectomy followed by a six-week course of radiotherapy, and a 20-hour implant of caesium into the vagina.

Mrs Thurman made a remarkable recovery, but was left with scarring following the surgery. She was placed on hormone replacement therapy. Not only could Mrs Thurman no longer have children, her marriage also sadly broke down after her treatment. She claimed damages on a provisional basis for personal injuries as a result of cervical cancer. She brought a claim based on the defendant's failure to diagnose:

- severe dyskaryotic cells on the smear of 8 January 1988;
- cervical carcinoma in March/April 1991 when the D&C was performed; and

---

[5] (1997) 36 BMLR 63.

- dysplastic squamous epithelium in the histology results from the D&C in 1991.

Liability for the first two allegations was admitted on 16 January 1997. The case went to trial before Mr Justice Hedley limited to determining the quantum of general damages and the provisional award.

After considering a number of factors related to Mrs Thurman's pain, suffering and loss of amenity, the judge awarded £50,000 in respect of general damages. She requested an award of provisional damages on the basis of the risk of the following potential future injuries:

(1) The likelihood of recurrences of cancer secondary to carcinoma of the cervix.
(2) Osteoporosis secondary to radiotherapy.
(3) Interference with the urinary function, secondary to radiotherapy.

Both parties agreed that in respect of particulars (2) and (3), the period specified for seeking further damages in the event that the described risk materialised was ten years from the date of the order. However, they were unable to agree this time figure for the first particular – the chance of recurrence of the primary cancer. The court ordered that there be no time limit within which the plaintiff could reapply for such damages:

> 'The defendants urge that there be some finality to their obligations and fairness requires an end-point to be fixed. The plaintiff submits that the risk, of recurrence, could materialise at any time and that the injustice to her of a time limit is greater than that to the defendants of not having one ... In this case I have come to the view that there should be no limit of time. There is no medical or other scientific evidence upon which any time limit could be sensibly based. In my judgment, therefore, the potential injustice to the plaintiff of an arbitrary time significantly outweighs that to the defendants of having no limit.'[6]

At least one judge has approached the awarding of provisional damages from a different perspective. In *Molinari* v. *Ministry of Defence*[7], Mr W. Crowther QC, sitting as a deputy High Court judge in the Queen's Bench Division, made an award of provisional damages in a non-medical negligence oncology case. *Molinari* involved an 39-year-old employee of the Royal Naval Dockyards who developed acute lymphoblastic leukaemia after exposure to ionising radiation at work. An award for provisional damages was requested on the basis that there was reason to believe that the plaintiff's

---

[6] *ibid*, at p. 66.
[7] [1994] P.I.Q.R. Q33; also reported at Kemp & Kemp, L3-091.

condition was likely to seriously deteriorate, a possibility in fact conceded by the defendants. The court agreed that the case appeared to be a classic case for provisional damages. However, the judge noted what in his view was a complication in section 32(a) of the Supreme Court Act 1981: what happens if the deterioration in the plaintiff's condition should logically translate into a decrease in the global damage award instead of an increase?

This extreme example is used to illustrate the point. Let us assume the case of a young man in his early twenties, with no dependants, who spends every penny that he earned on himself. He contracts a disease which produces a severe and permanent disability. There is a 50–50 chance that, within a year or two of judgment, he will suffer a relapse and, after a short and comparatively painless illness, will die. If damages were assessed in the traditional way, the effect of the chance of the relapse and death would reduce the damages significantly. The overall effect on the general damages would be to reduce them substantially. The damages for future loss would also be reduced significantly, because there would be a 50–50 chance that all the plaintiff was entitled to was damages in respect of the lost years, which in his case would be modest.

If provisional damages were awarded, the position would be entirely different. The damage would be assessed on the assumption that deterioration and death would not occur. The plaintiff would therefore recover his full loss of earnings and, if he deteriorated in the future, he could come back for further damages, notwithstanding the fact that his imminent death invalidated the basis of the original award.

Section 32(a) of the rules makes no provision for this eventuality. It does not, for example, provide for the original award to be reopened, or for the over-compensation to be calculated and offset against further damages. It seems that, in such an extreme case, the proper course might be for the trial judge to refuse an award of provisional damages on the grounds that the potential injustice to the defendants of such an award far outweighs the potential injustice to the plaintiff of a traditional award.[8]

The trial judge in *Molinari*, true to his word, then employed his self-stated test of balancing the respective injustices and, after analysing the options, concluded by granting the award of provisional damages:

> 'Putting the matter at its lowest, I have no doubt that any injustice that the defendants may suffer from an award of provisional damages is far outweighed by the potential injustice to the plaintiff in not making such an award and, accordingly, I propose to award provisional damages.'[9]

In the Appendix, we report important cancer cases which should help litigators with their assessment of damages.

---

[8] [1994] P.I.Q.R. Q33, at Q38.
[9] *ibid*, at Q39.

Chapter 7
Cancer: Basic Facts and Background

The diagnosis of cancer immediately conjures visions of death, brings terror, shatters lives and may leave its victims helpless and hopeless. This popular view of cancer is brought about in many instances by memories of the terrible death many years previously of an aged relative. But the treatment of cancer has changed, and a significant number of people with cancer are cured of their illness, whilst a further proportion may have their symptoms eased for a significant period of time. The issues of life quality weigh strongly on the minds of the physicians that treat cancer. Drugs that ease pain are used with a liberality that was unheard of 30 years ago, and new medicines have been developed that effectively relieve most of the worse symptoms of cancer.

Cancer and its causes

Cancer is common; each year in England and Wales 278,000 people are diagnosed as having cancer. In terms of causes of death, cancer comes second to heart disease. The reasons for the development of cancer remain mysterious but this doesn't prevent causes being broadly classified as genetic or environmental; in other words, what we are and what we do to ourselves.

It is known that there is a strong genetic basis to the development of a few cancers. Some kidney and retinal cancers are hereditary, and if you have more than two close relatives with breast cancer, your own chance of developing breast cancer is increased by a factor of two. Environmental causes of cancer may range from substances to which we are exposed in the work place to dietary causes. Occupational causes are significant; workers in the dye industry are at risk from bladder tumours, whilst asbestos workers have a very high incidence of a rare tumour called mesothelioma and an even higher incidence of lung cancer. Industrial compensation is awarded for the development of mesothelioma, because it is virtually entirely specific to asbestos exposure, but not for lung cancer, because asbestos acts as a co-carcinogen with cigarette smoke.

There is a strong relationship between diet and the development of cancers. It has been known for many years that vegetarians are half as likely to get cancer as meat eaters, but it remains unknown whether it is the meat itself that is the cause of cancer or whether it is the additives, which may include steroids, antibiotics, colourants and antioxidants. Surprisingly, not all food additives are bad. Stomach cancer has decreased in incidence over the last 30 years and this decrease is thought to be due to reducing agents, which are additives that prevent foods decaying and so decrease the effect of cancer-inducing food products on the gut.

Communicating

Medicine is full of jargon, which is useful for communication between doctors but makes life difficult for patients ... and lawyers! Clear communication is an absolute requisite for the perfect care of the patient and his family, and it is a paradox that language, the tool of communication, distances doctors from their patients.

When they talk to patients, many clinicians have little understanding of how alien their speech is, diffracted not only by jargon, but also by class. So few of us realise how far our conversation is removed from the easy language of non-medical folk. Talk of scans, chemotherapy, radiation therapy and median survival are poorly understood by the majority of people. The timorous patient is much too polite to ask his clinician to explain things in a language that he understands, and so for many patients the doctor's initial explanation of the disease and its effects, the treatment and its side-effects may be completely lost.

The time when a patient with cancer is given his diagnosis is terribly traumatic. In many instances, the patient is seized with fear and this renders any communication non-existent. The doctor may try and give some explanation of treatment and its chance for success. Because of this fear, what the patient hears may not be what the doctor says. There are other barriers to communication. It is common for the patient to remember something entirely different from what he has heard, because the subject matter is so difficult psychologically for him to deal with that the truth is often obliterated in his memory. Relatives and friends may ask the patient what the doctor said. Different explanations will be given them according to how the patient feels at the time and what the patient thinks his different friends and relatives should know. For all of these reasons, a story which may be at extreme variance to the truth may be provided to the lawyer by his client and will always have to be carefully interpreted. It is clear that communication is all, and in our own experience of litigation, it is obvious that failed communication is the basis for 95% of all claims.

Cancer and its symptoms

Medical students think they are developing every tumour. The reason for this is that many of the symptoms of cancer are entirely non-specific and represent part of a continuum with the normal symptoms of life. Not every headache is diagnostic of a brain tumour, nor every cough symptomatic of lung cancer. It is the GP's job to distinguish between non-specific and specific symptoms initiating the required tests in order to achieve a diagnosis. In the USA, where defensive medicine is the norm, virtually every symptom is investigated. In the UK, clinicians are taught to assess the significance of individual symptoms in the context of their association with other symptoms, and to place these symptoms in another bigger context – patients and their lives.

Patients with cancer may present with symptoms that point to an organ system malfunction or with non-specific complaints. Specific symptoms include the coughing of blood, which suggests the possibility of a lung cancer particularly if the patient is a smoker; altered bowel habit, which suggests the diagnosis of a bowel cancer; or blood in the urine, indicating the possibility of a tumour in the kidney or bladder. The bigger context into which the careful clinician puts these symptoms might be a smoking habit for the patient coughing blood, or exposure to industrial carcinogens for the patient with blood in his urine.

Patients with cancer may also present with symptoms that are not specific to any organ system, but are general and relate to the fact of cancer. These general symptoms include loss of appetite, weight loss, lethargy or pain in the bones. Loss of appetite and weight are thought to result from production by the tumour of chemicals that act on the brain to reduce appetite and also from the metabolic needs of the tumour itself – the tumour grows, and the body starves. Bone pain may be a result of the spread of the tumour to the skeleton and the pain comes from irritation of the nerves lining the tissues that surround the bone.

All of these specific and non-specific features need to be taken into the context of a patient, and it is the responsibility of the GP to define the significance of these symptoms. This he should do by carrying out the relevant examination and investigations and finally referring as necessary to a hospital specialist for more specific testing. The GP is not expected to carry out sophisticated examinations or to initiate complex investigations, but it *is* his job to carry out with thoroughness and a reasonable standard of competence the examination and investigations necessary to set in train the clinical care of a cancer patient.

Cancer and its signs

The clinician is trained to be a detective; illness is the crime and the patient is the scene of that crime to be inspected for clues. The stigmata of illness are called 'physical signs'. Each symptom and sign should be investigated by blood testing and radiological testing, the results of which are the objective evidence of disease. The following case exemplifies the processes required for diagnosis.

An elderly man complains that he is coughing blood, and he should be asked about his smoking history. An examination ought to be carried out of the hands and then the chest. Examination of the hands may show clubbing, which is diagnostic of lung or heart pathology. The doctor will next look in the patient's eyes to establish whether there is any paralysis of the nerves controlling movement of the eyes. These may be damaged by lung cancer, either as a result of the position of the cancer in the chest, where it can trap nerves, or as a result of spread of the cancer to the brain.

In his examination of the chest, the doctor will also carefully feel in the patient's armpits and neck to assess whether or not enlarged lymph glands are present. These glands may suggest spread of the lung tumour outside of the chest. The GP should initially examine the chest by asking the patient to breathe in and out; he will observe the patient's chest movements and the rate of flow of air through the patient's mouth. The movements of the chest with breathing will give him a clue as to possible pathology. For example, where there is collapse of the lung, there will be less movement on the collapsed side. He will assess the position of the trachea: this may be shifted from a mid-line position, indicating the possibility of a collapsed lung or the inappropriate presence of fluid pushing the trachea from its mid-line position.

Next the clinician will 'percuss' the chest, banging the tip of his second finger against the flat of the second finger of his other hand, which is placed tight against the patient's chest. He will listen to the sounds of the underlying structures in the lung, evaluating the qualities of the echo of his percussion note which tells him about the nature of these underlying structures. For example, fluid gives a dull echo whilst normal lung sounds hollow.

Having carried out these examinations, the doctor will listen to the movement of air through the lungs with his stethoscope, trying to identify whether or not there are crackles and wheezes: their presence indicates whether the underlying lung is aerated properly. Finally, information is obtained by asking the patient to repeat a phrase such as '99', and from the character of the transmission of these sounds the clinician's stethoscope will tell him of the nature of the underlying lung function.

At this point, having assessed the patient's 'history' and having carried out an examination, the GP will then go on to plan the relevant investigations. The patient's history of smoking and coughing of blood with signs of fluid in the lung should lead the GP to carry out a series of preliminary investigations that may lead to a provisional diagnosis. These test results will help him to make the appropriate hospital referral for further investigation and treatment. In this particular instance, the investigations of choice are a chest X-ray, a blood count in which the concentration of red cells, white cells and platelets are measured, and a further blood test to assess liver and kidney function.

Hospital referral

The results of these investigations will enable the GP to refer the patient on to the hospital specialist, which in this case would be a chest physician, for the further assessment and investigation of possible lung cancer. In his letter of referral to the hospital consultant the GP will relate the history of the patient's presenting complaint, describe the patient's past history and summarise the results of the investigations that have been organised. Finally, he will present to the hospital consultant his own views as to the possible diagnosis.

The receipt of such complete letters of referral are, unfortunately, quite unusual in hospital practice. However, the days are long gone when it was not at all uncommon to receive the following letter:

'Dear Doctor
Please see and advise
Yours sincerely'

The consultant will read the GP's letter and make an assessment of the significance of the symptoms reported. He will then advise the appointment clerks as to the urgency with which the patient needs to be seen at the hospital. Letters with insufficient information will not allow the consultant to make an accurate assessment of the clinical situation.

If the GP has indicated that a diagnosis of cancer is suspected, a hospital consultant will generally do his best to ensure that an early appointment is sent to the patient.

Hospital assessment

In out-patient departments, the majority of new patients are seen by the hospital consultant to whom that patient is referred. In busy clinical practice, where there may be 10 or 20 new patients in each clinic, a new patient might have to be seen by a more junior doctor whose duty it is to present the patient's case to the consultant for his view prior to the initiation of investigations. This presentation is generally done on an informal basis.

The consultant seeing a new patient with a suspected diagnosis of cancer will listen to that patient's story of his presenting complaint and take a full written note of that history. The notations of doctors working within the NHS tend to be fuller than those in the private sector, where the information recorded may solely take the form of a letter to the GP. At the initial discussion – the clerking – the patient with a suspected diagnosis of cancer should be asked specific questions about associated symptomatology, such as weight loss and pain, bleeding, cough and breathlessness, and questions about his general medical condition. Full details should be obtained about family history, occupation, past medical history, drug history and social history.

The answers to these questions may provide important clues as to the origins of the tumour and also may help in planning the future care of the patient with cancer. Thus, the finding of a strong family history of breast cancer would increase the consultant's index of suspicion that the patient's breast lump may be malignant. An occupational history of exposure to asbestos may lead to the suspicion that the patient's cough may be caused by a lung cancer or mesothelioma. A past history of heavy alcohol abuse may lead the clinician to suspect the development of a hepatoma within a cirrhotic liver. A knowledge of the social history will allow the clinician to plan discharges and organise social services according to the patient's needs.

So the doctor really is a detective taking clues from the patient's history in order to find a diagnosis. It is usual that the diagnosis comes from the history rather than from the clinical findings. The patient will next be examined, and just as the history should be thorough, so should the examination, which is only complete when all organ systems are examined. The reason for this is that medical clues can be obtained from each system as to the nature of the underlying illness and the effects of the underlying illness upon other systems. The clinician can then establish what treatments the patient will cope with. The patient should have cardiovascular, respiratory, abdominal, lymphatic and central nervous systems examined and the suspicions aroused by the history confirmed or refuted.

Our patient with a suspected diagnosis of lung cancer has been referred by his GP to a chest physician. The chest physician will note the history, establish that his patient was a smoker and on examination will find clubbing, an effusion in the chest and paralysis of the muscles of the patient's eye. The clinician will conclude from these findings that the patient has cancer of the lung which is inoperable, and furthermore will be able to predict the microscopic appearance of the tumour, which will be the squamous variant of lung cancer. He will know that the patient's median survival (life expectancy) is six months. All of this information becomes available to a good physician in a 20-minute interview with a patient.

A further example of this road to diagnosis is provided by the patient with an altered bowel habit. Such a patient should be similarly assessed by his GP and then referred to a specialist bowel surgeon. In this case, the assessment would only be complete if it includes a thorough abdominal examination. This requires that a rectal examination should be carried out; it is negligent practice not to do this in such a patient.

Hospital tests

The clues of histories and examinations are then followed by the consultant setting in train the investigations relevant to the patient's condition. These investigations aim to achieve a clinical and tissue diagnosis. In the case of our patient with a smoking history and cough, routine blood tests and chest X-rays should be carried out on the days of the clinic attendance. More complex radiological assessment such as CT imaging will be organised and carried out within a reasonable time-frame. Arrangements for bronchoscopy will be put in place to attain a tissue diagnosis. For the patient with altered bowel habit, a sigmoidoscopy and biopsy should be carried out in the clinic, which will be followed by routine blood testing, X-rays, scans and colonoscopy and finally admission for surgery.

Treatment

Having achieved a diagnosis within a reasonable time-frame, a plan for treatment should be made. This may involve the use of surgery, radiotherapy or chemotherapy and should involve referral by the consultant to a specialist, cancer surgeon or physician. Unfortunately, the provision of care in the UK is scandalously suboptimal. It is estimated that only 40% of all cancer patients see a specialist cancer consultant, which severely compromises the chance for cure and effective symptom control. The choice of referral depends upon the disease and its spread, and also the attitude of the patient's clinician to cancer. This is surprisingly important, because it is not always taken as routine that patients should be referred for cancer treatment; some non-specialist doctors prefer to care for the patient, thus denying them specialist care.

Stage and grade

Tumours are given a stage and grade and the difference between the two is often a matter of confusion for lawyers. 'Stage' means the extent of the spread as shown by scanning and X-rays, and 'grade' means the degree of agressiveness of the tumour as demonstrated microscopically. Staging is carried out by clinical and surgical means. Staging is classified according to the TNM system of the Union International Contre le Cancer (UICC). The T stage defines the tumour and its degree of spread, the N stage defines the involvement of lymph nodes and the M stage defines the presence or absence of distant metastases. The subscript P before the TNM staging of the tumour denotes that the patient has been surgically staged and that the staging has not relied upon clinical and radiological assessment.

Treatment and treaters

Surgery is used for tumours that have proven not to have spread beyond the primary site and that are considered to have a reasonable chance of cure by surgery. The reason surgery should be carried out by a specialist is that the patient is most likely to be cured by the doctor with the most experience, and furthermore is likely to have the least complications from the procedure. Unfortunately, in the UK, this is by no means the standard and it should be noted that the differences in outcome are most significant.

There are two different species of oncologist: the clinical oncologist is generally a non-academic who specialises in radiotherapy; the medical oncologist is usually an academic with an interest in cancer research who specialises in chemotherapy. Radiotherapy is used for local treatment of inoperable tumours such as those involving the brain. Treatment may involve the use of particle therapies such as electrons or of high-energy rays. Modern radiotherapy machines are termed supervoltage and this refers to their ability to provide focused high-energy treatments.

Chemotherapy is a systemic treatment given in the form of tablets or intravenous injections for a cancer that has spread from its original site, or for a tumour that is strikingly chemosensitive that has not spread. It is the treatment given, for example, for leukaemia and some variants of lung cancer.

Cure and palliation

The treatment of cancer can be considered to proceed with curative or palliative intent. Oncologists talk about complete and partial remission; about median survivals; and of five- and ten-year survivals. We talk about the toxicity of the therapy, and this we divide into expected, which we generally will discuss in full detail with our patients, and unexpected, which are those very rare side-effects occurring at a rate of less than 1%, whose details we tend rather patronisingly and in the interest of time not to burden our patients with.

Side-effects of treatment

Chemotherapy and radiation both have expected adverse effects. The side-effects of chemotherapy are caused by the non-specific poisonous effects of these drugs. Chemotherapy evolved from nerve gases developed for warfare. The drugs were rather paradoxically applied to human tumours because of the observation that these nerve gases were found to cause leukaemias in experimental animals. Chemotherapeutic agents damage normal cells as well as malignant cells. The most important of these damaging effects is upon the bone marrow, where lowering of blood counts may lead to infection and bleeding. Other common side-effects include baldness and damage to the ovary and testis causing loss of fertility. They also cause nausea and vomiting.

Over the last 20 years there have been attempts to reduce these toxic side-effects, the result of initiatives by pharmaceutical companies where new drugs without the toxicities of their parent molecules have been synthesised. In some areas of the UK, these new drugs may not be prescribable on the basis of their cost and this leads to an inequable variation in the quality of care throughout the country, the so-called 'postal code lottery'. Many of the side-effects of chemotherapy can be ameliorated by the use of other drugs. Thus, naturally occurring substances called growth factors, which stimulate the production of bone marrow cells, have been synthesised and their use may limit the development of bone marrow suppression, preventing infection and bleeding. Again, their prescription is varied throughout the country because of cost implications and differing opinions concerning their worth.

Radiation also has specific toxicities and these are generally predictable, although their extent may not be. If a tumour in the bladder is treated with radiation therapy then the development of diarrhoea towards the end of treatment is expected, because normal bowel in proximity to the bladder has been exposed to treatment. Radiotherapy to upper abdominal organs may cause nausea and vomiting, and to the brain, tiredness and headaches. The patient should be warned of all of these symptoms and shown what precautions to take in order to limit them.

Surgery has specific toxicities; for example, the patient operated on for a low rectal tumour may be rendered impotent by surgery, and a woman having a breast lump removed may develop tingling or burning in the scar.

These side-effects should always be explained to the patient. In many centres, the patient will be asked to sign a consent form, acknowledging that he has agreed to receive treatment, and also that the side-effects have been explained.

Cancer and litigation

The treatment of cancer is enormously complex and depends upon a trusting relationship between the patient and his doctor, a relationship that should be made secure by the knowledge that the best treatments will be given him by a doctor who is well informed and specialises in the treatment of that patient's particular condition. Mistakes can be made, and often these mistakes may not result from malignity or stupidity but rather from the human error to which we are all prone. We can all make mistakes. Generally, if these mistakes are acknowledged and explanations given, the patient and his family are able to accept this and deal with the consequences. In the authors' experience, it is almost invariable that it is only when this error has not been identified and explained in open discussion that litigation proceeds.

Causation is one of the most difficult aspects of litigation in cancer. It is extremely common that if an error has been committed there will be no loss of chance for prolongation of life. However, litigation often proceeds in ignorance of this matter, and it is usual that the only loss is one of a chance for relief of suffering.

Chapter 8
Breast Cancer

Epidemiology

In England and Wales, breast cancer is a common disease. Currently, 31,500 women are affected and 12,100 die as a result of this condition. The likelihood of the development of breast cancer is affected by a positive family history of breast cancer, increasing age, diet, social class and nulliparity. The incidence of breast cancer has increased significantly because of the introduction of breast screening, and with it mortality rates have decreased.

Presentation

Women with breast cancer generally present to their clinicians with a lump in their breast. On average, there is a delay of approximately three months between the woman first noting the mass in her breast and her seeing a hospital clinician. Alternative sources of referral are from breast screening programmes where mammographic detection leads to diagnosis in a previously unnoted breast lump. As a result of governmental concerns over the care of patients with breast cancer, the investigation and treatment of this disease has been prioritised. Patients in whom this condition is suspected are generally seen as out-patients within two weeks of receipt of the referral letter.

Out-patient diagnosis

A careful history should be obtained from the patient who is then examined. The mass may be thought to be benign or malignant. Benign lumps are more likely in younger women and tend to be painful, enlarging before menstruation. Malignant lumps tend to be more common in older women and are generally painless: only 30% of malignant breast lumps are painful.

Diagnosis is by clinical, mammographic and cytological means. After examination, mammography and aspiration cytology should be performed to further assess the significance of the breast lump. In a younger woman, ultrasonography rather than mammography is the radiological investigation of choice. If the clinical, mammographic or cytological features suggest malignancy, the woman should then proceed to surgery within two weeks of diagnosis.

In the 1990s there has been a tendency to develop one-stop clinics in which examination, cytology and mammography are all carried out on the same day.

Surgery

Surgery for breast cancer depends upon the clinical stage of the disease. If the mass is less than 5 cm in size and not fixed, the preferred treatment is lumpectomy. In a woman who is premenopausal, the procedure will also include axillary dissection. The reason for this is that if the lymph nodes are affected by a cancer, there is an advantage in this group of women to additional chemotherapy. In the node-negative woman there is a very much smaller advantage to additional chemotherapy. In an older woman, axillary dissection is not generally performed. The reason for this is that additional treatment with chemotherapy within this group of women is not dictated by lymph node status, because the advantage is much smaller than in younger women and the toxicity of the treatment outweighs these modest gains.

For a woman whose tumour measures 5–10 cm in size, the preferred surgical option is mastectomy with axillary dissection.

For more advanced breast cancer, treatment is much more contentious and elderly women are treated with hormonal therapy alone. In a younger woman, chemotherapy is given in the first instance to reduce the size of the tumour, and this may then be followed by radiation to the breast and nodal areas.

Stage and grade

Breast cancer, as with other tumours, is described according to grade and stage. There are two main pathological variants of breast cancer, ductal and lobular, and these are both graded as follows:

G1   Well differentiated
G2   Moderately differentiated
G3   Poorly differentiated

This grading was first described by Bloom and Richardson, and bears their eponyms. As one might expect, poorly differentiated tumours have a worse prognosis than moderately differentiated tumours, which have a worse prognosis than well differentiated breast cancer. Stage is defined according to the classification of the UICC, which is updated every ten years or so. The subscript P denotes a pathological staging.

T stage (primary tumour)

T1   Tumour less than 2 cm
T2   Tumour measuring between 2 and 5 cm
T3   Tumour measuring between 5 and 10 cm
T4   Tumour of any size extending into skin or chest wall

There are further T substagings not elaborated in this report.

N stage (nodal involvement)

N0   No nodes involved
N1   Mobile axillary nodes
N2   Fixed axillary nodes
N3   Involved supraclavicular or infraclavicular nodes

M stage (metastatic state)

M0   No metastases
M1   Spread to distant organs

There are many other staging systems.

Adjuvant radiotherapy

After lumpectomy, radiotherapy is given to the breast. This is done in order to reduce the risk of local recurrence of the tumour. Without radiation this risk is between 40 and 60%; with radiation the risk is reduced to approximately 4–6%, which is the same as that for more radical surgical procedures. Radiotherapy is generally given over a six-week period and requires daily attendance at hospital. The side-effects of radiation include tiredness and burning of the skin, which is generally mild. Rarely, more serious consequences of radiation are seen, which include damage to the brachial nerve plexus and, with more old-fashioned treatment machines and plans, damage to the coronary blood vessels.

Adjuvant hormonal therapy

Recently, there has been interest in the possibility of additional hormonal therapy given at the initial presentation of the illness. Treatment with tamoxifen has been shown to have an advantage in terms of disease-free and overall survival in postmenopausal women and is now given routinely to this group of patients. It has a much smaller effect in premenopausal women with breast cancer. It is usually recommended that treatment should extend for at least two years.

There have been reports of cases of endometrial carcinoma associated with the use of tamoxifen. The estimated risk is 1 per 20,000 women years of use.

Adjuvant chemotherapy

Adjuvant chemotherapy has a significant place in the management of breast cancer. It should be given in a chemotherapy day ward where nurses and support staff have the experience to deal with all of the problems associated with treatment. Standard chemotherapy using the Bonadonna CMF (cyclophosphamide, methotrexate, fluorouracil) programme is the treatment of first choice. Day one CMF programmes are less effective and it has never been proved that more intensive therapies have an additional advantage. Six courses of therapy are given over a six-month period. It is arguable whether any more intensive adjuvant therapies improve upon survival prospects.

Treatment of metastatic breast cancer

The treatment of metastatic breast cancer depends very much upon the age of the patient and the sites of metastasis. In older women whose metastases are in skin or in bone, the preferred treatment option is hormonal; the agent of first choice is tamoxifen. This is taken as a tablet and has little in the way of side-effects. Approximately 70% of women aged 70 respond to this therapy. In a premenopausal woman, hormonal therapy is generally ineffective and at the age of 30, just 10% of patients overall will respond to treatment. However, oophorectomy is generally the first therapeutic stratagem. If this fails, treatment with other modalities of therapy will then proceed.

In both pre- and postmenopausal women, radiation treatment is very effective in controlling pain, if bones are affected. If the lungs or liver are affected, then chemotherapy is required. Overall, 40–60% of patients respond to chemotherapy and this response is of a median duration of one year.

High-dose chemotherapy

Breast cancer responds to chemotherapy but inevitably, after responding, patients relapse and die. There have been attempts to maximise response rates by intensifying chemotherapy. High-dose treatments were popularised in the early 1980s. Response rates were found to be higher than for conventional treatment; however, toxicity was significantly worse, and death rates reached 20% as a result of the side-effects of treatment. Even more significantly, patients who responded and survived toxicity relapsed, and the median duration of response was no better than that expected with conventional treatment.

In the 1990s there has been an increase in the numbers of patients receiving high-dose chemotherapy for breast cancer. This has been possible as a result of the improvement in supportive therapy, principally bone marrow rescue either with stem cells or marrow. Mortality has decreased and now is 5% in the best centres. Overall, there has been no significant improvement in the expectation for survival for patients with metastatic breast cancer, and 20% of patients are alive at two years from transplantation.

It has been argued recently that these relatively good results are entirely the result of the selection of good-prognosis patients for treatment with high-dose therapy and that the same effects could be achieved with less intensive conventional therapy.

It may be that early intensive therapy given as adjuvant treatment for patients with poor-risk tumours will lead to improved survival, but this has not been shown in any randomised study.

Chapter 9
Ovarian Cancer

Epidemiology

Carcinoma of the ovary is a common tumour affecting nearly 4500 women annually and leading to the death of 3700 each year in England and Wales. Ovarian cancer is the fourth most frequent cause of cancer death in women. The average age at which the disease occurs is approximately 60 years. By far the most common pathological subtype of ovarian cancer is epithelial, and it is this group that this report describes.

Presentation

Patients with ovarian cancer usually present to their GPs with non-specific abdominal symptoms such as abdominal discomfort and swelling. There may be associated urinary frequency or postmenopausal bleeding. Patients with disseminated disease may have loss of appetite and weight. A patient with these symptoms should be examined by her GP and, if there is abdominal swelling or a pelvic mass, referred on to a specialist gynaecologist for his views as to the patient's management. The vast majority of patients present with advanced disease.

Investigations

A gynaecologist should see the patient in the out-patient clinic and take a full clinical history and conduct an examination. The examination should include a pelvic assessment. If the patient is thought clinically to have ovarian cancer, the investigations organised should include a full blood count, routine biochemistry, chest X-ray, a pelvic ultrasound and an abdominal pelvic CT scan together with measurement of serum levels of the glycoprotein CA-125. If there is no obvious evidence from these investigations for gross spread of the tumour outside of the abdominal cavity, the patient should then be booked for a laparotomy.

Surgery

Surgery should be undertaken in specialist centres, by a surgical gynaecological oncologist. At operation, the abdominal contents are examined and, where possible, tumour debulking should be undertaken. This should include removal of the omentum, ovaries, fallopian tubes and uterus with excision of all visible peritoneal deposits.

Pathology

The tumour should be examined by the pathologist and classified histologically into one of the types shown in Table 9.1.

Staging

An attempt will then be made to stage the patient's tumour. The staging used is the FIGO classification which is as follows:

Stage 1 Growth limited to the ovaries:
 (a) One ovary, no ascites
 (b) Both ovaries, no ascites
 (c) Tumour on ovarian surface or capsular rupture or ascites positive for malignant cell.
Stage 2 Growth involving one or both ovaries with pelvic extension.
Stage 3 Growth involving one or both ovaries with peritoneal implants or superficial liver metastases.
Stage 4 Tumour metastasing to liver parenchyma or pleura.

Treatment

Treatment is defined by the FIGO staging system.
 If the tumour is confined to one ovary, the gynaecological oncologist may choose to observe the patient after definitive surgery. In stage 1a and 1b ovarian cancer, there is no indication for additional therapies, as survival at five years is 95%. For patients with stage 1c disease, treatment is con-

Table 9.1 Histological classifications of ovarian cancer.

Epithelial	Sex cord/stromal	Lipid cell	Gonadoblastoma	Soft tissue	Germ cell	Unclassifiable	Metastatic
Serous	Granulosa				Dysgerminoma		
Mucinous	Androblastoma				Endodermal sinus		
Endometrioid	Gynandroblastoma				Embryonal		
Clear cell	Unclassified				Polyembryonal		
Brenner					Teratoma		
Mixed					Mixed		
Undifferentiated							
Unclassified							

troversial. The survival of this group is also excellent, and there may be no need for chemotherapy. However, adjuvant therapy may be indicated if the tumour is high grade.

Unfortunately, more than two-thirds of patients present with FIGO stages 2 and beyond. For these patients and patients with stage 1c disease, chemotherapy is indicated. Ovarian cancer is chemosensitive and there is a long history of the use of chemical agents in the treatment of this condition. The discovery of responsiveness to single-agent treatments led to the use of combination chemotherapy programmes. Intensive treatment using multiple-drug regimens was advocated throughout the 1970s and early 1980s.

In the early 1990s, it was thought that single-agent therapy carboplatin was just as effective as combination treatments in terms of overall survival, although there might be a minor advantage in terms of initial response rates and response duration to combination programmes. In the late 1990s, fashions have changed again and treatment involves the use of combination therapy. There is evidence from randomised studies that combination therapy with cisplatin and taxol has the highest response rates. Six courses of treatment are recommended.

Second-look surgery

In the 1980s there was considerable enthusiasm by clinicians for their patients to have a second-look laparotomy, which is a laparotomy at the end of chemotherapy where an attempt is made to further reduce tumour bulk. This is not considered to be as important in the 1990s, because the finding of residual disease at second-look laparotomy is associated with a very poor prognosis and debulking surgery in this context probably does not improve overall survival, although it does define the patient's chance of survival.

Prognosis

Approximately 80% of patients with advanced ovarian cancer respond to chemotherapy for ovarian cancer. The median survival for this group of patients is two and a half years, with 7% of patients surviving five years. Localised ovarian cancer constitutes less than 5% of all presenting patients. Patients with stage 1a and 1b ovarian cancer have an excellent outlook with a 95% chance of survival.

Tumour markers

Ovarian cancer secretes CA-125, a glycoprotein. Approximately 80% of patients with advanced ovarian cancer have elevated CA-125 levels. Raised

CA-125 levels may also occur in any gynaecological, pancreatic, breast, colon, lung or hepatocellular tumour. CA-125 levels are elevated in a number of benign conditions including endometriosis, pancreatitis, pelvic inflammatory disease and peritonitis. Changing levels may be used to monitor treatment.

Chapter 10
Cervical Cancer

Epidemiology

Carcinoma of the cervix annually affects approximately 3500 women in England and Wales and is the third commonest of the female genital cancers. This cancer is associated with evidence of viral infection, particularly the human papillomavirus, smoking, large numbers of sexual partners and low socio-economic status. The average age of a woman with cervical cancer is approximately 50 years.

Symptoms and investigation

Women with cervical cancer may present to their doctors with intermenstrual bleeding, postcoital bleeding or painful intercourse. There may frequently be a vaginal discharge, which can be bloody or offensive, or symptoms suggestive of a urinary infection such as urinary frequency or urgency. When the cancer has spread, common symptoms include back pain owing to enlarged abdominal lymph nodes or referred pain in the legs owing to involvement of the nerve plexuses of the pelvis. These symptoms may be accompanied by loss of weight.

When a woman presents to her doctor with these symptoms the management should be as follows. The GP should take a full history and examine the patient. The examination should include an assessment of the patient's general state of health together with palpation of the abdomen and a vaginal assessment. This may confirm the presence of a discharge and reveal a cervical mass.

The GP should then refer the patient to a gynaecologist who will repeat the examination, take smears from the cervix for cytological examination and then organise admission for examination under anaesthesia and cervical biopsy. The presence of a negative smear does not exclude a cancer. Colposcopy should be performed as an out-patient procedure prior to admission. This technique allows direct visualisation of the cervix with properly directed biopsies. After these assessments have been performed, and a histological diagnosis obtained, staging investigations should then be organised. These should include a full blood count, profile, chest X-ray and a CT scan of the abdomen and pelvis.

Staging and grading

Carcinoma of the cervix is staged as a result of these findings as follows:

Stage 0   Carcinoma in situ. Intraepithelial carcinoma grades 1–3.
Stage 1A Microscopic disease confined to the cervix.
Stage 1B Disease confined to the cervix and greater than stage 1A.
Stage 2A Carcinoma extending beyond the cervix without parametrial involvement.
Stage 2B Parametrial involvement.
Stage 3A Extension to the pelvic side wall.
Stage 3B Extension to the pelvic wall with hydronephrosis or a non-functioning kidney.
Stage 4A Extension beyond the true pelvis to adjacent organs.
Stage 4B Spread to distant organs.

The vast majority of cervical cancers are squamous cell tumours. These are graded as G1, G2 or G3 tumours according to their microscopic appearance. G1 tumours are well differentiated, G2 are moderately differentiated and G3 are poorly differentiated.

Treatment

The treatment of cervical cancer will depend upon the stage of disease. Stage 0 carcinoma of the cervix should be treated by cone biopsy or by surgical excision, stage 1A disease can sometimes be managed by cone biopsy or local excision, but usually by hysterectomy. Stage 1B and 2A cervical cancer is usually treated by either radical hysterectomy with pelvic lymphadenectomy or by pelvic irradiation. Both methods are equally effective in the long-term control of the disease. Stage 2B and 3 carcinoma of the cervix should be treated by pelvic radiotherapy and stage 4 with chemotherapy.

Prognosis

As a result of treatment, virtually 100% of patients with cervical intraepithelial neoplasia (CIN) disease are cured. Approximately 0.3% of women subsequently develop invasive carcinoma. If CIN is left untreated, then over a 30-year follow-up, 10–40% of patients will develop invasive cancer. The evidence for this is based on data from a single study carried out in New Zealand of untreated patients with CIN.

Approximately 5% of patients treated for stage 1A carcinoma of the cervix will progress to develop advanced disease. Between 65 and 85% of all patients with stage 1B and 2A carcinoma of the cervix survive five years after treatment by radical hysterectomy or radiation. The chance for a cure is smaller in stage 2B disease and the expectation is that approximately 50–65% survive with radiotherapy alone. Forty to sixty percent of patients with stage 3A disease and 25–45% of patients with stage 3B disease survive five years and are treated with radiotherapy and frequently with chemotherapy.

Patients with stage 4 cervical cancer do very poorly; it is very unlikely that cure will be achieved. Chemotherapy is the treatment of first choice; a number of agents have activity in the order of 15% and their combination is accompanied by some synergy of effect. The most commonly applied treatment programme involves the combination of cisplatin, methotrexate and bleomycin. About 30–40% of patients will respond to treatment but durable cures are rare. Chemotherapy is associated with toxicity and this includes nausea and vomiting, hair loss, infections and kidney failure. Because of the toxicities of treatment, an alternative approach is to palliate symptoms by treating with painkillers alone.

Terminal care

In the terminal phases of illness, patients with cervical cancer may have a number of problems which prove difficult to manage. These include fistulae from vagina to bladder and from rectum to vagina or bladder as a result of local progression of the tumour. Obstruction of kidney function may occur as a result of blockage of the ureters, either by enlarged lymph nodes or by tumour from the cervix growing within the pelvis to block the ureters. These situations can be treated surgically, in which case a colostomy or ileostomy may be formed to relieve bowel or ureteric obstruction, or radiologically, by passage of a stent to reverse obstructive damage to the kidneys.

Screening

Cervical cancer is a particularly unpleasant disease in that it affects young women and causes quite distressing local symptoms. A signficant proportion of patients can, however, be cured by radiotherapy or by surgery and, more importantly there is good evidence that effective screening can prevent the step-wise progression of cervical cancer through different stages of disease. In England and Wales, it is currently recommended that all women are screened by means of a cervical smear at five-yearly intervals. This recommendation is slightly different from that made by oncologists which is for three-yearly screening.

Chapter 11
Vulval Cancer

Introduction

Carcinoma of the vulva is a rare disease that generally affects elderly women. Approximately 750 new cases are reported each year in England and Wales. The causes of vulval cancer are not known but are thought to include chronic irritation and viral infection by human papillomavirus types 16 and 18. These viruses have been detected in vulval intraepithelial neoplasia which is a premalignant condition disposing towards the development of the tumour. A higher incidence of vulval cancer occurs in smokers as compared with non-smokers.

Symptoms

Patients with vulval carcinoma generally present with vulval itching and a change in the skin of the vulva which appears either white, red or dark brown. A proportion of patients with this disease present with dissemination of the tumour and may come to medical attention because of enlarged groin nodes.

Initial investigations and staging

The patient with a suspected diagnosis of vulval carcinoma should be referred to a gynaecological oncologist. In the clinic, a history will be taken and the patient will be examined. Staging investigations, including a blood count, renal function tests, chest X-ray and CT or MRI of the pelvis and abdomen, will be organised in order to define the initial treatment and assess the extent of disease dissemination.

Treatment

The treatment of vulval cancer should be carried out in specialist centres because the results are clearly superior to the results achieved by non-specialist centres. The main form of treatment is surgical and involves radical vulvectomy and skin grafting. The morbidity of radical vulvectomy is high and includes impaired psychosexual function. As a result, surgical techniques have been modified in order to produce fewer side-effects.

Grading and staging

Vulval tumours are staged using the FIGO classification.

Stage 1   Confined to vulva; less than 2 cm.
Stage 2   Confined to vulva; greater than 2 cm.
Stage 3   Extends beyond the vulva or involves unilateral regional nodes.
Stage 4a Involvement of rectum, bladder, urethra or pelvic bones or bilateral nodes.
Stage 4b Distant metastases.

Vulval carcinoma is almost exclusively squamous cell in origin and is graded as well, moderately or poorly differentiated. Other rarer vulval tumours include melanoma.

Prognosis

Unfortunately, most patients with vulval carcinoma present with late disease. However, early presentation is associated with a good prognosis. The five-year survival is as follows:

Stage 1   95%
Stage 2   85%
Stage 3   74%
Stage 4   31%

Vulval intraepithelial neoplasia

Vulval intraepithelial neoplasia is seen more commonly than it used to be. It is a premalignant condition of the vulva and occurs in a significant proportion of young women. Forty percent of patients are less than 40 years old. Patients with this condition generally present with vulval itching. The disease can be detected on clinical examination following the application of dilute acetic acid which leads to field change (change within the area).

The treatment of this condition is very difficult and is generally conservative, avoiding where possible the discomfort of mutilating procedures. If the lesion is small, excision biopsies are carried out. If the disease is multifocal, skin grafting may be required or laser therapy maybe applied. Recurrences are common, occurring in up to 50% of patients. The progression to invasive disease in those patients with a recurrence is also common and is reported in up to 20–30% of all patients.

Chapter 12
Cancer of the Larynx

Epidemiology

Carcinoma of the larynx is a relatively common condition in England and Wales. There are 1800 patients registered annually and four males are affected for each female. Tobacco is the most important aetiological factor in the development of carcinoma of the larynx; no occupational factors have so far been linked to its development.

Presentation

The vast majority of patients with carcinoma of the larynx present with hoarseness of the voice. Other typical presentations include changes in the character of the cough due to paralysis of the vocal cord, and the development of lumps in the neck due to spread of the cancer to lymph nodes.

Investigation

The patient with a suspected diagnosis of carcinoma of the larynx should be referred by his GP to an ear, nose and throat (ENT) surgeon. The appointment for out-patient review should be within two to four weeks of receipt of the medical referral. In the out-patient clinic, the ENT surgeon will make an attempt to visualise the larnyx by direct laryngoscopy. Staging investigations such as a CT scan of the neck and a chest X-ray will be organised together with routine blood testing.

Grade and stage

Carcinoma of the larynx is invariably squamous cell in origin and the microscopic appearances are graded as well, moderately or poorly differentiated. Staging, which indicates the degree of spread, is based on the TNM classification and is divided into glottic or supraglottic and subglottic categories.

Glottic tumours of the larynx

T staging (primary tumour)

T1 Tumour in one (T1a) or both (T1b) cords which are mobile.
T2 Extension to supraglottis or subglottis with mobile cords.
T3 Tumour confined to larynx with immobile cords.
T4 Extension beyond larynx.

Supraglottic tumours

T staging (primary tumour)

T1 Tumour confined to region and mobile.
T2 Extension and mobile.
T3 Tumour confined to larynx and fixed.
T4 Extension beyond larynx.

Subglottic tumours

T staging (primary tumour)

T1 Tumour confined to subglottis.
T2 Extension to one or both cords which are mobile.
T3 Tumour confined to larynx and fixed.
T4 Extension beyond larynx or destruction of cartilage.

N stage (nodal status)

N1 Homolateral mobile nodes.
N2 Contralateral or bilateral mobile nodes.
N3 Fixed nodes.

M stage (metastatic state)

M0 No metastases.
M1 Metastases present.

Treatment

Early-stage laryngeal carcinoma

Treatment is with radiotherapy, usually to a total dose of up to 6500 centigrays (Gy) in up to 35 fractions over a four- to six-week period.

Advanced laryngeal carcinoma

Patients with T3 and T4 carcinoma of the larynx have a relatively poor outcome in comparison to the outlook for early-stage cancer. Current treatment generally consists of neoadjuvant chemotherapy which is usually cisplatin based and is followed by radical radiotherapy or surgery.

Prognosis

The prognosis for early-stage laryngeal carcinoma is excellent. Ninety-five percent of patients with T1 carcinoma are cured by treatment and have good voice quality. The 5% that relapse are managed by laryngectomy which leads to cure in approximately 50% of patients. Late-stage carcinoma of the larynx is associated with a relatively poor prognosis. Initial response rates to chemotherapy are high – between 40 and 60% – but late survival is unusual.

Chapter 13
Lung Cancer

Epidemiology

In England and Wales, 42,000 people annually develop carcinoma of the bronchus. Approximately 31,000 are male and 11,000 are female. Carcinoma of the bronchus is the most common tumour of men and the second most common cancer of women. The overall prospects for survival are poor – 5–8% of patients survive five years from diagnosis. The most important cause for carcinoma of the bronchus is smoking, and the incidence of lung cancer is directly related to the number of cigarettes smoked. Although the overall incidence of smoking is decreasing within England and Wales at a rate of a little less than 1% per annum, there has been an increase in women smokers and in young smokers and this bodes poorly for the future. There are other risk factors for the future development of lung cancer, including exposure to asbestos and heavy metals, such as nickel, and fibrotic disease of the lung.

Presentation and investigations

Patients with carcinoma of the bronchus generally present with a cough or haemoptysis. This may be associated with weight loss and symptoms of metastatic cancer, such as bone pain or jaundice. Patients with chest symptoms suggestive of a diagnosis of carcinoma of the bronchus are generally referred promptly by GPs to a hospital specialist chest physician.

The physician should take a history and examine the patient where signs suggestive of a bronchial carcinoma may be elicited. These include clubbing and abnormalities in the chest. The chest physician should then organise a number of investigations, including full blood count, liver function tests, chest X-ray and sputum cytology. The purpose of examining the sputum is to look for cancer cells coughed up from the tumour. If the chest X-ray is abnormal, the patient will then proceed to fibreoptic bronchoscopy, by which narrowing of the airways by tumour may be observed. Biopsies and washings are then obtained and examined microscopically.

By these means a histological diagnosis should have been achieved. There are a number of different variants of carcinoma of the bronchus and these histological classifications are important in that they define the patient's further treatment. The main histological variants are squamous cell carcinoma, small cell carcinoma, adenocarcinoma and large cell carcinoma. For treatment purposes, tumours are described as being either small or non-small cell cancers. These constitute 95% of primary lung neoplasms.

Staging

A diagnosis having been made, the patient is then staged. Staging procedures are performed in order to define prognosis and treatment. Staging should include a radioisotope bone scan and liver ultrasound. In small cell carcinoma, examination of the bone marrow by aspiration and trephine is required. CT is helpful in assessing operability and in examination of the mediastinum.

As a result of these investigations the patient can be staged clinically and from the staging a decision made about treatment and prognosis. The TNM staging of the UICC is as follows.

T stage (primary)

- T1 Tumour is less than 3 cm in diameter.
- T2 Tumour is more than 3 cm in its greatest diameter and is at least 2 cm distant from the carina.
- T3 Tumour of any size that extends to adjacent structures or is less than 2 cm from the carina.

N stage (nodal status)

- N0 No evidence of regional nodal involvement.
- N1 Evidence of involvement of peribronchial or homolateral hilar lymph nodes.
- N2 Involvement of mediastinal lymph nodes.

M stage (metastatic state)

M0 No evidence of metastases.
M1 Metastases are present.

From the results of staging and histology it is possible to give a prognosis and define treatment.

Treatment

Non-small cell lung cancer

Non-small cell lung cancer may be treated with either surgery or radiation treatment. Surgery is only possible for those patients with limited-stage disease, that is T1N0M0 and T2N0M0 disease and a small number with T2N1M0 tumours. Surgery has a significant morbidity and mortality and operability depends upon lung function prior to resection together with cardiac status and the presence of other major illnesses. It is estimated that approximately 30% of patients with non-small cell carcinoma of the lung are able to be operated on successfully. The five-year survival for this group of patients is variably quoted at between 5 and 40%. An overview of 2675 patients gives a five-year survival of 30%. There is a subgroup variation in survival. For example, if those patients with adenocarcinoma are considered, the expectation is for survival ranging between 38 and 79%, and averaging 65%, at five years. Radical radiotherapy is considered for those patients who have operable disease by virtue of poor medical state. Five-year survival figures of 6% are reported in a review of 1487 patients. Conventionally patients receive 6000 cGy over a six-week period. More rapid treatment regimens are used particularly in the north of England and similar survival figures are found.

For the majority of patients with more advanced cancer, palliative radiotherapy is the only treatment option. This is given to patients who have symptoms as a result of their disease which might include haemoptysis, breathlessness or chest pain. Radiotherapy is given according to various prescriptions. Some radiotherapists advise a single dose of 1000–1500 cGy and others 3000 cGy in ten fractions over two weeks. Radiotherapy also, has side-effects and these include tiredness, oesophagitis and skin change. There is now considered to be a limited place for chemotherapy in this condition. Response rates for the most active regimens are in the range of 15–25%. The median survival of responding patients is six to seven months, offering no major survival advantage over palliative therapy. Combination therapy, using regimens such as MIC (mitomycin C, ifosfamide and cisplatin), is considered to be too toxic in view of the low response rates. Single-agent therapies using agents such as navelbine, vinorelbine or taxol have a role in the younger patient, and may be used as primary therapy in rendering operable the surgically inoperable patient.

Small cell lung cancer

Small cell lung cancer is an entirely different disease from non-small cell lung cancer. It is very rare for patients to have localised small cell lung cancer and approximately 95% of patients with small cell lung cancer have metastatic disease at presentation. For these patients radiotherapy and surgery are completely inappropriate. However, for the very small minority of patients who have clinically operable disease (1–5%), five-year survival is the result of treatment with both therapeutic modalities.

The most important modality of treatment for small cell lung cancer is chemotherapy. Conventionally the VAC regimen (vincristine, adriamycin and cyclophosphamide) produces some of the best results, and because of its simplicity of administration was one of the most favoured options until approximately two years ago. Approximately 80% of patients have an initial response to chemotherapy with this and similar programmes and this generally includes a complete remission rate of up to 60% of patients. The current chemotherapy programme of first choice is etoposide and cisplatin. Untreated, the median survival is three months but with treatment, 10–20% of patients will survive two years and 5% five years.

Chemotherapy has toxic effects including neutropenic sepsis, hair loss and nausea. Local radiotherapy to the primary site of the tumour is considered, because there may be some advantage in terms of local relapse rate. It used to be that patients with small cell lung cancer were also considered for prophylactic cranial irradiation because of the high incidence of cerebral relapse. Unfortunately, this procedure has very great toxicity and as a result is no longer a part of clinical practice. Small cell lung cancer is associated with many paraneoplastic syndromes, due to secretion by the tumour of specific growth factors and hormones. One of the commonest is hyponatraemia due to inappropriate secretion of antidiuretic hormone. This is treated by water restriction.

Chapter 14
Cancer of the Tongue

Epidemiology

Cancers of the tongue are rare in the West but have a high incidence in the developing world. This is because cancers of the tongue are associated with chewing tobacco and betel-nut together with the use of snuff. Other important factors in the development of cancer of the tongue are alcohol abuse, chronic infection of the oral cavity and syphilis. Cancer of the tongue is also associated with a premalignant condition called leukoplakia and with exposure to the human immunodeficiency virus. Until recently, 75% of patients were male but now the sex incidence is equal.

Presentation

Most patients with carcinoma of the tongue present with an ulcer that fails to heal. Other presentations are with symptoms suggestive of metastatic disease such as enlargement of lymph nodes. Patients with cancer of the tongue often present with very late-stage disease. The reason for this is that it is frequently seen in the socially deprived who have neglected their own personal care and have excessive exposure to the relevant carcinogens. A patient with a suspected diagnosis of carcinoma of the tongue should be referred to an oral surgeon with a specialist interest in this malignancy.

Grading and staging

Carcinomas of the tongue are almost invariably squamous cell tumours and they are graded as well, moderately or poorly differentiated. The disease is staged according to the extent of the local tumour and the presence of spread to nodes or distant sites.

T stage (primary tumour)

- T1 Tumour less than 2 cm
- T2 Tumour 2–4 cm
- T3 Tumour more than 4 cm
- T4 Local invasion of surrounding tissues

N stage (nodal status)

- N0 No nodes involved
- N1 Homilateral nodal involvement
- N2 Bilateral or contralateral nodal involvement
- N3 Fixed regional nodes

M stage (metastatic state)

- M0 No metastases
- M1 Distant metastases

Treatment

T1 and T2 tumours

The results of treatment with surgery and radiotherapy for early-stage carcinoma of the tongue are equivalent. The choice of treatment depends upon patient preference and also upon local practice. Although speech and swallowing are better preserved after radiotherapy, long-term side-effects are generally more severe because radiation causes atrophy of the salivary glands. The resultant failure of the production of saliva causes tooth decay. Radioisotope implants are often used for the treatment of small lesions in order to maximise dosages.

T3 and T4 tumours

The best approach to advanced tumours is the combination of radiotherapy with surgery.

Management of local regional lymph nodes

In the absence of clinically detectable metastases, patients who have tumours that are more than 3 mm thick are generally treated with adjuvant radiotherapy to regional neck nodes. In the presence of palpable lymphadenopathy, regional lymph node dissection is advised.

Prognosis

The prognosis for patients with T1 and T2 tumours is relatively good. The expectation is for local control in 70–85% of all patients. The prognosis is worse for patients with T3 cancers, with 30–55% of patients having local control. Patients with T4 tumours unfortunately are not cured. The prognosis for patients with nodal involvement is that 30% survive for five years.

Complications of treatment

The most significant complications of surgery are the impairment of speech and swallowing. This depends upon the exent of the surgery that is carried out but generally for patients who have had a hemiglossectomy speech and taste are preserved.

For radiotherapy, the situation is different. The salivary glands have received a significant dose of radiation and so saliva may not be produced. The result of this is poor oral hygiene and dental decay. As a result of therapy, the tongue may become fixed because of radiation fibrosis so that speech may become impaired.

Patients who are treated for this condition are subject to a high rate of additional complications which range from 5–30%, and these complications include second cancers and death from infection. Other rarer side-effects include late tissue necrosis with the formation of a fistula due to radiotherapy. Fistulae are usually managed conservatively.

Chapter 15
Cancer of the Oesophagus

Epidemiology

This cancer is increasing in incidence. Two men are affected to every woman. This cancer occurs in the over-60s and is associated with alcohol, tobacco and premalignant conditions such as Barrett's oesophagus and the Plummer Vinson syndrome.

Presentation

Cancer of the oesophagus is a tumour of the gullet. Patients with this malignancy characteristically present with difficulty in swallowing, with food tending to stick in their throats. This symptom may be accompanied by weight loss, chest pain or cough.

Investigation

The patient who presents with these symptoms to his GP should have a full history taken and be examined. The patient should then be referred up to a specialist thoracic or gastrointestinal surgeon who will repeat the history and examination and organise a number of investigations, including a full blood count, biochemical profile and chest X-ray. This will be followed by a barium swallow and fibreoptic oesophagoscopy.

The barium swallow may show a fixed narrowing of the oesophagus. The endoscopy may confirm this narrowing which can be directly visualised by this procedure. The level at which the obstruction is seen should be determined and biopsies taken of the lesion. The biopsies should be examined by a histopathologist who will describe the tumour as being either a squamous cell carcinoma or adenocarcinoma. Rare variants include lymphoma, sarcomas and small cell carcinoma.

Staging

Confirmation of the diagnosis of malignancy should be followed by CT scanning in order to stage the tumour and define operability. Tumour staging is performed according to the TNM classification.

T stage (primary tumour)

TX   Tumour stage unknown
T0   No tumour
T1S Carcinoma in situ
T1   Tumour infiltrates the submucosa
T2   Tumour invades muscularis
T3   Tumour invades inadventia
T4   Tumour extends to neighbouring structures

N stage (nodal status)

NX   Unknown
N0   No metastases
N1   Regional metastases

M stage (metastatic state)

MX   Metastases unknown
M0   No metastases
M1   Distant metastases

Pathology

The majority of tumours of the oesophagus are graded as well, moderately and poorly differentiated squamous cancers. Those tumours that are adenocarcinomous, arising at the junction of the oesophagus and stomach, should be regarded as gastric in origin, invading up from the cardia.

Treatment

The treatment of carcinoma of the oesophagus depends upon the stage and site of the tumour. If the tumour is confined to the oesophagus the patient, if medically fit, might be a candidate for oesophagectomy. This is an extremely complex and elaborate procedure and will not be discussed here further. If the patient is not fit for surgery, radiation may be the treatment of choice. Radical radiation dosages, i.e. an attempt at curative radiotherapy, is considered when the tumour is less than 5 cm in length. Larger tumours are very rarely curable with radiotherapy and for these tumours palliative procedures only are undertaken.

Treatment is designed to include the estimated macroscopic extension of the tumour, together with regional lymph nodes. CT planning is required. Treatment is delivered with the aim of sparing the spinal cord by using oblique as well as anterior and posterior fields. External beam radiation may be complemented by intracavity treatment. Treatment is given to a total dosage of approximately 6500 cGy over a six-week period. The complications of radiotherapy include pneumonitis, pericarditis, myocarditis and damage to the spinal cord. Oesophageal strictures may occur and are relatively common; these may require dilatation.

Prognosis

The survival of patients with carcinoma of the oesophagus is poor. With radiation alone, one-year survival is in the range of 30–60%, and with surgery is of the same order. The median survival is one year and the five-year survival for both surgery and radiotherapy is approximately 5%. Recurrence of carcinoma of the oesophagus is usually dealt with by oesophageal dilatation with passage of an Atkinson tube or equivalent. If this is not possible then a feeding gastrostomy is made. The median survival from local recurrence ranges between six weeks and three months.

Spontaneous regression is reported in almost all cancers. It is extraordinarily rare in carcinoma of the oesophagus.

Chapter 16
Gastric Cancer

Epidemiology

Gastric cancer is a relatively common malignancy in England and Wales. Each year nearly 13,000 men and women present with this condition. Gastric cancer is the sixth most common malignancy of men and women in England and Wales and constitutes approximately 5% of all cancers. The male/female ratio is 1.5 to 1. Little is known of the aetiological factors for gastric cancer. The average age of presentation is 65.

Presentation

Patients with gastric cancer generally present to their GP with symptoms of abdominal pain. Classically, the pain is epigastric and worse with meals. The differential diagnosis includes benign peptic ulceration. The GP should examine the patient and organise for routine blood tests to be carried out. These should include a full blood count and liver function tests. Such symptoms require investigation by a consultant physician and a hospital referral should be made.

Investigations

The patient with new peptic ulcer symptoms should be seen by a specialist gastroenterologist. The initial assessment will be carried out in the out-patient clinic. A detailed history should be obtained and particular attention should be paid to the possibility of metastases as suggested by a history of significant weight loss. The patient should be examined, and routine and more specialised tests organised. The routine tests should include a full blood count, liver function tests and chest X-ray. The more specialised investigations should include a gastroscopy with endoscopic biopsy of any apparent lesion and CT imaging of the abdomen. Having achieved a tissue diagnosis the results of the CT scan will be used to determine operability. Twenty years ago the vast majority of patients with gastric cancer presented with inoperable disease. Currently, approximately 50% are operable at the time of presentation of their tumour.

Initial treatment

The only significant chance for cure rests with surgery. There is considerable debate concerning the operative procedures of first choice. Old retrospective data suggested that survival is improved with total gastrectomy compared with subtotal gastrectomy, but randomised trials have shown equivalent survival with lesser complications for subtotal gastrectomy for carcinoma of the antrum as compared with total gastrectomy. For proximal lesions, total gastrectomy is the operation of first choice and leads to better long-term function and a low incidence of operative complications. Gastrectomy or partial gastrectomy should be accompanied by lymph node dissection. Currently, in the West, the consensus view is that surgery should be confined to the dissection of the perigastric lymph nodes rather than more extended lymph node dissection. However, in Japan, where carcinoma of the stomach is very common, improved survival has been obtained in patients by extensive lymphadenectomy.

Staging

The staging of gastric cancer is as follows.

Primary tumour (T stage)

- T0   No evidence of tumour.
- TIS Carcinoma in situ.
- T1   Tumour invades lamina propria.
- T2   Tumour invades muscularis.
- T3   Tumour invades adventitia.
- T4   Tumour invades adjacent structures.

Lymph nodes (N stage)

- N0   No nodes involved.
- N1   Perigastric nodes within 3 cm of primary tumour.
- N2   Perigastric nodes more than 3 cm from tumour.

Metastasis (M stage)

    M0 No metastases.
    M1 Distant metastases.

Stage grouping (Table 16.1)

Stage	Grouping		
0	T1S	N0	M0
IA	T1	N0	M0
IB	T1	N1	M0
	T2	N0	M0
II	T1	N2	M0
	T2	N1	M0
	T3	N0	M0
IIIA	T2	N2	M0
	T3	N1	M0
	T4	N0	M0
IV	T4	N2	M0
	Any T	Any N	M1

Pathology

Ninety-five percent of all gastric tumours are adenocarcinomas. The remainder are squamous cell cancers and lymphomas. Rarely, small cell cancers are reported.

Adjuvant therapy

There have been many studies of adjuvant treatment, investigating whether or not additional treatment confers a survival advantage. However, on balance no significant role for adjuvant radiation or chemotherapy has been proven.

Treatment of metastases in inoperable local disease

Patients with inoperable local disease and metastases may be treated with chemotherapy. Over the years, many treatment programmes have been introduced and the majority have contained 5-fluorouracil. There is considerable doubt as to whether or not combination therapy offers any improvement in response rates and the chance for survival as compared with single-agent 5-fluorouracil treatment.

In the 1970s, there was considerable enthusiasm for the introduction of combination therapy containing 5-fluorouracil, adriamycin and mitomycin C (FAM regime). This treatment schedule was initially reported as leading to responses in 40% of patients with a median duration of response of approximately nine months. Randomised trials have shown that the same order of response can be obtained with single-agent 5-fluorouracil with the same expectations of survival.

In the 1990s, there has been considerable support for combination chemotherapy using continuous-infusion 5-fluorouracil, epirubicin and cisplatin. Initially, a 70% response rate has been reported and the median survival of patients responding is seven months. The programme is well tolerated and offers patients a reasonable quality of life.

Survival

Approximately 10% of patients with gastric cancer survive five years. Long-term survival is only seen in patients who have had successful gastric surgery. The median survival of patients with advanced local disease or metastatic tumour is approximately six months.

Chapter 17
Cancer of the Pancreas

Epidemiology

Carcinoma of the pancreas has increased in incidence over the last decade and is now the fifth leading cause of cancer deaths. Two males are affected for every female. There is an increased risk of developing pancreatic cancer with age, and it has been suggested that excess coffee consumption predisposes to the development of cancer of the pancreas. Smoking is also associated with an increased risk of this disease of between two- and fivefold.

Symptoms and investigations

Patients with carcinoma of the pancreas present with many different symptoms. These include abdominal and back pain, weight loss, anorexia and fatigue. In many patients the disease is asymptomatic until their presentation with obstructive jaundice. Other less common presentations include superficial venous thrombosis and diabetes. Because of the position of the tumour, late presentation is very common.

The patient with a suspected diagnosis of pancreatic cancer should be referred by his GP to a general surgeon or a gastroenterologist and be seen in the out-patient clinic within two weeks of receipt of the GP's letter of referral. The clinician should organise a number of tests which include full blood count, renal and liver function tests, measurement of serum levels of the tumour marker C19.9, a chest X-ray and a CT scan of the abdomen. Abdominal ultrasonography is also helpful.

Investigation of the patient with pancreatic cancer is aimed at establishing the prognosis and defining operability.

After the initial tests have been carried out, the patient should proceed to endoscopic retrograde cholangiopancreatography (ERCP). At ERCP, cytology specimens may be obtained by suction of the pancreatic duct or biopsy. A failure to obtain a diagnosis by endoscopy should be followed by further investigation. Fine needle aspiration cytology under CT scan is usually successful at obtaining a tissue diagnosis.

Staging and grading

A commonly used staging system for pancreatic cancer is that of the Cancer Task Force, as follows:

Stage 1   No direct extension and no regional lymph node involvement.
Stage 2   Direct extension into adjacent tissue. No lymph node involvement.
Stage 3   Regional lymph node involvement with or without direct tumour extension.
Stage 4   Distant metastases.

Ninety percent of pancreatic tumours are adenocarcinomas of ductal origin and approximately 10% are acinar. Tumours are graded as well, moderately or poorly differentiated. Other rare tumours include endocrine malignancies.

Treatment

The initial treatment of a patient with pancreatic cancer depends on operability of jaundice. In a jaundiced patient, efforts should be made to treat the jaundice prior to attempting any surgical intervention. However, there is some discussion as to the advantages of this approach. The jaundice is usually due to obstruction of the biliary tree by the tumour and may be treated either by endoscopic stenting or by percutaneous transhepatic stenting of the biliary system.

Unfortunately, up to 90% of patients present with advanced disease and are surgically inoperable, and for these patients the value of stenting is controversial owing to the limited survival of this group.

For the small minority of patients with operable disease, as defined by preliminary investigation, referral should be made to a surgeon with expertise in pancreatic surgery. This is because pancreatic surgery is difficult and requires specialist skills. Better results and lower morbidity and mortality rates are observed by specialists. The operation of choice is the Whipple's procedure, which involves resection of the pancreas, distal stomach and upper duodenum.

Ten percent of patients with pancreatic cancer have operable disease. Surgery for pancreatic cancer was initially associated with a very high operability of approximately 25%. This has fallen in specialist centres to 5% with the expectation that 20% of patients will survive five years.

Treatment of inoperable disease

Patients with inoperable pancreatic cancer have a poor prognosis and treatment is palliative. The median survival is four months. Active treatment with chemotherapy may be advised. The most successful chemotherapy programmes have response rates of up to 40% but the median duration of survival of these responding patients is just one month more than might be expected without active treatment.

An alternative approach to the management of this condition is to treat symptoms by coeliac axis block. This procedure blocks the pain nerves from the pancreas and ensures good life quality. The technique requires skill and is relatively well tolerated.

Chapter 18
Cancer of the Colon

Epidemiology and presentation

Colon cancer is a major cause of cancer deaths in England and Wales and there are approximately 14,700 cases and 11,500 deaths annually. Patients with carcinoma of the colon present to their GPs with a history of altered bowel habit and rectal bleeding. This may also be accompanied by weight loss and abdominal pains. The GP should take a full history from the patient and examine him. These symptoms are suggestive of malignancy and, accordingly, an urgent referral should be made to a specialist bowel surgeon. The patient should ideally be seen within two weeks of receipt of the GP's referral letter.

In the out-patient clinic, the surgeon should take a full history from the patient and examine him. This should include a rectal examination which may show the patient to have melaena. Proctoscopy and sigmoidoscopy should be performed in the out-patient setting. Blood tests should be organised to include a full blood count, renal function and liver function tests. A chest X-ray should be carried out and a barium enema arranged as an out-patient procedure. The barium enema may show narrowing of the colon; in malignancy, this narrowing is typical and has the appearance of an apple core. Lower gastrointestinal endoscopy using a fibreoptic endoscope may then be organised and biopsies taken of the suspicious area.

Surgical management

The suspicion of malignancy having been raised, the patient should be worked up for surgery. As part of this work-up, an assessment should be made of operability by CT scanning. The CT scan will show whether or not there are enlarged lymph nodes within the abdomen and will also define the possibility of further spread to involve the liver. If there is no gross evidence of dissemination of the cancer, the patient should be admitted to hospital for laparotomy and colectomy.

At operation, a mid-line incision should be performed and the abdominal contents inspected. The tumour should be mobilised and removed together with a good margin of normal tissue. Ideally, the tumour should be inspected by a pathologist and frozen sections performed to ensure that the resection edges of the apparently normal gut contain no tumour. An end-to-end anastomosis is then made. If the patient is found to have less than three liver metastases at operation, an attempt should be made by the surgeon to remove these metastases. If there are more, no operative action needs to be taken, lymph node sampling should also be performed, the surgeon biopsying mesenteric glands so that the pathologist can provide information which affects the patient's management. The incision wound is then repaired. Providing no hepatic surgery has been performed, the patient should be ready to be discharged within seven days of the operation.

Tumour grade and stage

The tumour should be examined histologically. It is described as being either well, moderately or poorly differentiated. A Dukes stage is given and this reflects the degree of invasion of the tumour. Dukes stage A is when a tumour is confined to mucosa; Dukes stage B is when a tumour perforates the serosa; and Dukes stage C is when lymph nodes are affected. Tumours of the colon are also divided according to their anatomical subsites. These are the appendix, caecum, ascending colon, hepatic flexure, transverse colon, splenic flexure, descending colon and sigmoid colon.

The tumour can also be staged according to the TNM clinical classification system.

Primary tumour (T stage)

T0 No evidence of primary tumour.
T1 Tumour invades submucosa.
T2 Tumour invades muscularis.
T3 Tumour invades through muscularis.
T4 Tumour perforates the peritoneum.

Regional lymph nodes (N stage)

N0 No nodal involvement.
N1 Metastasis in one to three pericolic nodes.

N2   Metastasis in four or more pericolic nodes.
N3   Metastasis in any lymph node.

Metastatic state (M stage)

M0   No distant metastases.
M1   Distant metastases.

Adjuvant treatment

Following recovery from surgery, no additional treatment is recommended for patients with Dukes A or B disease. However, patients with Dukes C tumours should have adjuvant chemotherapy, because there is a survival advantage in this group of patients. Treatment should be with a 5-fluorouracil containing programme. There is considerable contention as to which is the optimal treatment schedule. In the USA but not in the UK, additional adjuvant therapy with levamisole should be considered. This is an immunomodulatory agent whose biological effects in colonic cancer are unknown. Treatment should continue for one year and is given on a fortnightly basis. Approximately 80–90% of Dukes A patients, 60–70% of Dukes B patients and 25–50% of Dukes C patients survive five years.

Management of metastatic disease

Metastatic colonic carcinoma has a poor prognosis and the current recommendation is for treatment with 5-fluorouracil and radiotherapy as appropriate. There is considerable debate as to whether or not the addition of folinic acid is of an advantage to the patient. The current consensus is that there is a benefit at least in terms of remission rates although not of overall survival.

Chapter 19
Cancer of the Rectum

Epidemiology

Rectal cancer affects 9300 people and causes 5700 deaths each year in England and Wales. The development of this tumour may be associated with premalignant changes and this can be associated with hereditary conditions. Diets high in fat and low in fibre lead to higher incidences of rectal cancer.

Presentation and initial assessment

Patients with rectal carcinomas generally present with a history of altered bowel habit, rectal bleeding and weight loss. A patient with such symptoms should be urgently referred by his GP to a specialist bowel surgeon who should organise an urgent appointment for the patient to be seen. The surgeon will take a history from the patient and examine him. This examination should include a rectal assessment digitally, by proctoscopy and sigmoidoscopy. If a mass is seen, this should be biopsied. A full blood count, liver function tests and renal function tests should be performed together with a chest X-ray and a barium enema. A CT scan or abdominal ultrasound should be performed in order to assess preoperatively operability, lymph node status and hepatic infiltration.

Surgery

The surgery performed depends upon the site of the carcinoma and a preoperative assessment of operability. Tumours of the upper and middle third of the rectum are treated by anterior resection. In this procedure, the rectum is mobilised from the sacral hollow and the tumour together with an adequate margin of normal tissue is removed. This normal margin ranges between 2 and 5 cm. The mesorectum and lateral pararectal tissue should be removed. The role of pelvic lymphadenectomy has not been clearly defined. Lesions of the lower third of the rectum are treated by abdominoperineal resection; the rectum is mobilised and the peritoneum at the base of the bladder or posterior vagina is incised. The lateral ligaments are divided and the anus excised, and a permanent colostomy is required.

Approximately 10–15% of patients will present with hepatic metastases. If there are less than four, these should be resected at the time of operation to remove the primary tumour, as this is thought to be associated with a good prognosis and the possibility of cure. This operation may be complicated by haemorrhage and infection.

Staging and grading

After surgery, the tumour is examined histologically. It is described as well, moderately or poorly differentiated according to the microscopic appearances and staged according to the Dukes system. Dukes stage A is when a tumour is confined to the mucosa. Dukes stage B is where the tumour perforates the serosa, and Dukes stage C is where lymph nodes are involved.

The TNM system is also used to stage rectal cancer, as follows:

Primary tumour (T stage)

T1 Tumour invades submucosa.
T2 Tumour invades muscularis.
T3 Tumour invades through muscularis.
T4 Tumour perforates visceral peritoneum.

Nodal status (N stage)

N0 No nodes involved.
N1 Metastasis in one to three perirectal lymph nodes.
N2 Metastasis in four or more perirectal lymph nodes.
N3 Metastasis in any distant lymph node.

Metastatic state (M stage)

MX Unknown
M0 No metastases
M1 Metastases present

Complications of surgery

A neurogenic bladder is very common after pelvic surgery but will usually recover within ten days. Sexual dysfunction in males is inevitable, and the most common problems are retrograde ejaculation and erectile impotence. Surgery is complicated by a significant mortality, with an incidence of 1–5%.

Adjuvant treatment

After the patient has recovered from surgery, he should receive pelvic radiotherapy. This is done because it has been shown in randomised studies that there is a decreased risk of pelvic recurrence of between 5 and 10%.

Prognosis

Five-year survival for Dukes stage A disease ranges between 88 and 93%, for Dukes stage B disease is between 70 and 80%, and for Dukes stage C cancer is between 30 and 40%.

Treatment of metastatic rectal cancer

Metastatic rectal carcinoma will respond to chemotherapy. Between 15 and 25% of patients will have a regression of metastases when treated with single-agent 5-fluorouracil. The median duration of response is approximately nine months but there are long-term survivors. Treatment is associated with little toxicity. There has been recent interest in the possibility that the activity of 5-fluorouracil may be potentiated by the use of folinic acid. In three of seven published trials this has been found to be so, but in none of these trials is there an overall survival advantage to the responding patients. Newer agents such as tomudex have recently been developed for the treatment of this condition but are probably less active than 5-fluorouracil.

Chapter 20
Renal Cancer

Epidemiology

Renal cell carcinoma is not a particularly common cancer and amounts to approximately 2% of deaths from malignancy in England and Wales; 2300 patients die annually of this disease. The causes of renal cell cancer are not clear. There is evidence for a genetic predisposition in a very small percentage of patients. The disease has an increased incidence in patients with Von Hippel–Lindau disease and tuberous sclerosis.

Presentation

Patients with renal cell carcinoma commonly present with pain in the loins or blood in the urine. Other symptoms include unexplained fevers, joint pains, symptoms due to anaemia or polycythaemia, a varicocele, generalised symptoms of malignancy such as weight loss and cachexia, and symptoms due to spread of the disease to metastatic sites such as brain, lung or bone. If the diagnosis of renal cell carcinoma is suspected by the GP, the patient should be sent on to a urologist.

Hospital investigation

The urologist will assess the patient in the out-patient clinic, taking a full medical history and conducting an examination. Investigations organised will include a full blood count, liver and renal function tests and a chest X-ray. Further investigation will include a CT scan of the abdomen and the thorax to define operability.

Surgery

If the patient has no evidence of spread of the disease then the urological surgeon will arrange for him to be admitted for nephrectomy. At operation, the kidney and vascular pedicle together with the ureter are removed. If there is enlargement of abdominal lymph nodes, the surgeon should attempt to dissect away these nodes.

Staging

The patient with renal cell carcinoma is staged according to the spread of the disease, as follows:

Primary tumour (T stage)

T1 Small tumour without enlargement of the kidney.
T2 Large tumour with deformity of the kidney outline.
T3 Extension of the tumour beyond the kidney.
T4 Involvement of neighbouring organs with the kidney cancer.

Lymph node status (N stage)

N0 No evidence of nodal involvement.
N1 Involvement of a single node.
N2 Involvement of multiple regional nodes.
N3 Fixed regional lymph node involvement.
N4 Juxta regional lymph node involvement.

Metastatic state (M stage)

M0 No evidence of metastases.
M1 Distant metastases present.

Treatment of inoperable or metastatic tumour

Management of an inoperable primary tumour

Locally advanced inoperable kidney cancer may cause significant symptoms which may be poorly controlled by systemic palliative measures.

These local symptoms may include haematuria, which may be so profound that regular blood transfusion is required, and loin pain, which may be poorly controlled with opiate analgesia. These symptoms can be treated by angioinfarction, where agents are introduced into the renal artery to occlude the tumour's blood supply. A number of different agents can be introduced into the renal artery, including steel coils and chemotherapy pellets. By these means, successful symptom palliation is achieved in approximately 70–80% of all patients. This procedure does have significant morbidity which includes a transient increase in pain, fever and occasionally shock due to the release of tumour products into the circulation. In hospitals where it is not possible to treat by angioinfarction, radiation to the kidney may be given.

Adjuvant therapy

Local radiotherapy to the tumour bed leads to no survival advantage and has significant morbidity and so is not recommended. Adjuvant chemotherapy and immunotherapy confer no survival advantage.

Treatment of metastatic kidney cancer

Chemotherapy

Chemotherapy is generally ineffective in the treatment of kidney cancer and the most active of the agents, which include the vinca alkaloids, produce responses in less than 10% of patients. Chemotherapy is generally not used in the treatment of this tumour.

Hormonal therapy

Initial reports of the efficacy of hormonal treatments in the management of kidney cancer have proven to be incorrect. Response rates of up to 30% were described to medroxyprogesterone acetate; however, this order of response has not been confirmed and the true response rate to hormonal agents is probably less than 2%. A wide variety of hormonal treatments have been used in this condition and include tamoxifen and flutamide in addition to the progestagens.

Immunotherapy

The most important of the therapies used for metastatic kidney cancer is immunotherapy. The first agents used were BCG and *Cryptosporidium parvum* but these have been replaced by interferons and interleukin 2. The overall order of response to interferon therapy is 15%. Approximately 5% of patients have a complete response with a median duration of seven months. In 1985, the results of treatment with interleukin 2 were first published, and 60% of patients with kidney cancer were reported to respond to treatment. This high response rate was not confirmed in subsequent studies which were, however, encouraging in that overall approximately 20% of patients were seen to respond to treatment. The most significant aspect of interleukin 2 treatment is that responses are durable, and those patients achieving a complete response are likely to be cured of their malignancy. In the original dosage regimen, the treatment had significant toxicities. These toxicities are fewer with subutaneous low-dose scheduling of interleukin 2 treatments. Currently interleukin 2 is given with interferon alpha.

Prognosis

Overall, 5–7% of patients with metastatic renal cell cancer survive five years from diagnosis. However, the median survival for patients with metastatic disease is nine months.

Chapter 21
Bladder Cancer

Epidemiology

Carcinoma of the bladder is common in England and Wales, and each year approximately 6900 men and women are registered with the disease and 4700 die. The average age at which patients with this condition present to their clinician is approximately 65 years.

Presentation and investigations

The initial symptoms include haematuria, dysuria and frequency of micturition. These symptoms are, unfortunately, commonly treated by GPs with antibiotics for a period of time prior to referral to a specialist. Referral should be promptly organised to a specialist urological surgeon. The patient will be seen in an out-patient clinic, a careful history taken and an examination made. The patient's symptoms should be investigated further by performing a full blood count, renal function tests, liver function tests, bacteriological and cytological examination of the urine to examine for the presence of infection and malignancy. An intravenous pyelogram (IVP) may be ordered to examine the urothelial tract radiologically, or an ultrasound investigation carried out.

These investigations should be organised promptly and the patient reviewed with the result within two to three weeks. The urologist should then organise for the patient to be admitted for cystoscopy. The patient is anaesthetised for this procedure and the urethra and bladder are carefully examined using a fibreoptic cystoscope. Any abnormal areas within the bladder should be biopsied together with areas of surrounding apparently normal-looking bladder. The urologist at cystoscopy may describe a normal-looking bladder or the presence of a papilloma or solid tumour. The suspicious areas are treated by diathermy and the pelvis carefully examined in order to describe the clinical staging of the tumour.

Tumour grading and staging

The tumour should then be examined pathologically and is given a grade according to differentiation, as follows:

G1 Well differentiated
G2 Moderately differentiated
G3 Poorly differentiated

Lesions are further characterised pathologically by their microscopic appearance as being either transitional cell carcinoma or squamous carcinoma. Approximately 90% of patients in England and Wales have transitional cell carcinomas. The rest are squamous carcinomas or adenocarcinomas. There may be squamous metaplasia present within a transitional cell carcinoma and this is indicative of a poor prognosis.

The tumour should also be staged according to the TNM classification as follows:

Primary tumour (T stage)

T1S Carcinoma in situ.
TA Papillary non-invasive tumour.
T1 Superficial tumour, not invading beyond the lamina propria.
T2 Tumour invading superficial muscle.
T3A Invasion of deep muscle.
T3B Invasion through bladder wall.
T4A Tumour invading prostate, uterus or vagina.
T4B Tumour fixed to the pelvic wall.

Nodal status (N stage)

N0 No lymph node involvement.
N1 Single regional lymph node involvement.
N2 Bilateral regional lymph node involvement.
N3 Fixed regional lymph nodes.
N4 Juxta regional lymph node involvement.

Metastatic state (M stage)

M0 No evidence of metastases.
M1 Distant metastases.

A subscript P is given to describe the pathological staging of the tumour.

Treatment of superficial bladder cancer

The majority of transitional cell carcinomas of the bladder present as superficial tumours. After resection by diathermy at cystoscopy, approximately 60% of these will recur. The recurrence rate is greater where there are multiple tumours, associated carcinoma in situ or poorly differentiated tumours. The outlook is best for solitary tumours, tumours with good histology and tumours without invasion of the lamina propria.

The recommendation for follow-up is slightly controversial but, in most practices, cystoscopy is performed three-monthly until the patient is tumour free and thereafter six-monthly for two years then yearly for three years. Practice varies throughout England and Wales.

If tumours are poorly controlled by cystoscopic diathermy but remain superficial, agents may be instilled into the bladder to try and control the disease. There are a number of different compounds used, including BCG, interferon, thiotepa, adriamcyin, mitomycin C, mitozantrone and epodyl. The consensus view is that diathermy and intravesical chemotherapy prevent the progression of superficial to locally advanced or metastatic disease in 40% of cases. However, overall, approximately 10% of patients with superficial tumours develop invasive disease. If there is associated carcinoma in situ, over 60% of patients will develop invasive cancer. BCG is the treatment of choice for carcinoma in situ and mitozantrone and mitomycin C are the most popular treatments of multifocal superficial tumours.

Treatment of invasive bladder cancer

The treatment of muscle-invasive carcinoma of the bladder is by radiation or with surgery. Both have similar efficacy in terms of the control of the disease and this varies according to clinical staging: 40–60% of T2 tumours, 25% of T3 tumours and 5% of T4 tumours are controlled by radiotherapy or surgery. In England and Wales, radiotherapy is the most widely practised treatment because it has limited morbidity and because patients are left with a bladder at the end of therapy. Radical cystectomy has a morbidity that varies between centres and may range up to 3% of patients. Radical radiotherapy is generally given to a total dose of 6500 cGy over a six-week period. Treatment may be given to the whole pelvis, focusing down upon the bladder towards the end of treatment, or may be given to the bladder alone. During radiotherapy the patient may get cystitis or proctitis. At the end of treatment he may suffer from a small shrunken bladder consequent to radiation fibrosis.

Treatment of metastatic bladder cancer

Bladder cancer that has spread beyond the bladder is conventionally treated with chemotherapy. There have been recent advances in the treatment of this disease such that new hope is now offered to patients with metastatic cancer. A number of different programmes are used for the treatment of this condition and include programmes which have the acronyms CMV (cyclophosphamide, methotrexate, vinblastine), MVAC (methotrexate, vinblastine, adriamycin, cisplatin) and MVMJ (methotrexate, vinblastine, mitozantrone, carboplatin). The results of treatment vary from centre to centre but the overall expectation is for an initial response in approximately 50% of patients, with a median duration of nine months. During the terminal phases of illness patients require specialist care for symptom palliation. The disease may spread to bone, lung or liver, and opiate analgesia or local radiotherapy may be helpful in easing symptoms.

Chapter 22
Prostate Cancer

Epidemiology

Carcinoma of the prostate is the second most common cancer of males in the Western world. The latest incidence figures suggest that in England and Wales 11,500 men were diagnosed as having prostate cancer in 1991 and that there were 8500 deaths. The disease has doubled in incidence over the last 20 years and will soon overtake lung cancer as the most common of male cancers. This is the case in the USA, where prostate cancer has now exceeded lung cancer as the commonest cancer of males.

Presentation and investigation

Patients with prostate cancer commonly present with urinary frequency, a poor urine flow or difficulty starting and stopping urination. Other associated symptoms on presentation of illness include bone pain, weight loss and general debility. The patient with symptoms such as these should be referred by his GP to a urologist.

The patient should be seen in the out-patient clinic initially, where a careful history should be taken, a full examination made, routine blood tests performed and levels of acid phosphatase and prostate specific antigen (PSA) assessed. In addition, plain X-rays of the chest and pelvis should be performed.

From the clinical findings an assessment can be made of the degree of prostate enlargement. If the prostate is malignant it is staged as follows:

Clinical staging and grading

T0 No tumour palpable.
T1 Tumour in one lobe of the prostate.

T2 Tumour involving both prostate lobes.
T3 Tumour infiltrating out of the prostate to involve seminal vesicles.
T4 Extensive tumour, fixed and infiltrating local structures.

If the X-rays show no evidence of metastases, a bone scan should be carried out. If the facilities are available, fine needle aspiration cytology should be performed on the prostate by the rectal route and a histological diagnosis established. In modern hospitals this might be performed by the radiologist rather than the urologist, who will carry out a prostatic ultrasound with needle biopsy of abnormal areas.

By this means, a grading of the tumour can be made. The system most commonly used is termed the Gleason grade, where '1' represents the most indolent form of prostate cancer and '9' the most aggressive.

Prostate specific antigen

PSA levels are not necessarily diagnostic of prostate cancer. Where levels are raised above 4 µg/l but less than 10 µg/l the chance of the patient having prostate cancer is approximately 25%. At levels over 10 µg/l the chance of diagnosing prostate cancer will have increased to 40%. Levels of this antigen may be elevated in benign prostatic hypertrophy.

Management

Early-stage tumours

The treatment of prostate cancer depends upon the clinical stage and is surrounded by controversy. Early-stage small-bulk prostate cancer, that is T1 and T2 disease, without evidence of spread may be treated by observation, radiotherapy or radical prostatectomy. The options for treatment depend upon the patient's overall state and preference. Observation involves regular follow up without treatment. Radiotherapy involves approximately six weeks of attendance at hospital for prostatic irradiation which is given in an attempt to sterilise the tumour. Radiotherapy has morbidity. Acutely, it may be associated with symptoms of cystitis and proctitis, and post-treatment it is associated with impotence in up to 70% of patients. Radical prostatectomy involves major abdominal surgery with removal of the prostate and associated draining lymph glands. It is a major operative procedure, but modern anaesthetic techniques and surgical advances have meant that the morbidity is limited. However, a degree of incontinence is reported in up to 25% of patients and impotence, which is under-reported by surgeons, occurs in up to 90% of patients. There is an operative mortality of less than 1%.

The reason that the patient can be offered the prospect of choice in determining what therapy he should have for early-stage disease is because observation, radiotherapy and radical surgery have all been shown to offer the patient the same overall chance for long-term survival, particularly for those patients with good histology tumours. The reason for controversy in this field is that there has been no randomised comparison of these three options involving significant patient numbers, and so this subject remains a matter for vociferous debate.

Locally advanced or metastatic cancer

When patients have locally advanced, that is T3 or T4, prostate cancer or metastatic disease, treatment involves the use of hormonal therapy. Again, this area is one of considerable debate and controversy. Hormonal therapy for this condition was first described in the 1940s when the disease was found to be dependent upon testosterone (produced by the testicles). For this reason, the first treatments offered in the 1940s were orchiectomy or oestrogen (female hormone) therapy.

Treatment

The results of treatment were first analysed in the 1960s by the Veterans Administration Co-operative Urological Research Group (VACURG). In their studies, the VACURG randomised patients to treatment with oestrogens or placebo or by orchiectomy or placebo. The overall survival of patients, treated or untreated, was the same and there was an excess mortality rate from cardiovascular deaths in the oestrogen-treated group. The reason for this is that oestrogens cause an increased coaguability of blood and increased blood volumes.

Because orchiectomy is barbaric and oestrogen therapy is associated with morbidity and mortality, medical treatments for this condition have been sought which are not barbaric and have no side-effects.

The most effective of these new treatments which has the least morbidity associated with its use is a group of compounds called the gonadotrophin-releasing hormone agonists. These include leuprorelin acetate, goserelin acetate and buserelin. They are currently given by monthly subcutaneous injection.

Effects of treatment delay

Later analyses of the VACURG study showed that all the patients treated by placebo were eventually given hormonal therapies by their primary care physicians. As the survival of both groups of patients, treated and untreated, was the same, the real conclusion of the study is that early, as compared with late, treatment offers the same prospect for survival. This important issue is currently undergoing re-investigation by the Medical Research Council (MRC) in a randomised prospective trial. The MRC trial has been published in a preliminary form. Early analysis has shown an increased risk of disease complications and a more rapid rate of death in those patients having delayed treatment.

Prognosis

Small-bulk localised disease

The outlook depends upon tumour grade. Observation, radiotherapy and surgery all lead to an equivalent survival of 80% at ten years for patients with low-grade tumours. Patients with poorly differentiated, high Gleason-grade tumours have a worse outlook with observation and radiotherapy than with surgery: only 15% of patients survive ten years. It is argued that patient selection influences this result, as fitter patients, who will invariably do better than less well patients, are selected for surgery.

Metastatic and large-bulk localised disease

It has been shown recently in two clinical trials that the addition of an anti-androgen to gonadotrophin-releasing hormone agonist therapy leads to an improvement in survival rate. The median survival for patients with metastatic tumours treated with combination anti-androgen therapy is three years, and for those treated with single-agent gonadotrophin-releasing hormone agonist or by orchiectomy it is two and a half years. These results remain controversial.

The prospects for survival for a patient with locally advanced disease without metastases is much better. The median survival of this group is four and a half years. It is not known whether there is an advantage to combination gonadotrophin-releasing hormone agonist and anti-androgen therapy in this patient group.

Prostate cancer is very responsive to treatment and 80% of patients improve subjectively. However, after a period of approximately one year, most patients who had metastatic cancer on presentation have clinical signs of relapse. In relapse, treatment is palliative and hinges upon the use of radiotherapy and steroids. Blood transfusion is often necessary.

Chapter 23
Testicular Cancer

Epidemiology and presentation

Testicular cancer affects 900 men each year in England and Wales. Patients present during the second and third decade of their lives, generally with pain and swelling of the testis. The major predisposing factor to the development of testicular cancer is maldescent of the testes.

Investigations

The patient with a testicular mass should be referred immediately to a consultant urologist. Following hospital referral a patient should be initially staged by routine haematology, biochemistry, radiology, including CT scan of the abdomen and chest, and measurement of alpha-fetoprotein and human chorionic gonadotrophin. He should then proceed to orchiectomy. This is performed through a groin incision; the testis is removed by the surgeon and cut in half.

Pathology and staging

There are four main types of testicular tumour: seminoma, teratoma, lymphoma and small cell carcinoma. Teratomas constitute approximately 75% of all testicular malignancies. They are classically cystic when examined by the naked eye and contain a variety of different elements which may include cartilage, muscle, bone or virtually any other tissue. Subtypes of teratoma are described, called undifferentiated, choriocarcinoma or differentiated. Seminomas constitute 20% of tumours. They are generally uniform in appearance and consist of large cells with darkly staining nuclei. Approximately 5% of all testicular tumours are lymphomatous, and their appearance is generally uniform but with some areas of necrosis. Less than 1% of tumours are of small cell origin. These tumours have no specific macroscopic features. The tumour is then examined microscopically and again there are classic appearances. The rest of this report considers teratoma and seminoma.

Having made a histological diagnosis, treatment is initiated and depends upon the stage at which the tumour has advanced. The following stages are described:

Stage I: Tumour confined to testes.
Stage II: Tumour spread to abdominal lymph nodes.
Stage III: Tumour spread to lymph nodes above the diaphragm.
Stage IV: Tumour invading organs other than lymph nodes such as liver or lung.

The disease is further substaged according to the size of the metastatic deposits and the number of pulmonary metastases. In the USA, retroperitoneal lymph node dissection is undertaken to stage testicular cancer. This is not part of medical practice in the UK.

Treatment

Tumour stage defines treatment. If the tumour is localised to the testis, two actions are available to the clinician. The first for both seminoma and teratoma is observation without further therapy. If this policy is followed then the likelihood of any further treatment being required is approximately 25% for teratoma and 17% for seminoma. The alternative is to treat with adjuvant radiotherapy or two courses of chemotherapy (in some centres) for seminoma, or with two courses of chemotherapy for teratoma, following which the prognosis is excellent with a 1–2% chance of relapse. It should be noted that almost all patients who develop progressive disease during the period of observation without treatment are salvageable by chemotherapy. Patients with stage I teratoma are generally referred for adjuvant chemotherapy using BEP (bleomycin, etoposide, cisplatin) chemotherapy; two to four courses are given.

The management of stage II disease is controversial. For stage IIa seminoma, the majority of clinicians in the UK would treat with radiotherapy, and for stage IIa teratoma, four courses of chemotherapy is likely to be given. For all patients with stage IIb disease, whether it is seminoma or teratoma, cytotoxic chemotherapy is given. Before the advent of cytotoxic chemotherapy for teratoma, the disease was invariably fatal. The development of effective chemotherapy programmes has brought about a revolution in the management of patients with malignancy, and now virtually all patients are cured by treatment.

Treatment with cytotoxic agents was originally introduced into medical practice by Li in the early 1960s. As a result, approximately 8% of patients with advanced disease were cured using a combination of agents that included actinomycin and chlorambucil. In the early 1970s, Samuels treated patients with vinblastine and bleomycin and produced remissions in approximately 50% of men treated. This treatment was of considerable toxicity because of the large dosages of vinblastine and bleomycin used and also because of the relative lack of support programmes for patients with neutropenic sepsis and thrombocytopenia which occur as a result of the use of these agents. In 1976, Einhorn introduced the BVP (bleomycin, vinblastine and cisplatin) programme for the treatment of malignant testicular tumours. This regimen was enormously successful and 70% of patients with advanced disease were cured.

Over the last decade, there have been refinements in the way that treatment has been given. Drug treatment which initially required six courses of five-day treatments has now been reduced to four courses of three-day treatments. Substitution of drugs within this programme to produce the modern three-day JEB (bleomycin, etoposide and carboplatin) programme has meant that toxicity has been limited, and the expectation is that 95% of patients with good-prognosis tumours and 48% of patients with poor-prognosis disease are cured.

At the end of treatment one problem may be that of persistent mass, by which is meant a residual tumour at the site of the original metastatic disease. The approach to this problem is to proceed to surgery, which may be very extensive and involve both thoracotomy and laparotomy. At surgery the residual mass of tumour is excised as completely as possible, and this may require dacron grafting of major vessels or removal of a kidney in order to take away the tumour completely. This operative procedure is extremely intricate. Histological examination of the removed tumour shows that in one-third of cases there is necrotic tumour, one-third are differentiated teratoma and another third are undifferentiated cancer. If necrotic tumour is found, no further action is taken. If undifferentiated tumour is found, further chemotherapy is given and 30–40% of patients will be cured by the combination of chemotherapy and surgery. In those patients who have differentiated tumour, it is important to remove the residual mass of the disease because over a five-year period, approximately 50% of differentiated tumours undergo further malignant change.

Side-effects of treatment

The effects of treatment are very closely monitored by measuring the serum levels of alpha-fetoprotein and human chorionic gonadotrophin. These are hormones secreted by teratomas and seminomas. If the tumour is being treated effectively the levels of these hormones in the blood will decay over a known period (three to five days for alpha-fetoprotein and approximately 12–36 hours for human chorionic gonadotrophin).

There are specific toxicities that relate to treatment. Cisplatin will cause renal damage, deafness, and a peripheral neuropathy which may manifest as numbness in the fingers or toes or complete loss of motor and sensory function in the limbs. Bleomycin unfortunately causes pulmonary toxicity, that is, an irreversible and progressive loss of lung function which is fatal, in approximately 2% of patients treated. The drug regimen used generally causes sterility (loss of functional spermatogenesis). However, in 80% of patients there is recovery of spermatogenesis which generally occurs at 18 months from the completion of treatment.

Retroperitoneal lymph node dissection has specific effects on sexual function which range from complete impotence to retrograde ejaculation. This phenomenon does not necessarily mean that the patient is functionally sterile because sperm can be collected and artificial insemination techniques employed to successfully fertilise the patient's partner.

Prognosis

The treatment of teratoma and seminoma is highly complex and requires patient managment in centres of excellence, where the delivery of chemotherapy and the maintenance of patients during neutropenic and thrombocytopenic episodes can be successfully achieved. In the best hands, 95% of patients with this disease are cured and this is without doubt a significant advance in medical science, as young men with this malignant tumour can be returned to an active life within the community following treatment.

Prognostic indices have been described in detail by many authors. One of the more commonly used is described by the International Germ Cell Cancer Collaborative Group. Patients are classified as having good-prognosis disease with five-year survival of 92–95%, intermediate-prognosis tumours with 72–80% five-year survival, and poor-prognosis tumours with 48% five-year survival.

Chapter 24
Non-Hodgkin's Lymphoma

Epidemiology

Non-Hodgkin's lymphoma is a common malignancy, and in England and Wales approximately 3500 patients die annually as a result of it. Twice as many males as females are affected by this condition.

Presentation

Patients present with glandular enlargement which may be accompanied by constitutional symptoms including weight loss, sweating and fever. Where the diagnosis of lymphoma is suspected, the patient should be referred to a specialist oncology centre by the GP.

Initial investigations in hospital

In the out-patient clinic, a careful history is obtained from the patient, who is then examined. The investigations organised should include a blood count, renal and hepatic function tests, chest X-ray, bone marrow aspiration and trephine and CT scan of the abdomen and chest. These investigations are done in order to define the extent of the disease.

Staging

From these investigations the clinical staging is obtained. This is defined as follows:

Stage 1 Disease confined to one lymph node or two contiguous lymph node groups.
Stage 2 Disease on one side of the diaphragm in lymph node groups that are separate.
Stage 3 Disease on both sides of the diaphragm.
Stage 4 Extranodal spread of lymphoma.

Lymphoma is further divided into substage A or B depending upon the absence or presence, respectively, of constitutional symptoms, which are fevers, sweats and weight loss.

Grading

Preliminary investigations having been organised, the patient should then proceed to a lymph node biopsy. This is to define the pathological diagnosis. There are many classification systems for non-Hodgkin's lymphoma, but the most practical is to describe the tumour as being low, intermediate or high grade. A low-grade tumour tends to have a follicular nature and to contain relatively inactive cells. A high-grade tumour contains cells that have a high index of mitotic activity and there is no follicular nature to the lymph node. An intermediate-grade tumour has some of the features of both high- and low-grade tumours.

Treatment and prognosis

Once the disease has been staged and pathologically defined, treatment can be instituted.

Low-grade non-Hodgkin's lymphoma

Low-grade tumours are generally disseminated. However, if they are localised, i.e. stage 1, small bulk, peripheral, and without B symptoms, the treatment should be radiotherapy. For stage 2–4 disease, treatment is with chemotherapy with oral alkylating agents such as chlorambucil, or with an intravenous chemotherapy programme known as CVP (cyclophosphamide, vincristine and prednisone). Chlorambucil has very little toxicity and its only side-effect at high total dosages is sterility. CVP leads to hair loss but is without significant morbidity. Both regimens may be associated with marrow toxicity which results in admissions with neutropenic sepsis or with thrombocytopenic bleeding.
Patients with stage 1 non-Hodgkin's lymphoma have a 95% chance of

cure with radiotherapy. The patient with disseminated low-grade lymphoma is not cured by treatment. Although 85% of patients achieve a complete response to therapy, this response is transient, and after a median period of 18 months the patient relapses and requires re-treatment. The average patient has four such episodes of response and relapse and finally, after a median period of seven and half years, will progress to high-grade lymphoma or die of infection.

High-grade and intermediate-grade non-Hodgkin's lymphoma

Paradoxically, high-grade and intermediate-grade lymphomas are more likely to be confined to one lymph node group than low-grade tumours and are curable. Stage 1 disease may be treated with radiotherapy. Some clinicians will then proceed to treat with adjuvant chemotherapy. Patients with small-bulk, stage 1 non-Hodgkin's lymphoma have a 95% chance of cure with radiation, and this chance is only minimally improved with chemotherapy. If the stage 1 disease is bulky, chemotherapy alone may be given.

Stage 2, 3 and 4 high-grade or intermediate-grade non-Hodgkin's lymphoma are treated with combination chemotherapy. The most effective and safest programme is called CHOP (cyclophosphamide, vincristine, prednisone and adriamycin). This produces a response in 40–60% of patients, a proportion of whom eventually relapse. Approximately 30–40% of patients are, however, cured by treatment. The toxicities of therapy include vomiting and hair loss and admissions with sepsis and bleeding.

Chapter 25
Hodgkin's Disease

Epidemiology

Hodgkin's disease is a tumour of lymph glands which is characterised histologically by the presence of Reed–Sternberg cells. In England and Wales, approximately 1500 patients a year present with Hodgkin's disease. The presentation can be with swelling of lymph glands, which is generally painless, or with constitutional symptoms which include profound sweating, fevers and weight loss exceeding 10% of body mass. These constitutional symptoms are termed B symptoms. More men than women present with Hodgkin's disease and there is a bimodal age distribution with peaks in the third and seventh decades. The importance of this condition is in its high possibility for cure.

Investigation and diagnosis

When a patient with Hodgkin's disease presents to his GP, a full history should be taken and an examination made. Examination may show the patient to have enlargement of the lymph nodes or of the liver or spleen. The GP should refer the patient with suspected Hodgkin's disease either to a surgeon or to an oncologist for further investigation.

In the clinic, a careful history should be obtained and an examination made. Investigations will be organised, including a full blood count and erythrocyte sedimentation rate (ESR), liver and renal function tests, a chest X-ray, CT scan of the chest and abdomen, and bone marrow aspiration and trephine. The patient will be reviewed with the results of these tests in the out-patient clinic and admission will then be organised for a biopsy of the lymph glands. The purpose of the investigations is to define the clinical stage of the disease and the purpose of the biopsy to make a histological diagnosis.

Tumour grade

The excised lymph node will be examined by a specialist pathologist. Four different histological variants of Hodgkin's disease are described: nodular sclerosing, mixed cellularity, lymphocyte predominant and lymphocyte depleted. Nodular sclerosing Hodgkin's disease is subclassified as grade I or II.

Tumour staging

The results of the staging investigations will help the clinician to determine the clinical stage of the Hodgkin's disease, and this in turn defines treatment. The stages are defined as:

Stage 1   One lymph node or two continguous lymph node groups are affected.
Stage 2   Two non-continguous lymph node groups on the same side of the diaphragm are affected.
Stage 3   Lymph node groups on both sides of the diaphragm are affected.
Stage 4   Extranodal spread to the liver, lung or bone and rarely to other sites occurs.

The tumour is further classified as being A or B, defining a lack or presence of constitutional symptoms, respectively. The staging is further defined by use of the subscipt S, which defines splenic involvement, or E, which defines extension to involve extranodal tissue in direct aposition to an enlarged lymph node group.

The purpose of staging is to define treatment groups. The current recommendations for treatment are as follows. Stage 1 and 2A disease are generally treated with radiation. The exceptions to this rule are where there is bulky lymphadenopathy or constitutional symptoms. In these instances, chemotherapy may be the preferred option. Stage 2B–4B disease is generally treated with combination chemotherapy.

Treatment and its side-effects

Radiation

Radiation treatment is generally given according to two well-defined treatment plans. Lymphadenopathy above the diaphragm is treated with mantle radiation, which includes the lymph node groups in the neck, axillae and chest, to a total dosage of 3500 cGy given over a period of four-to six-weeks. Infradiaphragmatic radiation is generally given in the inverted-Y distribution, which includes the para-aortic and iliac nodal groups. Treatment is given to a total dosage of 3500 cGy over a four- to six-week period.

Mantle radiotherapy may be complicated by radiation pneumonitis, which is characterised by a period of breathlessness and fever which responds to steroids. It is invariably accompanied by loss of saliva production and an oesophagitis. Infradiaphragmatic radiotherapy may be complicated by some minor bowel disturbance, but generally is well tolerated. Radiation is usually avoided in children and adolescents as it may lead to gross growth disturbance. Infradiaphragmatic radiation may cause sterility.

In patients with good-prognosis disease, the radiation fields may be reduced to reduce toxicity. Thus, extended field or mini-mantle treatments may be prescribed.

Chemotherapy

Combination chemotherapy for Hodgkin's disease was introduced in the mid 1960s. The original treatment regimen, which has the acronym MOPP, combined mustine, vincristine (oncovin), prednisone and procarbazine. These drugs are given intravenously and orally over a four-week period. The treatment is repeated six times. Treatment is associated with acute nausea and vomiting, sterility in 90% of males and 50% of females and the development of second tumours in approximately 5% of patients.

Chemotherapy treatments have been modified over the years in order to reduce side-effects. The current recommendation is for a programme called ABVD (adriamycin, bleomycin, vinblastine and dacarbazine). These drugs do not cause sterility or second malignancies, and are of obvious advantage in a disease where there is a high expectation of cure.

Randomised trials have shown an equivalence of ABVD to standard therapy with MOPP, and to hybrid therapies.

Bone marrow transplantation

High-dosage chemotherapy with either bone marrow transplantation or peripheral blood stem cell support is a relatively new and toxic treatment for drug-resistant Hodgkin's disease. The most commonly applied current programme in the UK uses 'mini-BEAM' or BEAM chemotherapy. Treatment is accompanied by either stem cell or bone marrow transplantation. Morbidity is high and, in certain groups, mortality reaches up to 30%. Long-term remissions occur in up to 40% of patients.

Prognosis

The results of treatment of Hodgkin's disease are considered to be one of the miracles of modern oncology, in that approximately 90% of patients with small-volume, early-stage disease are curable with radiation, and between 40 and 60% of patients with advanced disease are curable with chemotherapy. A poorer prognosis results from the presence of bulk disease, constitutional symptoms or poor-prognosis histology. The patient who is 'cured' as a result of treatment is unfortunately at risk from late relapse, and this may occur 15–30 years from diagnosis. This risk of late relapse is small.

Chapter 26
Melanoma

Epidemiology

Melanoma is a tumour of melanocytes, the pigmented cells of the skin. The incidence of melanoma is 10 per 100,000 of population and has increased by approximately tenfold over the last 30 years as a result of increased exposure to sunlight. Risk factors for the development of melanoma include being white, and having dysplastic naevi or familial melanoma.

There are four main clinical descriptions of melanoma: superficial spreading, nodular, lentigo maligna and acral lentiginous.

Presentation

Patients with malignant melanoma generally present with a history of a new mole, or change in an existing mole, which may bleed or itch.

Because of the public awareness of melanoma, generally there is quite rapid self-referral to GPs with these symptoms. The GP should examine the patient clinically and then refer him on to a consultant dermatologist or plastic surgeon for a specialist opinion.

Initial surgical treatment

On initial examination, the specialist will seek to confirm the diagnosis and, if there is no evidence for metastases, excise the primary lesion. This excision requires specialist surgery with wide excision of surrounding normal tissue. The reason for this relates to the incidence of local recurrence following inadequate resection and the delicacy of the surgery if the face is involved with the tumour.

Staging

Following excision and confirmation of the diagnosis histologically, staging investigations, which should include CT scanning, should be performed. As a result of surgery and staging procedures, the clinical stage can be defined as follows:

Clinical staging

Stage 1a Localised melanoma less than 0.75 mm thick.
Stage 1b Localised melanoma 0.76–1.5 mm thick.
Stage 2a Localised melanoma 1.6–4 mm thick.
Stage 2b Localised melanoma greater than 4 mm thick.
Stage 3   Limited nodal metastases involving only one regional lymph node group.
Stage 4   Advanced regional metastases or distant metastases.

The tumour can be staged according to the TNM classification of the UICC as follows:

T stage (primary tumour)

T_x Primary unassessable
T_{1s} Clark's level 1
P^I_1 Clark's level 2
P^I_2 Clark's level 3
P^I_3 Clark's level 4
P^I_4 Clark's level 5

N stage (lymph nodes)

N_x Unassessable
N_0 No nodes involved
N_1 Nodal metastases less than 3 cm
N_2 Nodal metastases greater than 3 cm

M stage (metastases)

M_x Unassessable
M_0 No metastases
M_1 Distant metastases

Pathological staging

The depth of invasion of a local tumour is the single most important prognostic factor in early-stage melanoma, as classified by Breslow thickness and by Clark's levels. These are pathology staging systems, as follows:

Clark's level 1   Melanoma confined to epidermis.
Clark's level 2   Penetration into papillary dermis.
Clark's level 3   Extension to reticular dermis.
Clark's level 4   Extension into reticular dermis.
Clark's level 5   Invasion of subcutaneous fat.

Breslow's staging system measures the vertical thickness of the primary tumour as follows:

Breslow thickness   Less than 0.75 mm
                    0.76–1.5 mm
                    1.51–3.99 mm
                    Greater than 4 mm

If regional metastases are evident, the management is relatively clearly defined and involves radical lymph node dissection. There are advocates of regional infusional programmes using cytotoxic chemotherapy, but the value of this is contentious. Radiotherapy may be used where localised disease is inoperable or as an adjuvant to surgery, reducing the bulk of the disease prior to definitive surgery.

Metastatic disease at distant sites should, if the patient is relatively fit, be treated with systemic therapy.

Treatment of metastatic melanoma

The outlook for patients with metastatic melanoma is poor. Patients generally have disease in multiple sites and the median survival is approximately four months. Treatment depends upon the patient, his fitness and the disease site. Single metastases in a lymph node or in a lung may be dealt with by surgical excision or radiotherapy. Patients with multiple disease sites are treated with chemotherapy or biological therapies, or a combination of the two. The most effective chemotherapeutic drugs are dacarbazine, the nitrosoureas and vindesine. The response rate to these compounds is in the range of 5–10%. Prolonged survival is very rare and the consensus view is that there is no advantage to the combination of single agents. Chemotherapy has side-effects; acute side-effects will include nausea and vomiting and there is a risk of neutropenic sepsis.

These side-effects are generally increased when a combination of drugs is used.

There has been an increased interest in the role of biological therapies. Within this group, the interferons lead to response rates of 10%; the median duration of response is approximately four months. More recently, adoptive immunotherapy using interleukin 2 and lymphokine activated killer (LAK) cells has been evaluated in melanoma. The high response rates initially reported have not been confirmed, and the true response rates are in the order of 10%, with a median duration of three months. Very rarely, spontaneous regression of metastatic disease occurs.

Prognostic factors

The most important prognostic factor is clinical stage, as reported in a group of 4000 patients treated in the USA and Australia. Approximately 90% of stage 1 patients, 60% of stage 2 patients and 30% of stage 3 patients survive ten years. The survival of stage 4 patients depends upon metastatic site: for patients with skin metastases only it is a median of seven months; for lung, one year; for brain, five months; liver, two months; and bone, six months.

Prognosis can also be described according to pathological staging. Depth of tumour invasion is the most important prognostic factor for localised melanoma. This can be described according to the Clark's level. Ten-year survival for a lesion less than 0.75 mm is 90% (Clark's stage 1); for a lesion 0.75–1.5 mm it is 80% (Clark's level 2); for a lesion 1.51–2.49 mm, 60% (Clark's level 3); for a lesion 2.5–3.99 mm, 50% (Clark's level 4); and for a lesion greater than 4 mm, approximately 30% (Clark's level 5).

Other important survival factors have been described from multifactorial analyses, and include the type of initial surgical management, pathological stage, ulceration, the presence of satellite nodules, anatomical location and, to a much lesser extent, patient's sex, age and tumour diameter. Lesions on

Table 26.1 Survival rates in melanoma based on metastatic rate.

Mitotic rate (mm^2)	Eight-year survival			
	Female		Male	
	Extremities	Axial	Extremities	Axial
0	0.86–0.99	0.61–0.98	0.67–0.98	0.35–0.95
0.1–6.0	0.64–0.98	0.32–0.94	0.38–0.95	0.14–0.84
>6	0.34–0.94	0.12–0.81	0.15–0.85	0.04–0.60

the feet and hands are said to have the poorest prognosis for any anatomical site.

The probability of survival has also been established on the basis of the tumour's metastatic rate (Table 26.1).

There are also odds ratios quoted for a number of independent predictors of survival (Table 26.2).

Table 26.2 Odds ratios for survival from melanoma.

Prognostic variable	Category	Odds ratio for survival
Mitotic rate	$0/mm^2$	11.69
	$0.1-6/mm^2$	3.49
	$>6/mm^2$	1.00
Tumour-infiltrating lymphocytes	Brisk	11.31
	Non-brisk	3.51
	Absent	1.00
Thickness	<1.7 mm	4.04
	>1.7 mm	1.00
Anatomic site	Extremities	3.8
	Axial	1.0
Sex	Female	2.92
	Male	1.0
Regression	Absent	2.79
	Present	1.00

Chapter 27
Carcinoid Tumours

Epidemiology

Carcinoid tumours are uncommon, with a reported incidence of 1.5 per 100,000 of population per year. Carcinoid tumours can develop in any organ derived from endoderm but occur most frequently in the appendix. They produce a number of metabolic products which lead to specific symptoms. These products are normally metabolised in the liver, and only produce symptoms when there is significant metastatic spread.

Presentation

Patients with carcinoid tumours are usually asymptomatic. These tumours are frequently diagnosed as a chance finding at post-mortem in patients who have died from other causes. Patients may present with symptoms due to the secretory products of their tumour if there is significant metastatic disease. These metabolic products cause diarrhoea, flushing and occasionally bronchospasm. These symptoms are so specific that there is little difficulty in making a diagnosis, which is often achieved in general practice. The patient with a suspected diagnosis of carcinoid should be referred to a specialist centre in view of the rarity of the condition.

Investigations in hospital

The presence of symptoms is likely to indicate that the patient with a carcinoid tumour has metastatic disease. The investigations of such a patient should be confined to establishing the extent of his disease and obtaining a histological diagnosis. The investigations required include a blood count, liver function test, chest X-ray, and a CT scan of the chest and abdomen. Twenty-four-hour urinary 5-hydroxyindoleacetic acid (5-HIAA) levels should be measured; 5-HIAA is the excretory product of the metabolites produced by carcinoids and results from the breakdown of 5-hydroxytryptamine (5-HT; serotonin).

Management

The striking feature of carcinoid tumours is their relatively benign course, and this benign course defines therapy. Treatment is aimed at palliating symptoms rather than at reducing tumour bulk. There are a number of therapeutic options.

Pharmacological control

These agents act to block the synthesis, release and peripheral blockade of circulating tumour products. The list of drugs used in the treatment of carcinoid symptoms include inhibitors of 5-HT synthesis such as para-chlorphenylalanine, peripheral 5-HT antagonists such as cyproheptadine, antihistamines, and inhibitors of 5-HT release such as somatostatin and its long-acting analogues. The most frequently used somatostatin analogue is octreotide, and this leads to a relief of symptoms in 80% of patients for a median duration of ten months.

Cytokines

Interferon has been used to treat patients with metastatic carcinoid tumours. Symptom relief will occur in 50–60% of patients. However, less than 5% of patients achieve any significant tumour regression. Treatment with interferon is associated with significant side-effects which may include flu-like symptoms, and for this reason it is not generally given.

Embolisation

When metastatic disease in the liver is extensive, hepatic artery embolisation may be considered. This involves selective cannulation of the artery with injection of embolic material. This will lead to sustained symptom relief in the majority of patients. There may be significant side-effects from embolisation, and so this procedure is not entered into without due consideration of the benefits.

Prognosis

The prognosis for patients with metastatic carcinoid tumour is excellent in comparison to that for most tumours. Patients with metastatic tumours commonly survive a very considerable time and the expectation, even in the presence of liver disease, is that approximately 50% of patients will survive five years and 20% ten years. In the absence of metastases, following resection of the primary, the outlook is excellent.

Chapter 28
Mesothelioma

Epidemiology

Mesothelioma is a fibrous tissue tumour arising mainly in pleura and peritoneum. Approximately three men are affected to each woman, and this relates to the importance of industrial exposure to the major carcinogen – asbestos.

The relationship of asbestos exposure to the later development of lung conditions was first noted in the 1910s by company doctors who observed the association in workers in the Cape Asbestos Factory in the East End of London. It was not until 1960 that the direct relationship between asbestos exposure and mesothelioma was finally established, and the risk of mesothelioma in asbestos workers is reported as being 8–13%.

Asbestos exposure may lead to pleural plaques, lung fibrosis, mesothelioma or small cell lung cancer. There is an additional risk to family members of patients, of asbestos-related lung disease which may occur many decades after the initial exposure.

Presentation and referral

Patients with mesothelioma generally present with breathlessness, chest pain, or general symptoms suggestive of disseminated malignancy such as weight loss. A history of asbestos contact can be obtained in 50–70% of such patients. Patients presenting with such symptoms should be referred by their GP to a specialist chest physician.

The specialist should take a careful history, making a particular note of industrial exposure, and examine the patient. Investigations should include full blood count, biochemistry and a chest X-ray. A blood count may be abnormal and show anaemia; the biochemistry may reveal abnormalities of liver function tests suggestive of infiltration; and the chest X-ray may show pleural plaques suggestive of previous asbestos contact, a pleural effusion or lung infiltration.

Diagnosis and staging

The diagnosis of mesothelioma usually requires open pleural biopsy and is unlikely to be obtained by less invasive procedures such as cytological evaluation or needle biopsies. Mesothelioma may not always have a classical histological appearance and the differential diagnosis includes adenocarcinoma. Light microscopy may be helped by electron microscopy which shows characteristic changes. After the diagnosis of mesothelioma has been confirmed pathologically, the patient with mesothelioma is staged as follows:

Stage 1   Disease confined to pleura with or without extension to ipsilateral lung, pericardium or diaphragm.
Stage 2   Disease invading the chest wall or mediastinum, the oesophagus, heart or lymph nodes.
Stage 3   Disease invading through to the peritoneum or opposite lung.
Stage 4   Distant metastases.

Staging is generally achieved with the aid of CT and defines treatment.

Treatment

In a fit patient with stage 1 disease, radical surgery may be recommended. Radiotherapy has little role because of its toxicity and ineffectiveness in controlling the course of the disease.

The treatment of more advanced state mesothelioma aims at symptom palliation rather than cure, because of the low order of responsiveness of this tumour to conventional therapy and the limited survival of the patient (approximately 18 months).

Chemotherapy is given to patients with this condition. However, the response rates to single agents is of the order of 15% without a survival advantage to treatment, as compared with palliative measures such as pleural aspiration. The most effective agents are adriamycin and cisplatin, which are very toxic. There is no advantage to combinations of chemotherapeutic agents, but many disadvantages arise from the increased treatment-related toxicity of combination therapy.

Immunotherapy is an alternative and newer approach. In a recent series of patients treated with intrapleural interferon gamma, responses were reported in 40% of patients. Responses were seen only in those patients with early-stage disease. There is anecdotal evidence that interferon alpha is effective in mesothelioma; however, there is little published information.

Prognosis

The outlook for patients with mesothelioma is poor. The median survival for patients with advanced disease is 18 months.

Chapter 29
Myeloma

Epidemiology

Myeloma is a plasma cell neoplasm which is characterised by the excessive production of a monoclonal immunoglobulin, infiltration of the bone marrow and skeletal deposits. Every year in England and Wales, 2500 patients develop myeloma. Approximately three males are affected for every two females and the mean age at diagnosis is 70 years.

Presentation

Patients with myeloma classically present with symptoms of bone pain or anaemia. Rarely they may present with complications relating to the disease. The patient with such symptoms should have a number of basic investigations organised by his GP. These should include a full blood count and ESR, renal function tests, serum calcium estimation, immunoglobulin levels and urine testing for Bence–Jones protein. A full blood count may show an anaemia and the peripheral blood film may show rouleauing of red cells. The ESR will characteristically be very high and the renal function tests may be deranged. The patient may have hypercalcaemia and there will usually be a monoclonal immunoglobulinaemia accompanied by reciprocal depression of the remaining immunoglobulins. These findings should lead to the referral of the patient with myeloma to the haematologist or oncologist for staging and treatment.

Hospital review

In the out-patient clinic, a full history should be taken and the patient examined. The abnormal clinical findings may be of anaemia and bone pain. In addition to the investigations organised by the GP, the examining clinician should order a bone marrow aspiration and trephine and a skeletal survey. The bone marrow aspirate may show infiltration with an excess of plasma cells. The skeletal survey will often show the characteristic changes of myeloma, which are widely disseminated, punched-out lytic lesions. The patient may also be found to have one of the specific complications of myeloma upon presentation; these include renal failure and hypercalcaemia, and are discussed in more detail below.

Diagnosis

The diagnosis of myeloma is dependent upon three major criteria: a biopsy that confirms plasmacytoma; bone marrow plasmacytosis with greater than 30% plasma cells; and a monoclonal gammopathy exceeding 3.5 g/dl. Minor criteria include bone marrow plasmacytosis between 10 and 30%, monoclonal gammopathy and lytic bone lesions.

Staging

Staging of myeloma is defined as follows:

Stage 1 Haemoglobin is greater than 10 g/dl and calcium is normal. Plain X-rays should show either normal bones or solitary plasmacytoma. The monoclonal production rate should be less than 5 g/dl for IgG or less than 3 g/dl for IgA. The urinary light chain component should be less than 4 g per 24 hours.

Stage 3 Haemoglobin is less than 8.5 g/dl, serum calcium is greater than 12 mg/dl. The monoclonal production rate is greater than 7 g/dl for IgG and greater than 5 g/dl for IgA. The urinary light chain production should be more than 12 g per 24 hours.

Stage 2 An intermediate stage between stages 1 and 3.

Treatment

The treatment of myeloma depends upon the use of cytotoxic chemotherapy. For many years, the gold standard of treatment was therapy with melphalan and prednisone. Treatment is given orally and responses are seen in up to 60% of patients. The median survival is 2.5 years. More recently, there has been interest in the use of combination chemotherapy for the treatment of myeloma; in randomised trials, there has been greater success with such treatment than with standard therapy. Currently the conventional first-line therapy for myeloma consists of adriamycin, carmustine (BCNU), cyclophosphamide, melphalan and prednisone. In such treatment programmes, responses are seen in up to 70% of patients. The median survival, however, is only marginally better at approximately 32 months.

There has been interest recently in the possible advantages of additional therapy with interferon alpha. This is given at a dosage of 3 megaunits subcutaneously three times per week. It has been claimed that with interferon alpha, the median disease-free survival has been increased. This is extremely contentious and remains a matter for medical dispute.

Palliative treatments are also significant in this condition and the most important of these is radiation therapy, given to palliate bone pain.

Response assessment

Response in myeloma is assessed using the South West Oncology Group (SWOG) criteria. A complete response is described as resolution of all lytic metastases, a decrease to 25% or less of the paraprotein levels in blood and to 10% or less of the paraprotein in urine. A partial response is where there is a decline in immunoglobulin production rates to less than 50% of their pretreatment values.

Complications of myeloma

There are several complications of myeloma which require urgent treatment. The first is renal failure, which may have a number of causes including direct infiltration, precipitation of Bence–Jones protein, amyloidosis, hypercalcaemia and hyperuricaemia. This generally resolves with treatment of the underlying condition.

Hypercalcaemia is very common in myeloma. This is steroid sensitive and may require treatment with bisphosphonates and hydration.

Cord progression is commonly seen in myeloma. This occurs as result of direct infiltration of the vertebral bodies with myeloma cells. Patients present with acute paralysis or root symptoms and require either surgical decompression or urgent radiation therapy.

Chapter 30
Soft Tissue Sarcomas

Epidemiology

Soft tissue sarcomas are tumours of the connective tissue, which supports the body and includes muscles, tendons, fat and synovial tissue. These tumours represent less than 1% of all malignancies. They have an incidence of approximately 1–2 per 100,000 per annum. There are no known aetiological factors, although rarely they do occur as second malignancies in areas of the body that have been previously irradiated.

Presentation and initial investigations

Most soft tissue sarcomas occur in the limbs and they present to the clinician with localised swelling. The patient with such a swelling should be examined by his GP who, if he suspects a tumour, should refer the patient on to an orthopaedic surgeon. The orthopaedic surgeon should take a full history from the patient and then make arrangements for the patient to proceed to excision biopsy of the mass.

Pathology

The resected specimen should then be examined by a histopathologist who will attempt to classify it. The most helpful classification of soft tissue tumours is into tumours of fibrous tissue, fibrohistiocytic tumours, adipose tissue tumours including liposarcomas, tumours of muscle, tumours of blood vessels, tumours of lymph vessels, tumours of synovium, tumours of mesothelium, tumours of peripheral nerves, tumours of autonomic ganglia, tumours of paraganglionic structures, tumours of cartilage and bone-forming tissue, tumours of pleuripotential mesochyme, and tumours of uncertain histogenesis and unclassified soft tissue tumours – this group is extremely numerous and there are at least 50 different subtypes.

These classifications in turn may be divided into benign and malignant conditions. Benign tumours do not generally metastasise and microscopic examination shows a low mitotic rate. Malignant tumours have a high mitotic rate and do tend to metastasise. Approximately one-third of tumours are low grade and two-thirds are high grade.

Staging

There are many different staging systems used to compare these tumours which take into account the degree of spread, the mitotic state and the size of the tumour. Some staging systems are based upon sites of disease alone. All of these systems are very complicated and are not particularly helpful for the clinician whose practical management of the condition depends upon whether or not the tumour is high or low grade and whether or not there is spread of the disease.

Treatment of the primary tumour

There is considerable discussion as to what is the appropriate management of a soft tissue sarcoma. Low-grade tumours which by definition should not have spread should be treated by surgical excision alone and local control should be achieved in 85–100% of patients. The situation is different for those patients with high-grade tumours and there is debate as to whether surgery alone, surgery combined with radiation, or surgery, radiation and chemotherapy is the correct approach.

Surgery

There is little argument that surgery is necessary and the operation of first choice should be one that allows a reasonably wide margin of normal tissue to be excised with the tumour. If a good procedure is carried out, such as muscle compartmental excision, the local failure rate is 7–18%. If less radical procedures such as excision biopsy are performed then the local failure rate is approximately 50%. More radical procedures such as amputation have a lower local recurrence rate of approximately 5%. Over the last decade there has been an increased trend toward radical compartmental excision with limb-sparing procedures.

Adjuvant chemotherapy and radiation

After definitive surgery has been performed, the need for radiation and chemotherapy is assessed. Radiation is not given for low-grade tumours. In high-grade tumours, radiotherapy has an advantage in terms of reduced local recurrence rates in extremity lesions where effective dosages can be given without risking vital structures. Local radiation has no effect upon the progression of distant metastases. Because patients with high-grade sarcomas are at great risk from progression of their cancer to a metastatic state, adjuvant chemotherapy has been investigated in a number of trials. The original studies, which were non-randomised, showed an advantage to combination chemotherapy. This result has not held up and the consensus view is that adjuvant chemotherapy has no advantage in terms of five-year survival. However, this remains very much a subject for debate and is given in many centres.

Treatment of metastatic sarcoma

The treatment of metastatic soft tissue sarcomas require the use of chemotherapy. The most effective single agent treatments lead to responses in 15–35% of patients. Attempts are made to capitalise on this by the use of combination chemotherapy programmes. A slight increase in response rates has been found by some groups of clinicians; however, this advantage is much debated. Many cancer doctors would advocate the administration of single-agent chemotherapy to their patients simply because combination therapies maximise toxicities and do not provide a significant advantage. Others would argue that combination regimens are still to be recommended, using three-drug programmes such as VAC (vincristine, adriamycin and cyclophosphamide). Overall, 20–30% of patients respond, and one-third of those patients who have a complete response may be long-term survivors.

Chapter 31
Thyroid Cancer

Epidemiology

Thyroid cancer is uncommon and accounts for less than 0.5% of all cancer deaths. The worldwide incidence is very varied, ranging from 12 per 100,000 in Iceland to 1 in 100,000 in England and Wales. Thyroid cancer affects many more women than men, with a ratio of 4:1. The disease has a bimodal distribution, occurring with increased incidence in the third and fourth decades and in the over-60s. Thyroid cancer is associated with exposure to radiation, low dietary iodine, and in association with inherited genetic conditions.

Presentation

Patients with thyroid cancer generally present with a mass in the thyroid. It is not uncommon for patients to present with lymphatic spread. It is unusual for patients to present with late-stage disease.

Diagnosis

Patients with a suspected diagnosis of carcinoma of the thyroid should be referred for a surgical opinion to a specialist head and neck surgeon. On presentation to the out-patient clinic, the patient will be examined for the possibility of dissemination of the tumour and a number of base-line investigations will be organised, including blood count, thyroid function tests, liver function tests, chest X-ray and CT scanning of the neck and chest. An ultrasound of the thyroid should be carried out and technetium scanning performed.

Management

The majority of surgeons in the UK will carry out fine needle aspiration cytology or a needle biopsy of the thyroid mass before proceeding to definitive surgery. The surgical procedure undertaken depends on the operative findings, and frozen section information from pathology is generally required during this procedure. The majority of patients in the UK are treated for thyroid cancer by total or subtotal thyroidectomy. It is important that an experienced surgeon carry out this procedure because of the risks of hypoparathyroidism, resulting from removal of the parathyroid glands and damage to the recurrent laryngeal nerves which may lead to vocal cord paralysis.

Stage and grade

Having proceeded to surgery, the pathologist should now examine the histological appearances of the thyroid tumour. There are three main types of thyroid cancer: follicular, papillary and anaplastic variants. There are two other rarer thyroid malignancies, which are medullary carcinoma of the thyroid and thyroid lymphoma. Thyroid tumours are staged according to the UICC criteria.

T stage (primary tumour)

- T0 No evidence of primary tumour
- T1 Unilateral tumour
- T2 Bilateral tumour
- T3 Extension beyond the gland

N stage (nodal status)

- N0 No nodal involvement
- N1 Homolateral nodal involvement
- N2 Contralateral or bilateral nodal involvement
- N3 Fixed nodes

M stage (metastatic state)

- M0 No metastases
- M1 Distant metastases

Postoperative management

Postoperative treatment with radioactive iodine-131 should be considered for patients with thyroid cancers. Treatment is given to those patients who have a poor prognosis or have small-bulk metastases as demonstrated by radioactive iodine scanning. Treatment with thyroxine is recommended for all patients with well-differentiated thyroid cancer that is driven by thyroid-stimulating hormone, a pituitary hormone. External beam radiotherapy to the neck should be considered for those patients with anaplastic carcinomas who have a high incidence of recurrence and a poor outlook.

Prognosis

The prognosis depends upon tumour stage and grade. Anaplastic carcinomas of the thyroid are associated with a poor prognosis; these tumours are associated with a median survival of two to six months. Only rarely will survival exceed 12 months.

In contrast, patients with well-differentiated papillary and follicular cancers of the thyroid have an extremely good prognosis. These tumours are exceedingly slow growing, often with a doubling time of more than one year and a clinical course that extends over many decades. The expectation for patients with well-differentiated papillary carcinoma of the thyroid is for an 80% survival at 30 years, and for follicular thyroid lymphoma, for 60% survival at 30 years.

Chapter 32
Chemotherapy Extravasation

Chemotherapy extravasation is the extrusion of chemotherapeutic agents out of the venous system into the surrounding tissue. This may lead to necrosis, the extent of which is varied.

There are certain agents that are much more likely to cause this problem than others, including adriamycin, mustine and the vinca alkaloids.

Certain precautions are generally taken to minimise the risk of extravasation. Unless venous access is a considerable problem, chemotherapy is generally given into a vein in the hand or forearm. Treatment is usually given concomitantly with a fast-running infusion of saline; this allows rapid clearance of the drug locally and also provides information as to whether or not the cannula is inserted into a vein or if there is extravasation. Chemotherapy is not given into the antecubital fossa unless there are major problems with venous access and there is a medical emergency requiring immediate treatment. This is because local swelling following extravasation cannot be clearly seen. In the rare cases where chemotherapy has to be given into the antecubital fossa, if at all possible a plastic cannula rather than a metal butterfly should be used. This should be securely taped and the elbow should be extended using a splint to limit movement.

Extravasation is generally accompanied by immediate swelling around the vein together with pain and discomfort, but this is not necessarily the case and it may occur after treatment has been discontinued. If extravasation is suspected, immediate action is required to limit tissue damage. The treatment options include injection of steroids and hyaluronidase, local cooling using ice packs and topically applied dimethyl sulphoxide (DMSO) which prevents the development of this problem. DMSO has been shown to be the most effective of all of these treatments at reducing chemotherapy extravasation damage.

Unfortunately, despite early treatment of extravasation injuries, a significant proportion of patients develop local necrosis which can be extremely debilitating and miserable, often requiring extensive plastic surgery, lengthy hospitalisation and delay in chemotherapy.

Appendix
Cases

To date there have been difficulties in quantifying general damages. The reasons generally given are twofold: first, there is a general dearth of reported decisions relating to the litigation of claims focused on oncology issues; second, those cases that have been reported are found in a number of different reporting sources.

This absence of a sizeable body of case law has traditionally meant that a certain amount of extrapolation and assumption has been exercised by both practitioners and the judiciary in assessing damages in claims involving the consequences of cancer care. Often, when the injuries to the victim of a cancer-based claim are the same as those found in other areas of personal injury litigation, the task of extrapolating general damage awards is not taxing and is consistent.

Many times, however, the injuries related to oncology claims are unique. In such situations, attempts to assess general damages by resorting to analyses of non-oncology-based cases can prove both unhelpful and misleading.

What follows is intended to be a helpful summary of some of the more noteworthy decisions in cancer cases where damages are discussed.

Cervical cancer cases

1. *Thurman* v. *Wiltshire and Bath Health Authority* **(1997) 36 BMLR 63**
   Date of judgment: 4 February 1997
   Court: Queen's Bench Division
   Before: Judge Mark Hedley

   Summary

   Plaintiff suffered invasive cervical cancer. Allegations of negligence in the interpretation of a Pap smear test. Failure to detect abnormal cells. Provisional damages.

Facts

The plaintiff was aged 24 when a routine cervical smear in 1988 was reported as normal. She had her first child in June 1990. In January 1991, she began to have heavy and frequent vaginal bleeding. She was referred for a D&C and was subsequently told that the histology results were clear. From January 1992, the plaintiff again noticed some vaginal blood loss, but did not consider it serious. In May 1992, she was confirmed as pregnant. Bleeding continued during the early stages of her pregnancy.

In June 1992, the plaintiff saw a gynaecologist as the bleeding had become heavier. Following a colposcopy and biopsy, the diagnosis revealed that her cervix was 'almost completely destroyed by a tumour'. The only treatment was a termination of her 12-week pregnancy, a Wertheim's hysterectomy followed by a six-week course of radiotherapy and a 20-hour implant of caesium into the vagina.

The plaintiff made a remarkable recovery, but was left with scarring following the surgery. She was placed on hormone replacement therapy (HRT). She cannot have any more children and her marriage sadly broke down after her treatment.

The plaintiff claimed damages on a provisional basis for personal injuries as a result of cervical cancer. The claim centred on the defendant's alleged failure to diagnose:

(a) severe cyskaryotic cells, from the smear on 8 January 1988;
(b) cervical carcinoma in March/April 1991 when the D&C was performed; and
(c) dysplastic squamous epithelium in the histology results from the D&C in 1991.

Liability for allegations (a) and (c) was admitted on 16 January 1997. The trial was limited to determining the quantum of general damages and the provisional award.

Assessment of general damages

The judge considered the following factors when determining the appropriate level of quantum for general damages:

(1) Development of invasive cancer with radical surgery, radiotherapy and a caesium implant.
(2) Abortion of the fetus, which would have been her second child.

(3) Loss of reproductive function, when the family was incomplete and the new partner did not have children of his own.
(4) Loss of hormones, thus the plaintiff now needs HRT.
(5) The plaintiff cannot wear some summer clothes due to permanent abdominal scarring.
(6) A deformed and shortened vagina, which interferes with the plaintiff's enjoyment of intercourse.
(7) Psychological suffering.

Taking all of these circumstances into account, the judge awarded £50,000 for Mrs Thurman's pain and suffering, and loss of amenity.

The provisional damage claim

The plaintiff requested an award of provisional damages on the basis of the risk of the following potential future injuries:

(1) The reoccurrence of cancer secondary to carcinoma of the cervix.
(2) Osteoporosis secondary to radiotherapy.
(3) Interference with the urinary function, secondary to radiotherapy.

The plaintiff and the defendant agreed that in respect of particulars (2) and (3) the period specified for seeking further damages in the event that the described risk materialised was ten years from the date of the order. However, they were unable to agree this time figure for the first particular – the chance of recurrence of the primary cancer. The court ordered that there be no time limit within which the plaintiff could reapply for such damages.

The total damages awarded, including interest, amounted to £60,305.

Comment

This case is noteworthy for two reasons. First, the plaintiff was successful in obtaining a generous finding from the court of the time limit within which she could apply for provisional damages in the event of a recurrence. The lifetime limit reflects a cautious and sympathetic approach to the plaintiff's concerns.

Second, the legal advisors for the plaintiff successfully faced the challenge of managing the claim when the plaintiff expressed a wish to not be advised of information regarding her prognosis. This required careful planning to ensure that the case and trial proceeded appropriately without possibly exposing the plaintiff to information she had expressly indicated she did not wish to know.

2. ***Wallace* v. *Portsmouth and South East Hampshire Health Authority* (1995)** Clinical Risk – *AVMA Medical and Legal Journal* (1996) 2(2), 62

Summary

Plaintiff suffered invasive cervical cancer. Alleged failure by health authority to further investigate and treat abnormal cervical smear test results.

Facts

The plaintiff was originally referred to hospital by her GP after requesting to be sterilised in the wake of an abnormal Pap smear result. The plaintiff did indeed undergo a sterilisation and a colposcopy on 4 September 1992. However, a cervical biopsy also planned for that same operation was not performed. Some abnormal cells were cauterised, but nothing further was done.

A follow-up smear test in March 1993 revealed severe dyskaryosis. However, the hospital failed to react to this abnormal result. At a further follow-up appointment in September 1993, it was revealed that the plaintiff was suffering from invasive cervical cancer. She was then referred to St Bartholomew's Hospital where examination confirmed a stage 2B cervical carcinoma.

The plaintiff underwent four weeks of intensive radiotherapy, followed by brachytherapy which consisted of a radioactive caesium insertion in November 1993. Fortunately the plaintiff was reported to have responded well to the treatment. She was prescribed HRT after her radiotherapy, and her overall prognosis in terms of survival was very good.

Proceedings were issued on 17 October 1994. The defendants admitted liability on 8 November 1994.

Damages

The plaintiff accepted a total payment into court of £15,500, which was made on 11 September 1995. The case report does not express what proportion of these damages was in respect of general damages.

3. ***Hughes, deceased* v. *Chester Health Authority* (1995)** Clinical Risk – *AVMA Medical and Legal Journal* (1995) 1(6), 219
Date of Settlement : September 1994

Summary

Failure to diagnose adenocarcinoma of the cervix, following a series of smear tests.

Facts

Between 1982 and 1987, the plaintiff had 14 cervical smear tests. One such test, in 1982, showed numerous severely dyskaryotic cells, consistent with carcinoma in situ. Another test taken four months later showed some minor dyskaryosis. This report was marked 'this is an abnormal result and should be drawn to the doctor's attention'. However, the gynaecologist wrote to the doctor, merely stating that the smear test was not far off normal.

The subsequent smear tests were reported as negative and one was reported as benign. The last report, on 7 December 1987, was negative. In August 1988, the plaintiff attended a different hospital where a fungating tumour in the cervix was diagnosed. A further biopsy showed squamous cell carcinoma.

On 20 September 1988, a Wertheim's hysterectomy was carried out but unfortunately the plaintiff was found to have metastatic carcinoma. A course of radiotherapy and chemotherapy commenced in 1989, but the plaintiff nonetheless died on 22 January 1990.

The deceased's husband instructed solicitors. They contended that the actions taken by the consultant gynaecologist were inadequate because no colposcopy or cone biopsy was undertaken until it was much too late, despite the repeatedly abnormal cervical smears.

Damages

Total damages: The claim was settled with total damages of £120,000.
General damages: The parties agreed a sum of £35,000 for the deceased's pain and suffering.

4. **B. v. *Medway Health Authority* (1995) Health Care Risk Report (1996) 2(3), 2**
Date of hearing: 1995

Summary

Failure to diagnose cervical cancer, resulting in death.

Facts

Mrs B had two smear tests, both of which were interpreted as negative and normal. The cancer was diagnosed in July 1991. Mrs B underwent several surgical procedures including a colostomy performed in November 1991. She underwent radiotherapy and chemotherapy. She experienced pain and drowsiness, despite large doses of morphine.

In August 1993, Mrs B died at the age of 34. During the three years prior to her death, she had suffered from the symptoms of cancer, heavy periods, kidney failure, bowel and abdominal pains and general malaise.

The defence conceded that the cervical cancer should have been diagnosed in 1988. It was admitted that had action been taken at that time, there would have been a 95% chance of survival with proper treatment. They conceded liability and a total payment, into court, of £200,000 was made shortly before the trial.

Damages

After a two-day hearing, the plaintiff was awarded £214,000. General damages were £45,000.

5. ***Cathryn Shorrock v. Crewe Health Authority* (1993) *AVMA Medical and Legal Journal* (1993) 4(2), 13; *PMIL Letter* (1993) 9(5), 36**
Date of settlement: 1993

Summary

Failure to report Pap smear which strongly suggested cervical cancer resulting in critical delay of 12 months in treatment and, eventually, death.

Facts

In May 1989, the plaintiff, then aged 30, was examined at hospital. A biopsy was undertaken which revealed no evidence of malignant disease. However, a smear test taken on the same day revealed abnormal endocervical cells and dyskaryotic cells, strongly indicative of stage 1B carcinoma. The result of the smear test was never revealed to the GP or the patient.

In September 1989, a doctor in the gynaecological clinic reviewed the plaintiff. This doctor noted that both the May 1989 biopsy and cervical smear had been normal. The plaintiff was then discharged and recommended to have annual smear tests with her GP.

In February 1990, the plaintiff reported a history of postcoital bleeding to her GP. He referred her to hospital, where the consultant noted carcinoma of the cervix on 15 May 1990. He also noted that the smear test from May 1989 was CINiii (CIN grade 3) with abnormal endocervical cells. Further investigations showed adenocarcinoma of the cervix with lymph node metastasis. A Wertheim's hysterectomy was performed on 30 March 1990. The plaintiff had extensive radiotherapy and chemotherapy, but unfortunately her condition deteriorated and she died on 16 November 1992.

It was alleged that if the hospital had correctly reported and acted upon the May 1989 smear test, the plaintiff would have still required a Wertheim's hysterectomy, but the postoperative radiotherapy and chemotherapy would not have been necessary. The expert medical evidence obtained by the plaintiff confirmed that but for the alleged negligence she would have had an 85% chance of survival.

Due to the failure to act upon the smear test, the plaintiff underwent unnecessary pain and suffering involved with radiotherapy and chemotherapy, which gave rise to colic and diarrhoea. She suffered from nausea, vomiting, weight loss, loss of hair and hallucinations. She needed HRT and had considerable psychological distress.

The expert medical evidence was obtained quickly following disclosure of the case notes. The health authority admitted liability before proceedings were issued. Significantly, an interim payment was made to the plaintiff before her early death in November 1992. The claim was settled after proceedings were issued.

Damages

The plaintiff's husband continued the action following her death. The heads of claim were as follows:

(1) Damages for the deceased's pain, suffering and loss of amenity;
(2) bereavement damages;
(3) funeral expenses;
(4) miscellaneous special damages;
(5) value of husband's care and attendance;
(6) plaintiff's loss of earnings;
(7) interest;
(8) future loss of dependency.

The claim was settled with damages of £140,000 plus the value of repayable benefits. The case report made no reference to what portion of the settlement figure was allocated to general damages.

Breast cancer cases

1. *Pawson v. St Helens and Knowsley Hospitals NHS Trust* **(1996) Clinical Risk –** *AVMA Medical and Legal Journal* **(1996) 2(4), 133**
   Date of settlement: 1 February 1996

   Summary

   The plaintiff suffered breast cancer. Mastectomy following misdiagnosis of cancer.

Facts

The 45-year-old plaintiff discovered a lump in her right breast in November 1991. The plaintiff was informed that she had a malignant tumour and that the whole of her right breast must be removed. A mastectomy was carried out on 13 December 1991. After the operation, further analysis of her breast tissue revealed that no cancerous cells ever existed.

The plaintiff underwent reconstructive surgery of her breast in April 1994. She has been left with extensive scarring to the reconstructed breast and a prominent scar on the left breast due to its reduction. Her breasts are considerably smaller than before and she has had difficulties accepting the changes to her body.

Damages

The case report notes that the plaintiff accepted a total sum of £40,630, plus interest accrued on the money paid into court.

Special damages amounted to approximately £9,200. It is likely that at least the major portion of the balance of £31,000 is to be allocated for general damages.

2. *Harling v. Huddersfield Health Authority* (1992) Kemp & Kemp L8-150
   Date : February 1992
   Court : Leeds District Registry

Summary

Mastectomy following incorrect diagnosis of cancer.

Facts

The plaintiff, aged 53 at the date of the order in 1984, underwent a mastectomy with the removal of her left breast, following an incorrect diagnosis of cancer made without any evidence of malignancy. She was actually suffering from florid mastitis.

Five subsequent operations were performed to reconstruct the left breast and reduce the size of the right breast. The left breast is badly disfigured, the right breast is moderately so. The left breast is flattened with two scars of twelve and four inches. The right breast sags with two scars of ten and three inches. The nipples and areolae of both breasts have been removed.

The plaintiff suffered from depression, anxiety, frustration and embarrassment. Further surgery is unlikely to improve the proportions of the breasts.

Damages

General damages: £36,400
Total damages: £40,000

3. ***D'Arcy v. Stockport Health Authority* (1992) *AVMA Medical and Legal Journal* (1992) 3(4), 14**
   Date of payment into court: 1989

Summary

Mastectomy following incorrect diagnosis of cancer.

Facts

In January 1972, the plaintiff, then aged 45, underwent a mastectomy with the removal of her right breast. Histology subsequently showed fibrocystic hyperplasia, with no evidence of malignancy.

The plaintiff suffered a complete loss of her right breast with ugly scarring and some loss of feeling in her back. She had problems adapting to the loss of her breast and the use of the prosthesis. She no longer went swimming or sunbathing and was embarrassed by her condition.

The plaintiff took action after reading of a similar case in a newspaper in May 1988. In October 1989, independent medical evidence revealed that the operation in 1972 was negligent. A complete right mastectomy should not have been undertaken, without first carrying out a tissue diagnosis and excision biopsy.

Damages

The plaintiff accepted a payment into court of £15,850.

4. ***Vaughan v. Paddington and North Kensington Area Health Authority* (1986) Kemp & Kemp L8-171**
   Date: 23 October 1986
   Before : Mr Justice Boreham

Summary

Double mastectomy following a negligent diagnosis of cancer.

Facts

The female plaintiff was aged 49 at the date of the trial. She was diagnosed as suffering from cancer of the breast in August 1981. In September 1981, operations were performed by agents of the defendants, St Mary's Hospital, to remove both breasts.

After the operations, the right breast became infected and the left breast bled profusely. The left breast continued to bleed until December 1981. The prostheses in both breasts were consequently removed. The plaintiff was very distraught, worried and upset, especially as she was continually in and out of hospital.

In July 1982, the plaintiff had plastic surgery which considerably improved the scarring on her chest and back, but was unable to reconstitute her nipples.

In February 1984, an examination by the Royal Marsden Hospital revealed that the plaintiff never had cancer. The defendants later that year admitted that the plaintiff never had cancer and in July 1986 finally admitted negligence.

The left breast is now replaced by a paddle of skin measuring seven by four inches. The right breast is now replaced by an elipse of skin measuring three by eight inches. There are two scars on the plaintiff's back, of eight and nine inches in length. The left side scar has spread in its central area to a width of one inch. The scars cannot be improved with any further surgery.

The plaintiff is now 'moderately disabled'. Since the operations, she has suffered great pain and restricted movement of the back and arms, especially on the left side. It is unlikely that she will ever regain normality. She will be unable to continue her pre-1981 job as a chambermaid, unless it is involves entirely light work.

Damages

General damages: £25,000
Total damages: £79,000

5. ***Judge v. Huntingdon Health Authority* [1995] 6 Med LR 223; Kemp & Kemp, L8-160; *Times Law Reports*, 9 March 1995; Clinical Risk – AVMA *Medical and Legal Journal* (1995) 1(3), 127**
Date of judgment: 28 November 1994
The High Court
Before: Mr R. Thitheridge QC, sitting as a deputy High Court judge

Summary

The plaintiff had breast cancer. She alleged that a failure to make a prompt diagnosis of the cancer resulted in an otherwise avoidable mastectomy.

Facts

The 33-year-old plaintiff discovered a lump in her breast. She subsequently consulted her GP, who referred her to a consultant surgeon with a letter suggesting its removal. The consultant examined her on 8 June 1989 and reassured her that everything was normal. He discharged her without further investigation or review.

The lump continued to grow in size and she again visited her GP. The plaintiff then saw the same consultant surgeon again on 1 March 1990. The lump was finally excised on 21 March 1990. Histology results revealed invasive ductal carcinoma with lymphatic permeation and bone metastases.

The plaintiff alleged negligence in failing to properly investigate and excise the cancer lump. The failure to promptly diagnose and treat her meant that she went from an 80% chance of surviving the cancer and having a normal expectation of life, to a 0% chance.

Held

The surgeon was negligent in failing to pay sufficient attention to the plaintiff's complaint and to the GP's referral letter. The lump was present on 8 June 1989, and the defendant failed to detect it when he should have. He should have arranged to see the plaintiff for a review.

Failure to make either fine needle biopsy or ultrasound available to the surgeon was not negligent, but that non-availability made it more important to ensure that there was no error or mistake in diagnosis.

The surgeon's negligence in failing to detect the lump resulted in the plaintiff losing an 80% chance of cure.

Damages

The plaintiff accepted an out-of-court settlement of £215,000.

6. **Taylor v. West Kent Health Authority [1997] 8 Med LR 251**
Date of judgment: 2 February 1997
Court: Queen's Bench Division
Before: Mr Justice Maurice Kay

Summary

Negligent delay in diagnosing breast cancer and to provide chemotherapy, which caused the plaintiff to die 18 months before she would have died otherwise.

Facts

The plaintiff noticed a lump on her breast and subsequently attended hospital on 9 January 1989. The cytology report on 10 January 1989 suggested a biopsy to confirm the diagnosis of fibroadenoma or fibrocystic disease. However, no biopsy was performed.

Two subsequent six-month reviews were carried out in July 1989 and January 1990, where the plaintiff was assured that everything was normal.

On 26 February 1990, the plaintiff's GP found swelling on the left breast and referred her to a consultant surgeon. The surgeon's report noted 'probable carcinoma'. The plaintiff was referred for radiotherapy, which commenced in May 1990. Metastasis was apparent by November 1990. She continued to receive radiotherapy and was finally given chemotherapy in July 1991. She eventually died on 23 December 1991.

Held

As to negligence:
No reasonable clinician would have interpreted the cytology report as excluding malignancy.

The registrar's interpretation and report failed to achieve the requisite standard of care. The plaintiff should not have merely received six-monthly reviews, especially as the cytology report suggested that the clinicians carry out further investigations.

It is probable that further appropriate investigation would have led to a diagnosis of carcinoma at that time.

The failure to provide adjuvant chemotherapy in 1990 amounted to breach of the relevant duty of care.

As to causation:
The plaintiff's tumour was particularly aggressive. Thus, even if she had received the appropriate diagnosis and treatment in 1989, she would still have died at about the same time as she did.

On a balance of probabilities, the negligent failure to provide the plaintiff with adjuvant chemotherapy in 1990, caused her to die 18 months before she would have done anyway.

Damages

To be assessed.

Other cancers

1. ***Cadwallader v. Anderson* (1993) *PMIL Letter* (1993) 9(8), 58**
   Date of settlement: 1992/3

   Summary

   Plaintiff developed testicular cancer. He alleged that a failure to appropriately examine the testicle when he complained of a lump in his testicle delayed the diagnosis and prolonged his pain and suffering.

   Facts

   The 29-year-old plaintiff consulted his GP in April 1988, complaining of a lump in his right testicle. He consulted him again on several occasions between April and July 1988. Eventually the GP referred him to a consultant urological surgeon who diagnosed malignant teratoma. The plaintiff underwent an orchiectomy on 26 July 1988.

   The plaintiff alleged that the GP was negligent in not examining his testicle during the visits of 28 May, 21 June and 8 July. As a result, the GP failed to put himself in a position to make a proper professional judgement about the plaintiff's condition. Had a proper examination been made, the orchiectomy would still have been necessary, but the plaintiff's additional pain and suffering would have been avoided. The plaintiff sought damages for his pain, suffering and loss of amenity for the period before he was referred for the orchiectomy operation.

   Procedural history

   The plaintiff complained to the Medical Services Committee, who initially absolved the GP of liability. On appeal, however, they found that the GP's failure to examine the testicle on 28 May, 21 June and 8 July had put him in a position of being unable to exercise proper professional judgement.

   Damages

   The claim was settled following the commencement of proceedings with the plaintiff accepting damages of £1,350.

2. ***Eaton v. Dale* (1993) *AVMA Medical and Legal Journal* (1993) 4(4), 12**
   Date of settlement: July 1993

Summary

Failure by the GP to diagnose a malignant tumour, consequently increasing the plaintiff's pain and suffering.

Facts

The plaintiff, aged 25, became pregnant in early 1990. In March 1990, she consulted her GP with a complaint of pain in her right knee. The GP said it was a torn tendon without any examination and prescribed no treatments. The pain increased over the next two weeks and the plaintiff consulted the GP again. He examined the knee through her trousers and diagnosed a Baker's cyst. He told her that X-rays could not be taken because of her pregnancy.

The pain increased in severity over the next four weeks and began to interfere with her walking. In May 1990, she visited the GP again, who examined the knee in the same manner and confirmed it was a Baker's cyst. He prescribed paracetamol and a cream to rub into the knee. She visited the GP for a fourth time when stretch marks appeared on the knee and the pain increased further. Again, the GP said nothing could be done because of the pregnancy.

The plaintiff was now very concerned and was seen privately on 23 August 1990. The examination revealed a growth on the knee and not a Baker's cyst. A biopsy on 31 August 1990 revealed a malignant tumour. On 31 October 1990 the tumour was removed. A course of chemotherapy and radiotherapy commenced after her son was born. Despite the treatment further metastatic deposits were found in her right leg and she finally died on 7 March 1992.

Before her death, the plaintiff made complaints to the Medical Services Committee about the GP. In June 1991, the GP was found to have breached his terms and conditions of service owing to his failure to examine her knee and refer her to a specialist. However, expert evidence from a clinical oncologist revealed that her tumour was highly aggressive and was unlikely to have been curable even if treated when she first reported the symptoms.

Nonetheless, the plaintiff claimed damages for the pain and suffering experienced during the four-and-a-half-month delay. During this period she had a swollen knee, problems sleeping, ineffective pain relief and difficulty walking.

Damages

The plaintiff's husband continued the action following her death and the claim was settled with damages, for pain, suffering and loss of amenity, in respect of the four-and-a-half-month period, of £4,000.

3. ***Lewis v. Liverpool Health Authority and Royal Liverpool University NHS Trust* (unreported)**
    Date of settlement: 1997

    Summary

    Failure to diagnose adenoid cystic carcinoma, consequently increasing the plaintiff's pain and suffering.

    Facts

    The plaintiff was under the care of the Royal Liverpool Hospital from 1985 until 1992, with a history of continuing pain in the face and left ear. During this period she underwent various investigations and tests. In November 1992, adenoid cystic carcinoma was finally diagnosed. The local invasion was now so severe that surgery to remove the tumour had to be abandoned.

    The plaintiff underwent chemotherapy, which could not be completed due to the adverse and painful side-effects. Future treatment is only likely to be palliative.

    The plaintiff alleges that her condition should have been diagnosed in September 1987, rather than at the end of 1992. The tumour would still have been beyond operative cure in 1987, but a prompt diagnosis would have led to far more effective management of her condition. She would have been spared five years of excessive pain and suffering, uncertainty, psychological trauma and chronic sepsis.

    Procedural history

    Proceedings were issued in December 1995. Expert evidence was exchanged in April 1997 and the trial was arranged for 23 June 1997.

    Damages

    Total damages: £31,000 (including special damages and interest).
    General damages: The claim was settled with a contemplated award of £25,000 for the five-year period of avoidable pain and suffering.

4. ***SH v. Salford Health Authority* (unreported)**
    Date of settlement: 1991

    Summary

    The estate of the plaintiff alleged failure to diagnose terminal lung cancer with metastatic disease which caused unnecessary pain and suffering.

Facts

The plaintiff attended Hope Hospital in April 1990, where a chest X-ray indicated that neoplastic disease seemed likely with either metastatic disease or two separate primaries. However, no steps were taken to confirm the possible diagnosis. She was treated for stress-related back pain at the pain clinic.

A second chest X-ray was carried out in July 1990. The report suggested that the appearances were strongly suspicious of carcinoma and recommended that an isotope scan be carried out, which was not done.

In August 1990, the plaintiff was seen privately, where the consultant suspected a pulmonary primary lesion with metastatic disease. In September 1990, this diagnosis was confirmed by a bone scan and X-rays.

On 18 September 1990, the plaintiff was admitted to Christie Hospital, where she received a single dose of palliative radiotherapy. On 15 November 1990, she died suffering from lung cancer with extensive bone metastases.

At the time of her death, the plaintiff had extensive cancer which could not have been cured, even if diagnosed earlier. However, the possibility of lung cancer with metastatic disease should have been investigated by medical staff after the first X-ray. Had they done so, the plaintiff could have received palliative radiotherapy and appropriate pain relief in April 1990, which would have rendered her 90–100% pain free.

Procedural history

Proceedings were issued by the plaintiff's husband as administrator of her estate.

Damages

General damages: The claim was settled with an award of £3,500 for the four to five months of pre-death avoidable pain and suffering.
Total damages: £3,500

5. ***Crawford v. North Manchester Health Authority* (1996) Clinical Risk – *AVMA Medical and Legal Journal* (1997) 3(4), 123; Health Care Risk Report (1997) 3(8), 2**
Date of settlement: December 1996

Summary

Failure to diagnose a malignant kidney tumour.

Facts

On 11 March 1991, the deceased, then aged 43, saw her GP complaining of pain in her right hypochondrium. On 18 March, she attended hospital for X-rays and an ultrasound scan. No abnormality of the pancreas, spleen or right kidney was found, but the report stated that a small cyst was present in the left kidney in its upper pole.

The GP reassured the plaintiff, but in fact she was suffering from a hypernephroma – a malignant kidney tumour – which remained undiagnosed until November 1992. By the time of the diagnosis, the deceased's illness was terminal and she died on 17 July 1993.

Proceedings were issued in March 1994, alleging negligence in relation to taking insufficient views of the left kidney. The plaintiff's case was that, had the condition been diagnosed at the time of the first ultrasound scan in March 1991, she would have undergone a nephrectomy and on the balance of probabilities she would not have developed metastasis. This is because up to 80% of patients with this condition survive if the diagnosis is achieved early.

Case history

The defendants made a payment into court of £10,000, which was rejected. In March 1996, an open admission as to negligence and causation was made.

Damages

General damages: The plaintiff's assessment was £25,000–£30,000.
Total damages: The case was settled with total damages of £57,500.

6. **Clifford v. Portsmouth and South East Hampshire Health Authority (1995) Health Care Risk Report (1995) 1(5), 2**
Date of payment into court: 1994/5

Summary

Failure to diagnose carcinoma of the colon, resulting in the patient's death.

Facts

In May 1989, the plaintiff, then aged 54, returned to England from Spain because of his deteriorating health. X-rays taken in Spain showed carcinoma of the colon. He was referred to hospital by his GP. He underwent a barium enema and gastroscopy. It was decided that he had a sigmoid volvulus with a long redundant loop, although malignancy was not ruled out.

He returned to Spain, but on 10 June he was admitted to hospital with a perforated carcinoma of the colon. He underwent an emergency colonectomy and splenectomy and developed peritonitis and became seriously ill.

The plaintiff sufficiently recovered to return to England, but developed metastases on the liver and died on 9 February 1992.

The plaintiff's widow commenced proceedings against the defendant health authority. It was the plaintiff's case that, had a prompt and proper diagnosis of carcinoma of the colon been made, the deceased could have had a planned colonectomy prior to perforation and his quality of life and life expectancy would have been significantly improved.

Case history

The case was settled following a payment into court, four weeks before the trial.

Damages

General damages: The sum of £20,000 can be attributed to the plaintiff's pain and suffering prior to his death.
Total damages: £50,000

7. ## MW v. Bolton Health Authority and Another (1995) AVMA Medical and Legal Journal (1993) 4(2), 12
Date of settlement: 1994/5

Summary

Incorrect diagnosis of cancer.

Facts

The plaintiff was 67 years old at the date of the negligence. In 1986, the plaintiff mentioned pain above the base of her spine during an out-patient appointment in hospital. Following X-rays, a provisional diagnosis of cancer was made. The diagnosis was wrong, as the X-rays actually showed a long-established congenital bone abnormality.

The plaintiff was prescribed morphine tablets and informed that she had secondary cancer, which was terminal. She was advised to reside at a nursing home, due to the level of care she would now require. She was given radiotherapy and spent a total of two years and four months in the nursing home. She was often heavily sedated with morphine and suffered from nausea and vomiting. She believed that she was terminally ill. She lost her whole independence, especially as she had given up her home and most of her possessions.

In 1989, the GP at the nursing home reviewed her records and discovered the error in the diagnosis. She was discharged from the nursing home in April 1989 and returned to the care of her family. She was now no longer self-dependent and had to move to high-dependence accommodation near her relatives.

In addition to the social disturbance and effects of morphine caused by the wrong diagnosis, the radiotherapy had (a) effectively destroyed the integrity of the hip joint, such that an arthoplasty was carried out in 1992, and (b) created a 10% risk of neuropathy or myelopathy over the ten years from the date of the dosage.

Case history

Proceedings were commenced, but the defendants indicated a wish to negotiate on a 'without prejudice' basis. No admission of liability was ever made. The defendants initially offered a sum of £17,500.

Damages

Total damages: The offer was increased to £30,000 and the plaintiff accepted.

8. ### Whiteford v. Hunter (1950) 94 Sol Jo 758, HL
   Date of judgment: 16 November 1950
   Court: House of Lords
   Before: Lord Porter, Lord Normand, Lord Oaksey, Lord MacDermott and Lord Reid

Summary

Plaintiff was inaccurately and incorrectly diagnosed as suffering cancer.

Facts

In 1992, the plaintiff, an American consultant engineer, was diagnosed with cancer and informed that he had a short time to live. Consequently, he closed his practice in England and returned to America. He was there found to be suffering from chronic cystitis and a diverticulum of the bladder, but not cancer.

He sued the defendant for the negligent diagnosis.

Case history

Mr Justice Birkett awarded the plaintiff £6,300 damages. The Court of Appeal reversed the decision and the plaintiff appealed.

Arguments

The plaintiff's argument was based on the facts that no cystoscope was used before opening the bladder, and no specimen of the growth was taken in order to test microscopically whether or not it was cancerous.

The defendant argued that his actions conformed to the skilled practice of the profession. Two surgeons gave evidence in support of this assertion. No specimen could have been taken using a cystoscope, unless it were fitted with a rongeur instrument. Such an instrument was rarely used in England at the time of the cystoscopy and was not possessed by the defendant.

Held

The appeal was dismissed.

9. ***Mills v. British Rail Engineering* (1991) PMIL Letter (1991) 7(8), 58**
Date of judgment: 4 July 1991
Court: Bristol High Court, Mr Justice Schiemann

Summary

An asbestos environment caused lung cancer, resulting in the death of an employee.

Facts

This action was brought by the widow of the deceased. The deceased was an employee of British Rail Engineering, where he worked in an asbestos environment. He started feeling ill towards the end of 1989, when he became breathless and found it difficult to breathe. He first saw his GP in January 1990. In February 1990, he was informed by his GP that he had a short expectancy of life, due to lung cancer. He was given four courses of chemotherapy in the year before his death. He was in hospital for three days at a time. He vomited, his hair fell out and his cough got worse. His wife and family looked after him until his death.

Damages

General damages: An award of £ 20,000 was made for pain and suffering, including loss of expectation of life.
Total damages: £85,669.85 (including interest).

10. **Molinari v. Ministry of Defence, [1994] P.I.Q.R. Q33, Kemp & Kemp, L3-091**
    Date of judgment: 6 December 1994
    Court: Queen's Bench Division
    Before: Mr W Crowther QC sitting as a deputy High Court judge

Summary

Plaintiff was diagnosed with acute lymphoblastic leukaemia, after exposure to radiation whilst an employee in the Royal Naval Dockyard.

Facts

The plaintiff, aged 39 at the date of the trial, was employed by the defendants as a fitter/turner at the Royal Navy Dockyard, Chatham, between 1970 and 1983. He was made redundant in 1983 and became a self-employed double glazing consultant.

In September 1990, he began to suffer from loss of appetite, and pain and swelling in the left calf. A bone marrow biopsy was carried out and he was diagnosed with acute lymphoblastic leukaemia. He received chemotherapy both as an in-patient and an out-patient.

He went into remission, but in February 1991 there was a relapse and he was readmitted to hospital. He underwent further chemotherapy, which led to a further remission. In April 1990, he received a bone marrow transplant and total body irradiation. In July 1991, he contracted pneumonitis, a potentially fatal lung disease, but survived. He remained on chemotherapy until the trial and will take penicillin for the rest of his life.

The plaintiff's suffering was horrendous. He had suffered as a result of his illness and its treatment. He has lost weight and his physique has deteriorated. His skin is thin and dry and he has lost his hair. He suffers from weakness, tiredness, lack of energy, and a cancer-related psychological order, chronic anxiety. He will develop cataracts in both eyes, which will require surgery, and is now sterile. He suffers from a discharge of unpleasant mucus in the mouth, which he has to constantly spit out.

Case history

The defendants admitted that the leukaemia was caused by exposure to radiation and admitted liability.

Damages

Total damages: £165,594

General damages: A provisional award of £40,000 was made for pain and suffering and loss of amenity, on the basis of no further relapse occurring.

11. ***Stokes* v. *Guest Keen and Nettlefold (Bolts and Nuts) Ltd* [1968] 1 WLR 1776, 112 Sol Jo, 821**
    Date of judgment: 4 October 1968
    Court: Queen's Bench Division
    Before: Mr Justice Swanwick

Summary

The plaintiff was diagnosed with scrotal cancer from exposure to mineral oil.

Facts

The deceased's widow issued proceedings against the defendants, after her husband died from scrotal cancer in February 1966. She alleged that:

(1) The cancer was caused by a long exposure to mineral oil, whilst the deceased was working as a tool-setter in the defendants' factory.
(2) The defendants were negligent as they knew or should have known of the risk of cancer.
(3) The defendants had failed to warn the deceased of the dangers to which he was exposed.
(4) The defendants had failed to instruct him in the precautions to be taken to prevent or minimise the effects of the oil.
(5) The defendants had failed to provide six-monthly medical examinations.

Held

The scrotal cancer was induced by the exposure to mineral oil, as there was a causal link between a long exposure to contact with mineral oil and the occurrence of skin cancer.

Damages

Total damages: £10,000

12. *Reay v. British Nuclear Fuels plc* and *Hope v. British Nuclear Fuels plc* [1994] 5 Med LR 1

Court: Queen's Bench Division
Before: Mr Justice French

Summary

An important decision in environmental, rather than medical negligence, law. Was paternal preconception irradiation (PPI) the material cause of (a) leukaemia in Dorothy Reay and (b) non-Hodgkin's lymphoma (NHL) in Vivien Hope?

Facts

Dorothy was born on 8 October 1961 and died on 2 September 1962. The cause of her death was early acute lymphatic leukaemia (ALL). The first plaintiff, Elizabeth Reay, claimed damages for the trauma suffered by the conception, birth and death of her leukaemic daughter Dorothy.

The second plaintiff, Vivien Hope, was born on 10 May 1965. In June 1988, she was diagnosed with NHL. She claimed damages for the past and future suffering and disability caused by NHL.

The court was not concerned with the amount of damages, as the figures had been agreed subject to liability. Negligence was also not in question, due to statutory liability under the Atomic Energy Authority Act 1954.

The court was only concerned with causation. The plaintiffs claimed that PPI caused mutation in spermtagonia, which via paternal sperm causes a predisposition to ALL and/or NHL in the next generation. This claim was primarily based on a report by Professor Gardner.

The dispute as a whole centred around four main issues:

(1) Occupational dosimetry – the doses of ionising radiation received by George Reay and David Hope during their respective employments at Sellafield.
(2) Environmental dosimetry – the doses of ionising radiation received by the members of both families, from radiation in the environment caused by emissions from Sellafield.
(3) Epidemiology – whether the Gardner study can show a link between PPI of fathers working at Sellafield and ALL and/or NHL in the next generation.
(4) Genetics – whether a possible biological mechanism by which radiation emitted from Sellafield could have materially contributed to one or both diseases.

Held

The plaintiffs failed to establish, on the balance of probabilities, that PPI was a material contributory cause of (a) leukaemia in Dorothy Reay and (b) NHL in Vivien Hope.

Glossary

Adjuvant chemotherapy. Additional chemotherapy given immediately after surgical treatment in an effort to confer a survival advantage.

Anastomosis. A joining together of tissues, usually bowel.

Angioinfarction. Insertion of coils, balls or sponge into an artery to block blood flow to a tumour or bleeding blood vessels.

Anterior resection. Resection of large bowel through the anterior route.

Arthroplasty. Excision of articular portions of a joint.

Aspiration cytology. Removal of cells by means of a needle and syringe.

Axillary dissection. Removal of lymph nodes in the armpit.

Biopsy. Removal of a small piece of tissue for microscopic examination.

Bronchoscopy. Examination of the trachea and upper airways by endoscopy.

Chemotherapy. Treatment with chemical substances.

Clerking. Initial discussion with a patient, so called because in the medieval period the patient's history was inscribed by a medical clerk.

Clubbing. Curvature of the fingernails and nail bed occurring in chest and cardiac conditions.

Coeliac axis block. Block of the nerves that sense pain in the upper abdomen.

Colectomy. Surgical removal of the colon.

Colonoscopy. Attachment of large bowel to skin in the abdominal wall.

Crackles and wheezes. Added sounds heard on listening to the movement of air through the lungs.

CT scan. A computerised scan that allows the accurate definition of body parts.

Cure. A reasonable chance of achieving survival in the cancer patient.

Cyanosis. Failure to oxygenate blood adequately.

Cystoscopy. Examination of the urethra and bladder.

Cytology. Microscopic examination of cells for purposes of diagnosis.

Diathermy. Burning of tissue with an electric current, carried out in operative procedures to stop bleeding.

Dysuria. Pain on passing urine.

Effusion. Escaped fluid in a body cavity.

Endoscopy. The use of fibreoptic or rigid tubes to examine internal structures such as bowel or bronchi.

Extravasation. Leakage into tissue of cytotoxic chemotherapy.

Feeding gastrostomy. A procedure whereby the stomach is attached to the anterior abdominal wall and a feeding tube inserted through the skin into the stomach.

FIGO staging system. An international classification system used to describe the spread of cancer.

Five-year survival. Percentage of patients alive five years after the initiation of treatment.

Gastrectomy. Removal of the stomach.

Gastroscopy. Examination of the stomach by endoscopy.

Grade. Degree of aggressiveness of a tumour, as demonstrated microscopically.

Gray. A unit of radiation.

Haematuria. Blood in the urine.

Haemoptysis. Blood in the sputum.

History. A patient's story, i.e. background, lifestyle, etc.

Laparotomy. Surgical incision into the abdominal cavity, to examine the abdominal contents.

Lumpectomy. Surgical removal of a breast tumour ('lump') and surrounding tissue.

Lymphadenectomy. Removal of lymph nodes.

Mammography. Soft tissue X-ray of the breast.

Mastectomy. Removal of the breast.

Median survival. The time-point at which 50% of patients are alive and 50% are dead, i.e. average life expectancy.

Melaena. Altered blood in faeces.

Metastasis. Distant spread of a tumour to involve other organs.

Mitosis. The division of cells.

Morbidity. Incidence of symptoms and adverse effects resulting from disease or treatment.

Mortality. Incidence of death resulting from disease or treatment.

Myelopathy. Degeneration of the spinal chord.

Neoadjuvant chemotherapy. Chemotherapy given before treatment of a tumour by surgery or radiotherapy in an effort to improve results and prevent metastasis.

Nephrectomy. Removal of the kidney.

Neurogenic bladder. Loss of nervous control of the bladder.

Neuropathy. Degeneration of nerves.

Neutropenic sepsis. Infection resulting from marrow suppression during chemotherapy.

Omentum. Fat surrounding the bowel.

Oncologist. Specialist giving cancer treatment.

Oophorectomy. Removal of the ovaries by radiotherapeutic, surgical or medical means.

Orchiectomy (also sometimes orchidectomy). Removal of the testicles.

Organ system. A grouping of structural units responsible for a particular function(s), e.g. the heart and blood vessels, or the lungs and airways.

Palliation. Treatment to relieve symptoms without a significant prospect for cure.

Pap smear. Method of staining cells for microscopic examination.

Percutaneous transhepatic stenting. Insertion of a tube to dilate the biliary system, inserted through the skin.

Planning CT scans. Scans carried out in order to plan radiotherapy delivery.

Proctitis. Inflammation of the lower rectum.

Proctoscopy. Examination of the lower rectum by endoscopy.

Radiation fibrosis. Scarring following radiotherapy.

Radical cystectomy. Removal of the bladder and pelvic lymph nodes.

Radical vulvectomy. Removal of vulval tumour *en bloc* with external genitalia with primary closure.

Radiotherapy. Treatment with penetrating radiation.

Reed–Sternberg cells. Cells that occur in Hodgkin's disease.

Relapse. Return of symptoms after apparent recovery.

Remission. Resolution of symptoms and physical signs.

Resection. Surgical removal of any portion or part of the body.

Retrograde ejaculation. Ejaculation of sperm backwards into the bladder during intercourse.

Salvage surgery. Removal of a recurrent tumour.

Second-look laparotomy. A laparotomy at the end of chemotherapy where an attempt is made to further reduce tumour bulk.

Sepsis. Destruction of tissues by bacteria or their toxins.

Sigmoid volvulus. Twisted bowel.

Sigmoidoscopy. Examination of the lower rectum by endoscopy.

Stage. Extent of the spread of a cancer, as shown by scanning and X-rays.

SWOG criteria. Definitions used in myeloma.

Technetium scanning. A form of radioisotope imaging.

Ten-year survival. Percentage of patients alive ten years after the initiation of treatment.

Thoracotomy. Surgical opening of the chest to examine the internal structures.

Thyroidectomy. Removal of the thyroid gland.

TNM classification. A method of staging tumours.

TPR charts. Temperature, pulse and respiratory rate charts completed by nursing staff.

Trachea. The main tube that takes air to the lungs.

Trephine. A term usually applied to bone marrow examination and meaning a core of marrow.

Table of Cases

Anderson v. Davis [1993] PIQR 287 24
B v. Medway Health Authority (1995) Health Care Risk Report 2(3), 2
.... 180–81
Barnett v. Chelsea and Kensington Hospital Management Committee
    [1969] 1 QB 428; [1968] 1 All ER 1068 20
Bolam v. Friern Hospital Management Committee [1957]
    2 All ER 118, 1 WLR 582 8
Bolitho v. City and Hackney Health Authority (1997), *New Law Digest*
    Commercial Communication 163, 13 November 1997; *Times Law Report*,
    27 November 1997 .... 8, 13, 28–30
Bonnington Castings Limited v. Wardlow [1956] 1 All ER 615; 1 All ER, HL
    25
Cadwallader v. Anderson (1993) *PMIL Letter* (1993) 9(8), 58 188
Cassidy v. Ministry of Health [1951] 2 KB 343 6
Cathryn Shorrock v. Crewe Health Authority (1993) *AVMA Medical and
    Legal Journal* 4(2), p. 13; *PMIL Letter* 9(5), p. 6 .... 35, 181–2
Clark v. MacLennan [1983] 1 All ER 416 27
Clifford v. Portsmouth and South East Hampshire Health Authority (1995)
    Health Care Risk Report (1995) 1(5), 2 192–3
Crawford v. North Manchester Health Authority (1996) Clinical Risk –
    AVMA Medical and Legal Journal (1997) 3(8), 2 191–2
D'Arcy v. Stockport Health Authority (1992) *AVMA Medical and Legal
    Journal* (1996) 3(4), 14 184
Davis v. Taylor [1974] AC 207 24
Defrietas v. O'Brien [1995] 6 Med LR 108, CA 12
Doyle v. Wallace, CA 18 June 1998 24
Eaton v. Dale (1993) *AVMA Medical and Legal Journal* (1993) 4(4), 12
    188–9
Harling v. Huddersfield Health Authority (1992) Kemp & Kemp L8-150
    183–4
Hope v. British Nuclear Fuels plc [1994] 5 Med LR 1 198

Hotson v. East Berkshire Area Health Authority [1987]
AC 750; 2 All ER 909, HL 21
Hucks v. Cole [1968] 4 Med LR 393 .... 9, 14
Hughes, deceased v. Chester Health Authority (1995) Clinical Risk – *AVMA Medical and Legal Journal* 1(6), 219 179–80
Judge v. Huntingdon Health Authority [1995] 6 Med LR 223; Kemp & Kemp L8-160; *Times Law Reports*, 9 March 1995; Clinical Risk – *AVMA Medical and Legal Journal* (1995) 1(3), 127 .... 23, 185–6
Lewis v. Liverpool Health Authority and Royal Liverpool University NHS Trust (unreported) 190
M W v. Bolton Health Authority and Another (1995) *AVMA Medical and Legal Journal* (1993) 4(2), 12 193–4
Mallett v. McMonagle [1970] AC 166 23
Maynard v. West Midlands Regional Health Authority [1984] 1 WRL 634
.... 10
McGhee v. National Coal Board [1973] 1 WLR 1 26
Mills v. British Rail Engineering (1991) *PMIL Letter* (1991) 7(8), 56
.... 195–6
Molinari v. Ministry of Defence [1994] P.I.Q.R. Q33; Kemp & Kemp L3-091
.... 76, 196–7
Page v. Smith [1995] 2 All ER 907, HL 74
Pawson v. St Helens and Knowsley Hospitals NHS Trust (1996) Clinical Risk – *AVMA Medical and Legal Journal* (1996) 2(4), 133 182–3
R v. Bateman [1925] 94 LJKB 791 5–6
Reay v. British Nuclear Fuels plc [1994] 5 Med LR 1 198
Roe v. Minister of Health [1954] 2 QB 66 .... 11, 16
S H v. Salford Health Authority (unreported) 190–91
Sidaway v. Governors of the Bethlem Royal Hospital [1985]
1 All ER 643; AC 871, HL 15
Stokes v. Guest Keen and Nettlefield (Bolts and Nuts) Ltd [1968]
1 WLR 1776, 112 Sol Jo, 821 197
Sutton v. PSFBP [1981] *Times Law Report*, 7 November 1981 72
Taylor v. West Kent Health Authority [1997] 8 Med LR 251 ... 73, 186–7
Thurman v. Wiltshire and Bath Health Authority (1997) 36 BMLR 63
.... 75, 176–8
Vaughan v. Paddington and North Kensington Area Health Authority
(1986) Kemp & Kemp L8-171 184–5
Wallace v. Portsmouth and South East Hampshire Health Authority (1996) Clinical Risk – *AVMA Medical and Legal Journal* 2(2), 62 179
Whiteford v. Hunter (1950) 94 Sol Jo 758, HL 194–5
Wilsher v. Essex Area Health Authority [1986] 3 All ER 801; [1988]
AC 1074, HL 7, 25

Index

actinomycin 145
Action for Victims of Medical Accidents (AVMA) 35
adenocarcinoma 116
adenoid cystic carcinoma 190
adriamycin 111, 137, 138, 121, 149, 152, 163, 167, 170, 174
after-the-event legal expenses insurance 3
alpha-fetoprotein 145, 146
anastomosis 126
angioinfarction 133
anti-androgen therapy 142
antihistamines 160
asbestos 78–9, 162
  case law 195–6
aspiration cytology 89, 123, 172
Atkinson tube 117
avascular necrosis 22
AVMA (Action for Victims of Medical Accidents) 35

Baker's cyst 189
balance of probabilities 21, 22, 23
barium enema 125
barium swallow 115
Barrett's oesophagus 115
BCG 133, 137
BEAM chemotherapy 152
Bence-Jones protein 165, 167

bisphosphonates 167
bladder cancer 135–8
bleomycin 100, 144, 145, 146, 152
Bolam test 8–10
Bonadonna CMF programme 91
bone marrow aspiration 147, 166
bone marrow transplantation 152
bone pain 80, 165, 167
breach of duty 7–15
  consent to treatment 15–17
  delay or failure to diagnose cancer 18–19, 23
  expert's brief 68
  treatment or clinical management of cancer patients 19
breast cancer
  adjuvant chemotherapy 91
  adjuvant hormonal therapy 91
  adjuvant radiotherapy 90–91
  case law 182–7
  delayed diagnosis 23, 30–31
  epidemiology 88
  high-dose chemotherapy 92
  out-patient diagnosis 88–9
  pre-action disclosure of records 55–6
  presentation 88
  stage and grade of tumour 89–90
  surgery 89

treatment of metastatic cancer
    91–2
Breslow's staging system 156
bronchoscopy 109
budgeting 46
buserelin 141

cancer
  case management *see* case
      management
  causes 78–9
  clinical examination 81–2
  communicating with the client
      79–80
  hospital assessment 82–4
  hospital referral 82
  hospital tests 84
  symptoms 80
  treatment options 11, 41, 84, 85
    bladder cancer 137–8
    carcinoid tumours 160
    cure and palliation 85–6
    gastric cancer 119
    Hodgkin's disease 151–2
    laryngeal carcinoma 107
    lung cancer 110–11
    melanoma 154–5, 156–7
    mesothelioma 163–4
    myeloma 166–7
    non-Hodgkin's lymphoma
        148–9
    oesophageal cancer 117
    ovarian cancer 94, 96
    pancreatic cancer 123–4
    prostate cancer 140–42
    renal cancer 132–4
    side-effects *see* side-effects
    soft tissue sarcomas 169–70
    stage and grade of tumour 84–5
    testicular cancer 144–6
    tongue cancer 113–14
carboplatin 138, 145
carcinoid tumours 159–61
carmustine 167

case law
  adenoid cystic carcinoma 190
  asbestos-related lung cancer
      195–6
  breast cancer 182–7
  cervical cancer 176–82
  colon cancer 192–3
  failure to diagnose 188–9
  incorrect diagnosis 193–5
  ionising radiation 196–7, 198–9
  kidney cancer 191–2
  leukaemia 196–7, 198–9
  lung cancer 190–91, 195–6
  non-Hodgkin's lymphoma 198–9
  scrotal cancer 197
  testicular cancer 188
case management 32, 48
  background reading 39–41
  basis of the patient's complaint
      37
  budgeting 46
  enlisting assistance from the
      defence lawyer 34–5
  first interview 41–4
    information to obtain 44–7
  identity of the patient's cancer
      37–8
  initial details 36–7
  instructing experts 59–60
    alleged delay or failure to
        diagnose 60–62
    alleged inappropriate or
        inaccurate radiotherapy 62–4
    letter of approach 64–5
    letter of instruction *see* letter of
        instruction
  medical brief 56–8
  motivation behind compensation
      claims 33–4
  patient's current condition 38
  persons attending the first
      meeting 38–9
  pre-action disclosure 48–51
    breast cancer cases 55–6

checking and sorting disclosed material 53–5
GP's records 52–3
histopathological results 55
hospital records 51–2
lung cancer cases 56
screening 36–7, 39, 58
time factors 33, 38
causation 20–21
duty and causation 28–31
expert's brief 68–70
allegations of delay or failure to diagnose 61–2
alleged inappropriate or inaccurate radiotherapy 63–4
loss of a chance 21–5
material contribution 25–7
cervical cancer
case law 176–82
epidemiology 98
prognosis 99–100
screening 100–101
smear tests 7, 75–6, 98–9
staging and grading 99
symptoms and investigation 98–9
terminal care 100
treatment 99
chemotherapy 85
bladder cancer 137, 138
breast cancer 91, 92
carcinoid tumours 160
cervical cancer 100
colon cancer 127
extravasation 174–5
gastric cancer 120–21
Hodgkin's disease 152
lung cancer 110–11
melanoma 156
mesothelioma 163
myeloma 166–7
non-Hodgkin's lymphoma 148, 149
renal cancer 133

side-effects 86, 87, 111, 145–6, 148, 149, 152, 156
soft tissue sarcomas 170
testicular cancer 144–5
chlorambucil 145, 148
cisplatin 96, 100, 110, 121, 138, 144, 145, 146, 163
Clark's levels 155, 156, 157
clubbing 81, 108
coeliac axis block 124
colon cancer 125–7
case law 192–3
colonoscopy 84
colposcopy 99
communication 6, 79–80
compensation claims 34
conditional fee agreements 3
cone biopsy 99
conflicting opinions 9–11, 12–13, 14–15, 17
consent to treatment 15–17
cord progression 167
croup 28
Cryptosporidium parvum 134
CT imaging 84, 131, 147, 160
cyclophosphamide 91, 111, 138, 148, 149, 167, 170
cyproheptadine 160
cystectomy 137
cystitis 140
cystoscopy 135, 137
cytokines 160
cytotoxic chemotherapy 144–5, 156

dacarbazine 152, 156
damages 22, 30–31, 71
general damages 71–4
provisional damages 74–7
delayed diagnosis 18–19, 23, 30–31
instructing experts 60–62
delayed treatment 141–2
dermatitis 26–7
diagnosis 79–80 (*see also* symptoms)
breast cancer 88–9

clinical examination 81–2
Hodgkin's disease 150
hospital assessment 82–4
mesothelioma 163
myeloma 166
thyroid cancer 171
diagnostic failure 18–19, 23, 30–31
  case law 188–9
  instructing experts 60–62
diathermy 136, 137
diet 79, 128
dimethyl sulphoxide (DMSO) 174
disclosure of documents *see* pre-action disclosure
Dukes stages 127, 130
duty of care 5–7
  breach of duty 7–15
    consent to treatment 15–17
    delay or failure to diagnose cancer 18–19, 23
    expert's brief 68
    treatment or clinical management of cancer patients 19
  duty and causation 28–31
dysuria 135

embolisation 160
endoscopic retrograde cholangiopancreatography 123
endoscopy 115, 119, 125
environmental causes of cancer 78–9
epidemiology 40, 78–9
  bladder cancer 135
  breast cancer 88
  carcinoid tumours 159
  cervical cancer 98
  colon cancer 125
  gastric cancer 118
  Hodgkin's disease 150
  laryngeal carcinoma 105
  lung cancer 108
  melanoma 154
  mesothelioma 162
  myeloma 165
  non-Hodgkin's lymphoma 147
  oesophageal cancer 115
  ovarian cancer 93
  pancreatic cancer 122
  prostate cancer 139
  rectal cancer 128
  renal cancer 131
  soft tissue sarcomas 168
  testicular cancer 143
  thyroid cancer 171
  tongue cancer 112
  vulval cancer 102
epirubicin 121
epodyl 137
erythrocyte sedimentation rate (ESR) 150, 165
etoposide 144, 145
expert evidence 9–11, 12–13, 14–15, 17
  instructing experts 59–60
    alleged delay or failure to diagnose 60–62
    alleged inappropriate or inaccurate radiotherapy 62–4
    letter of approach 64–5
    letter of instruction *see* letter of instruction
extravasation 174–5

failure to diagnose 18–19, 23, 30–31
  case law 188–9
  instructing experts 60–62
fast-track litigation highways 2
FIGO staging system 94, 96
fine needle aspiration cytology 30, 172
fine needle biopsy 23, 30, 123, 172
5-fluorouracil 91, 121, 127, 130
flutamide 133
folinic acid 127

follicular thyroid lymphoma 173
funding 2, 46

gastric cancer 79, 118–21
gastrointestinal endoscopy 125
general damages 71–4
genetic causes of cancer 78
Gleason grades 140, 142
glottic tumours 106
gonadotrophin-releasing hormone agonists 141, 142
goserelin acetate 141
GP's records 52–3 (*see also* pre-action disclosure)
grade of tumour or cancer 40, 84–5
   bladder cancer 136–7
   breast cancer 89–90
   cervical cancer 99
   colon cancer 126–7
   Hodgkin's disease 151
   laryngeal carcinoma 106
   non-Hodgkin's lymphoma 148
   pancreatic cancer 123
   prostate cancer 139–40
   rectal cancer 129–30
   thyroid cancer 172
   tongue cancer 112–13
   vulval cancer 103

haematuria 133, 135
hair loss 111, 148, 149
hepatic artery embolisation 160
histopathological results 6, 7, 75–6, 84, 98–9
   pre-action disclosure 55
Hodgkin's disease 150–53
hormonal therapy
   breast cancer 91
   prostate cancer 141, 142
   renal cancer 133
hospital records 51–2 (*see also* pre-action disclosure)
hospitals
   assessment procedure 82–4

   carcinoid tumours 159–60
   myeloma 165–6
   non-Hodgkin's lymphoma 147
   renal cancer 131
   liability 6–7
   referrals 82
   risk management 50
human chorionic gonadotrophin 145, 146
hyaluronidase 174
5-hydroxyindoleacetic acid (5-HIAA) 160
hypercalcaemia 165, 166, 167
hysterectomy 99

ifosfamide 110
immunogobulinaemia 165
immunotherapy 133–4, 157, 163–4
impotence 140, 146
infradiaphragmatic radiation 152
insurance 3
interferons 134, 137, 160, 163–4, 167
interleukin 2 134, 157
International Germ Cell Cancer Collaborative Group 146
interview techniques 41–4
   information to obtain 44–7
intraepithelial neoplasia
   cervical 99–100
   vulval 103–4
intravenous pyelogram 135
ionising radiation 76
   case law 196–7, 198–9

kidney cancer 131–4
   case law 191–2

laparotomy 96, 145
laryngeal carcinoma 105–7
legal aid 2, 46
letter of instruction 65
   anticipating opposing arguments 70
   conclusion 70

expert's brief 67
  proving causation 68–70
  questions on breach of duty 68
explanation of records and documents 66
factual or medical history 67
introduction 65–6
list of supporting documents 66
leukaemia 76–7
  case law 196–7, 198–9
leuprorelin acetate 141
levamisole 127
liability
  allegations of delay or failure to diagnose 60–61
  alleged inappropriate or inaccurate radiotherapy 62–3
litigation 1–4, 87
  alternatives 43–4
  case management *see* case management
loss of a chance 21–5
lung cancer
  asbestos exposure 162
  case law 190–91, 195–6
  diagnosis 81–2, 83–4
  epidemiology 108
  pre-action disclosure of records 56
  presentation and investigations 108–9
  staging 109–10
  treatment options 110–11
lymph nodes 98, 105, 114, 119
  Hodgkin's disease 150–51
lymphadenopathy 151
lymphoblastic leukaemia 76–7
  case law 196–7
lymphokine activated killer (LAK) cells 157
lymphomas 143, 144, 147–9

mammography 89

mantle radiation 151–2
material contribution 25–7
mediastinoscopy 10
medical negligence
  breach of duty 7–15
    consent to treatment 15–17
    delay or failure to diagnose cancer 18–19, 23
    treatment or clinical management of cancer patients 19
  causation 20–21
    duty and causation 28–31
    loss of a chance 21–5
    material contribution 25–7
  damages *see* damages
  duty of care 5–7
    duty and causation 28–31
  litigation 1–4, 87
    alternatives 43–4
    case management *see* case management
medical opinion 9–11, 12–13, 14–15, 17
medical records
  pre-action disclosure *see* pre-action disclosure
medical textbooks 41
melanoma 154–8
melphalan 166, 167
Merck Manual 41
mesothelioma 78–9, 162–4
metastasis
  bladder cancer 138
  breast cancer 91–2
  colon cancer 127
  gastric cancer 120–21
  liver 160
  melanoma 156–7
  prostate cancer 141
  rectal cancer 130
  renal cancer 133–4
  soft tissue sarcomas 170
  testicular cancer 144

methotrexate 91, 100, 138
mitomycin C 110, 121, 137
mitozantrone 137, 138
monoclonal gammopathy 166
multi-track litigation highways 2
mustine 152, 174
myeloma 165–7

nausea 149, 156
navelbine 111
necrosis 22, 175
negligence *see* medical negligence
nephrectomy 132
neutropenic sepsis 111, 145, 146, 148, 156
nitrosoureas 156
non-Hodgkin's lymphoma 147–9
   case law 198–9
non-small cell lung cancer 110–11

octreotide 160
oesophageal cancer 115–17
oesophagitis 152
oestrogen therapy 141
omissions 13–14, 28, 29–30
oncovin 152
oophorectomy 92
oral alkylating agents 148
orchiectomy 141, 142
ovarian cancer 93–7

palliative treatment 85–6
   bladder cancer 138
   lung cancer 110
   mesothelioma 163
   myeloma 167
   pancreatic cancer 124
   prostate cancer 142
   renal cancer 132–3
pancreatic cancer 122–4
Pap smears 7, 75–6, 98–9
papillary thyroid carcinoma 173
peripheral blood stem cell support 152

pleural aspiration 163
Plummer Vinson syndrome 115
pre-action disclosure 48–51
   breast cancer cases 55–6
   checking and sorting disclosed material 53–5
   GP's records 52–3
   histopathological results 55
   hospital records 51–2
   lung cancer cases 56
prednisone 148, 149, 152, 166, 167
private treatment 6
procarbazine 152
proctitis 140
proctoscopy 125
progestogens 133
prognosis
   carcinoid tumours 161
   cervical cancer 99–100
   gastric cancer 121
   Hodgkin's disease 153
   laryngeal carcinoma 107
   melanoma 157–8
   mesothelioma 164
   oesophageal cancer 117
   ovarian cancer 96
   prostate cancer 142
   rectal cancer 130
   renal cancer 134
   testicular cancer 146
   thyroid cancer 173
   tongue cancer 114
   vulval cancer 103
prostate cancer 139–42
prostate specific antigen 140
provisional damages 74–7
pyelogram 135

quantum 22, 30–31

radiation 76
   case law 196–7, 198–9
radiation fibrosis 114
radiation pneumonitis 152

radiological assessment 84, 109, 131, 147, 160
radiotherapy 85
  allegations of inappropriateness or inaccuracy 62–4
  bladder cancer 137–8
  breast cancer 90–91, 92
  Hodgkin's disease 151–2
  lung cancer 110
  melanoma 156
  myeloma 167
  non-Hodgkin's lymphoma 148, 149
  prostate cancer 140–41, 142
  rectal cancer 130
  side-effects 86, 87, 110, 114, 151–2
  soft tissue sarcomas 170
  testicular cancer 144
  thyroid cancer 173
records
  pre-action disclosure *see* pre-action disclosure
rectal cancer 128–30
Reed-Sternberg cells 150
referral procedure 82
renal cancer 131–4
  case law 191–2
retinopathy of prematurity 26
retro-peritoneal lymph node dissection 144, 146
retrolental fibroplasia 26
risk management 50

scrotal cancer 197
second-look surgery 96
second opinions 9–11, 12–13, 14–15, 17
seminomas 143, 144, 146
side-effects
  chemotherapy 86, 87, 111, 145–6, 148, 149, 152, 156
  radiotherapy 86, 87, 110, 114, 151–2

surgery 86–7, 114
sigmoidoscopy 84, 125
small cell lung cancer 111
smear tests 7, 75–6, 98–9
smoking 79
  cervical cancer 98
  laryngeal carcinoma 105
  lung cancer 82, 108
  vulval cancer 102
soft tissue sarcomas 168–70
somatostatin 160
South West Oncology Group (SWOG) 167
specialist opinion 12–13
sputum cytology 109
squamous cell carcinoma 116, 136
stage of tumour or cancer 40, 84–5
  bladder cancer 136–7
  breast cancer 89–90
  cervical cancer 99
  colon cancer 126–7
  gastric cancer 119–20
  Hodgkin's disease 151
  laryngeal carcinoma 106
  lung cancer 109–10
  melanoma 155–6
  mesothelioma 163
  myeloma 166
  non-Hodgkin's lymphoma 147–8
  oesophageal cancer 116
  ovarian cancer 94
  pancreatic cancer 123
  prostate cancer 139–40
  rectal cancer 129–30
  renal cancer 132
  soft tissue sarcomas 169
  testicular cancer 143–4
  thyroid cancer 172
  tongue cancer 112–13
  vulval cancer 102, 103
standard of care 8, 11–13
  consent to treatment 15–17
standard of proof 21
stem cell transplantation 152

sterility 146, 152
steroids 167, 174
stomach cancer 79, 118–21
subglottic tumours 106–7
supraglottic tumours 106
surgery 85
   bladder cancer 137
   breast cancer 89
   colon cancer 125–6
   gastric cancer 119
   lung cancer 110
   melanoma 154–5, 156
   ovarian cancer 94
   prostate cancer 140–41, 142
   rectal cancer 128–9, 130
   renal cancer 132
   side-effects 86, 114
   soft tissue sarcomas 169
   testicular cancer 145
   thyroid cancer 171
symptoms 80 (*see also* diagnosis)
   bladder cancer 135–6
   breast cancer 88
   carcinoid tumours 159
   cervical cancer 98–9
   colon cancer 125
   gastric cancer 118
   laryngeal carcinoma 105
   lung cancer 108–9
   melanoma 154
   mesothelioma 162
   myeloma 165
   non-Hodgkin's lymphoma 147
   oesophageal cancer 115
   ovarian cancer 93
   pancreatic cancer 122–3
   prostate cancer 139
   rectal cancer 128
   renal cancer 131
   soft tissue sarcomas 168
   testicular cancer 143
   thyroid cancer 171
   tongue cancer 112
   vulval cancer 102

tamoxifen 91, 133
taxol 96, 111
teratomas 143, 144, 146
terminal care
   bladder cancer 128
   cervical cancer 100
test results 6, 7, 75–6, 84, 98–9
   pre-action disclosure 55
testicular cancer 143–6
   case law 188
testosterone 141
textbooks 41
thiotepa 137
thoracotomy 145
thrombocytopenia 145, 146, 148
thyroid cancer 171–3
TNM clinical classification system 85
tomudex 130
tongue cancer 112–14
transitional cell carcinoma 136
treatment options 11, 41, 84, 85
   bladder cancer 137–8
   carcinoid tumours 160
   cervical cancer 99
   consent 17
   cure and palliation 85–6
   gastric cancer 119
   Hodgkin's disease 151–2
   laryngeal carcinoma 107
   lung cancer 110–11
   melanoma 154–5, 156–7
   mesothelioma 163–4
   myeloma 166–7
   non-Hodgkin's lymphoma 148–9
   oesophageal cancer 117
   ovarian cancer 94, 96
   pancreatic cancer 123–4
   prostate cancer 140–42
   renal cancer 132–4
   side-effects *see* side-effects
   soft tissue sarcomas 169–70
   stage and grade of tumour 84–5
   testicular cancer 144–6

tongue cancer 113–14
trephine 147, 166
tuberous sclerosis 131
tumour markers 96–7

ultrasonography 23
  breast cancer 89

Veterans Administration Co-
  operative Urological
  Research Group (VACURG)
  141
vicarious liability 6–7

vinblastine 138, 145, 152
vinca alkaloids 133, 174
vincristine 111, 148, 149, 152, 170
vindesine 156
vinorelbine 111
vomiting 149, 156
Von Hippel-Lindau disease 131
vulval cancer 102–4

washings 109
Woolf Reforms 2

X-rays 84, 109, 131, 147, 160

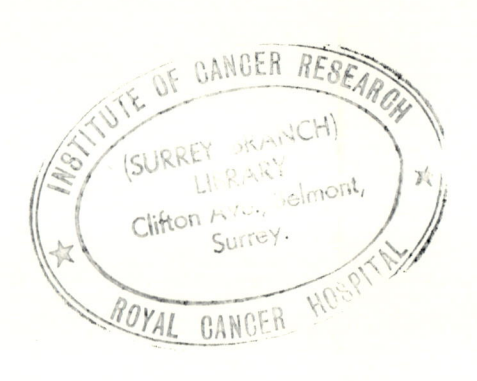